THE NOBEL MEMORIAL LAUREATES IN ECONOMICS

The Nobel Memorial Laureates in Economics

An Introduction to Their Careers and Main Published Works

Howard R. Vane

Professor of Economics, School of Accounting, Finance and Economics, Liverpool John Moores University, UK

Chris Mulhearn

Senior Lecturer in Economics, School of Accounting, Finance and Economics, Liverpool John Moores University, UK

Edward Elgar
Cheltenham, UK • Northampton, MA, USA

Published by
Edward Elgar Publishing Limited
Glensanda House
Montpellier Parade
Cheltenham
Glos GL50 1UA
UK

Edward Elgar Publishing, Inc.
136 West Street
Suite 202
Northampton
Massachusetts 01060
USA

A catalogue record for this book
is available from the British Library

Library of Congress Cataloguing in Publication Data
Vane, Howard R.
    The Nobel Memorial laureates in economics : an introduction to their careers
    and main published works / Howard R. Vane, Chris Mulhearn.
        p. cm.
    Includes bibliographical references.
    1. Economists—Biography. 2. Nobel Prizes—Biography. 3. Economics—
History. 4. Nobel Prizes—History. I. Mulhearn, Chris. II. Title.

HB76.V36 2005
330'.092'2—dc22
[B]
                                                                          2005046187

ISBN 1 84376 600 0 (cased)

Typeset by Manton Typesetters, Louth, Lincolnshire, UK.
Printed and bound in Great Britain by MPG Books Ltd, Bodmin, Cornwall.

Contents

CONTENTS

Preface

Today, students who graduate with a degree in economics do so with a thorough grounding in theory, methods of economic investigation and policy application. Sadly, at least in our experience, an ever-increasing number have little awareness of when many of the key ideas and building blocks which underlie their studies were first put forward and subsequently developed. This situation in part reflects the widespread disappearance of history of economic thought courses from both undergraduate and postgraduate degree programmes. Among other explanatory factors is the seemingly more instrumental approach taken by many students who are reluctant to engage in wider reading and instead focus their efforts on a limited number of set textbooks in order to pass their exams and gain a passport to higher earnings. As long-standing teachers of the discipline, this state of affairs is one that we have reluctantly come to acknowledge. Recognition of a situation, however, does not entail acquiescence. The main aim of this book is to provide an *introduction* to the careers and main published works of the Nobel Memorial Laureates in Economics for undergraduate and postgraduate students. In doing so, we hope to give students a better understanding of some of the key figures and their major insights which have helped mould the present state of economics. The vignettes may also encourage the reader to sample some of the Laureates' original works and thereby gain a better understanding of the context in which their ideas were first put forward. As Mark Blaug, who has kindly written a foreword to the book, notes 'economic knowledge is path dependent. What we now know about the economic system is not something we have just discovered, but it is the sum of all discoveries, insights and false starts in the past' (Blaug, 2001, p. 156). In our view, students are far better placed to understand economics if they have some awareness and appreciation of the origins and development of the main fields within the discipline. We hope that this book will provide a few pieces in the missing jigsaw of students' knowledge of the recent history of economic ideas.

Howard R. Vane and Chris Mulhearn

Foreword

If you visit any place where economists hang out in the first two weeks of October, you are likely to witness a heated debate about the probable next winner of the so-called Nobel Prize in Economics because the actual winner is usually announced in the third week of October. Most economists have strong views about their favourite candidate, not so much because the Prize is a popularity contest, but because they realise that the winner is not just a particular individual but also a particular style of doing economics, or a particular type of economics represented by the works of the winning Nobel Laureate.

There is a widespread misunderstanding, even among professional economists, of how the decision to award the Nobel Prize in Economics is actually made. The stereotypical view, sometimes expressed by financial journalists, is that a small cabal of Swedish economists pick the winners based on little more than their own knowledge of where economics is going and where it ought to go from then on. But as Howard Vane and Chris Mulhearn carefully explain in the opening chapter, the Nobel Prize in Economics rewards specific discoveries rather than outstanding achievements over a lifetime, as if economists, like inventors applying for a patent, must establish their originality to be eligible for an award. It is actually doubtful that economics as a discipline is characterised by novel discoveries rather than conceptual clarifications or different ways of pouring old wine in new bottles. Be that as it may, if as an economist you have an axe to grind, you are bound to associate it with the writings of one or more economists and, even if such views are dismissed as alien to a 'hard' science like economics, you are likely to think that some economists express the 'hardness' of 'real science' better than others and will therefore favour some names for the Nobel Prize over others. If you are a heterodox economist and view the mainstream with disdain for whatever reason then, of course, who actually wins the Nobel Prize in Economics is a matter of life and death. I hope that I have now said enough to explain why the Nobel Prize in Economics is more keenly anticipated and debated by economists than the Oscar Film awards are debated by cinema buffs.

If the awards were really in the hands of a small group in Sweden, as some lovers of conspiracies believe, a small group outside the worldwide professional community of economists, then the fury of the arguments would be all too easy to understand because the Nobel Prize in Economics would then represent outside interference in the House that Economists Built. But as our two authors quite rightly point out, the awards are actually based on consultations with professors of economics in all the Scandinavian countries, professors of economics in leading American and European universities, nominations by a long list of leading economists in the fields concerned, and even nominations by a number of non-economists if the works of nominated candidates are interdisciplinary. So, any notion that the Prize is awarded conspiratorially by a small elite is just nonsense. Besides, there is a high correlation between the Nobel Prize awards in any year and purely objective measures some years earlier, such as high citation counts in the leading economic journals, awards of medals and election to the presidency of professional associations of economists, and so on, and all these are judgements made within the subject by the scholarly community of economists.

However, if that were the whole story, the Nobel Prize in Economics might be thought of as icing on the cake, which could not possibly have an independent effect on economics. In that case, however, it would be difficult to understand why economists get so hot under the collar every October. But the fact of the matter is that a high correlation is not the same thing as the certainty that when x occurs y will also occur. Every now and then, the Nobel Prize in Economics is not simply the endorsement of the mean judgement of the profession but a genuine shock that sends the subject off in a new direction. As our authors argue, most of the Nobel Laureates have been either US citizens, or affiliated to an American university, or received their doctorates at one of 14 top-ranking universities, or won a prestigious award from a professional association of economists, and only four of the 55 Nobel Laureates to date have failed to meet any of these criteria, namely, Hicks, Hayek, Kantorovich and Selten. So, at least in those four cases, the Nobel Prize came as a real surprise to economists and made a real difference to economics, although it must be admitted that even here the prize was a shared prize and what was awarded and thereby promoted was a field of economics or type of economics personified by the Laureate in question (general equilibrium theory in the case of Hicks, non-formalised interdisciplinary thinking in the case of Hayek, activity analysis in the case of Kantorovich and game theory in the case of Selten). The Nobel Prize can make a difference, albeit only a small one.

If it is indeed a small difference, perhaps it would be better for economics if it were abolished altogether as some economists, for example, Milton Friedman, have suggested. First, it produces superstars in economics with all the kudos and high earnings of superstars – the Nobel Prize in Economics includes a monetary award, which, depending on the state of the stock market, can approach or exceed $1,000,000 – and this implies invidious comparisons that are extremely hurtful to the near-winners. Second, it promotes the idea that economics is a 'hard' science like physics and chemistry, which is one of the sources of the distrust of economists among neighbouring social scientists, such as sociologists, political scientists, anthropologists and even psychologists (a genuinely 'hard' social science). Perhaps economists would be a little less arrogant about other subjects without the Nobel Prize in Economics and, surely, that would be a good thing? Nevertheless, and on balance, I would hate to see the Nobel Prize in Economics disappear. It is good for economics to get a little jolt now and then from a partially-outside institution like the Nobel Prize Committee. Some of those jolts were deplorable in my judgement. Some were much needed and entirely appropriate. If I told you which was which, you would know exactly what I thought was right or wrong with modern economics. This is one way of defining the significance of the Nobel Prize: the more one cares about economics as a subject, the more one cares about the next winner.

Mark Blaug
University of Amsterdam
The Netherlands

Acknowledgements

With special thanks to The Nobel Foundation for granting the authors and publisher a one-time non-exclusive permission to use the photos of the Nobel Memorial Laureates which they kindly supplied.

The authors would also like to thank NTC Economic and Financial Publishing, Washington, DC, USA and Henley-on-Thames, UK for permission to reproduce their article, 'The Nobel Memorial Prize in Economics', which appeared in *World Economics*, January–March 2004.

The Nobel Memorial Prize in Economics: A Biographical Overview

Historical Background

Alfred Nobel (1833–96) was a Swedish inventor and industrialist who made a fortune largely from the manufacture of dynamite and other explosives. He left most of his money in trust and, according to the terms of his will,

> the capital, invested in safe securities by my executors, shall constitute a fund, the interest on which shall be annually distributed in the form of prizes to those who ... shall have conferred *the greatest benefit on mankind*. (emphasis added)

More specifically, Nobel's will states that five prizes should be awarded to the persons who have:

- 'made the most important discovery or invention' in Physics;
- 'made the most important discovery or improvement' in Chemistry;
- 'made the most important discovery' in Physiology or Medicine;
- 'produced the most outstanding work in an ideal direction' in Literature;
- 'done the most or the best work for fraternity between nations, for the abolition or reduction of standing armies and for the holding and promotion of peace congresses' (Nobel Foundation, 2004).

In 1900 the executors of Nobel's will established a private institution, the Nobel Foundation, to manage his bequest and to coordinate the work of the various prize-awarding institutions. The five original Nobel Prizes in Physics, Chemistry, Physiology or Medicine, Literature and Peace have been awarded annually since 1901.

It was not until 1968 that the Sveriges Riksbank (Bank of Sweden), as part of its tercentenary celebrations, instituted a sixth award: 'the Bank of Sweden Prize in Economic Sciences in Memory of Alfred Nobel'. The Economics Prize is then technically not a Nobel

1

Prize, as it was not part of the terms of Nobel's will, rather it is a Nobel Memorial Prize funded by the Bank of Sweden on the basis of a perpetual annuity. However, the Prize is popularly known as the Nobel Prize in Economics. The Prize is awarded annually by the Royal Swedish Academy of Sciences (which also awards the Prizes in Physics and Chemistry) in accordance with the same basic principles and rules as the original five Nobel Prizes. According to the statutes, 'the Prize shall be awarded annually to the person who has carried out a work in economic science of the eminent significance expressed in the Will of Alfred Nobel drawn up on November 27, 1895'. This means that it rewards specific discoveries, achievements or breakthroughs in economic science, rather than outstanding economists. First awarded in 1969, the Prize consists of a gold medal, a diploma bearing a citation and a sum of money (in recent years approximately $1 million).

Nomination and Selection Process
The work in handling nominations and the selection of the Nobel Memorial Laureates in Economics is largely undertaken by the Economics Prize Committee of the Royal Swedish Academy of Sciences. Each year invitations to nominate candidates for the Prize in Economic Sciences are sent to:

1. Swedish and foreign members of the Academy;
2. members of the Economics Prize Committee;
3. recipients of the Prize in Economic Sciences;
4. permanent professors in relevant subjects at universities and colleges in Sweden, Denmark, Finland, Iceland and Norway;
5. holders of corresponding chairs in at least six universities or colleges, selected for the relevant year by the Academy to ensure the appropriate distribution between different countries and their seats of learning; and
6. other scientists from whom the Academy may see fit to invite proposals.

Source: Nobel Foundation (2004).

The Prize Committee investigates the nominations it receives (1 February being the latest date of receipt) and commissions studies by specially appointed experts of the most prominent nominated candidates. It then submits its recommendations in the form of a report (including the expert studies) to the Social Science Class of the Academy. In keeping with the statutes of the Nobel Foundation, information about the nominations is confidential and cannot be disclosed for a period of 50 years. The full Academy meets in mid-October to decide the final choice of Laureates (a maximum of three economists can be awarded the Prize in any one year) by a secret ballot. The Academy's final award decision, which must be made not later than 15 November, is usually reached after it has met in mid-October. The deliberations and votes of the Academy are kept secret. The annual presentation of the award – along with the Prizes for Physics, Chemistry, Physiology or Medicine, and Literature – is made in a formal ceremony, presided over by the Swedish Royal Family, at the Stockholm Concert Hall on 10 December, the anniversary of Alfred Nobel's death.

The Nobel Memorial Laureates in Economics
Over the 1969–2004 period, 55 economists have been awarded the Prize. Single awards have been made on 20 occasions and joint awards on 16 occasions. In the case of joint awards, the Prize has been shared between two economists on 13 occasions and between three economists on three occasions. Table 1 provides summary information on the 55 Nobel Memorial Laureates in Economics including:

- their year and country of birth; and citizenship if different from country of birth (column 3);
- the university where they received their first degree and the year of its award (column 4);
- the university where they received their higher degree and the year of its award (column 5);
- their university/institutional affiliation at the time of the award of the Prize (column 6);
- their broad field of study (column 7); and
- the citation for which they received the Prize (column 8).

In what follows we use the summary information contained in Table 1 to comment on a number of characteristics of the awards.

Economics Prize Awards by Classification
It is possible to categorise the awards in a number of ways. For example, Lindbeck (1985) adopts a classification involving:

1. general 'basic' economic theory (e.g., Samuelson: 1970);
2. theoretical contributions concerning specific aspects or sectors of the economy (e.g., Friedman: 1976);
3. powerful new methods of economic analysis: their development and application (e.g., Leontief: 1973);
4. more nearly 'pure' empirical research (e.g., Kuznets: 1971); and
5. non-formalised innovative thinking (e.g., Myrdal and Hayek: 1974).

More recently Lindbeck (2001) has utilised a classification involving:

1. general equilibrium theory (e.g., Samuelson: 1970);
2. macroeconomics (e.g., Friedman: 1976);
3. microeconomics (e.g., Stigler: 1982);
4. interdisciplinary research (e.g., Becker: 1992); and
5. new methods of economic analysis (e.g., Leontief: 1973).

In both cases, Lindbeck (1985; 2001) acknowledges that because of the overlapping and 'multidimensional nature of scientific contributions' any classification is 'rather arbitrary'.

The classification we have chosen to adopt (see column 7 of Table 1) embraces eleven *broad* fields of study, in line with courses frequently taught within university degree programmes, namely:

1. microeconomics (e.g., Stigler: 1982);
2. macroeconomics (e.g., Friedman: 1976);
3. public economics (e.g., Buchanan: 1986);
4. financial economics (e.g., Merton and Scholes: 1997);
5. development economics (e.g., Schultz and Lewis: 1979);
6. international economics (e.g., Ohlin and Meade: 1977);
7. economic growth (e.g., Solow: 1987);
8. methods of economic investigation (e.g., Stone: 1984);
9. macroeconometrics (e.g., Klein: 1980);
10. econometrics (e.g., Heckman and McFadden: 2000); and
11. economic history (e.g., Fogel and North: 1993)

While the broad fields we have adopted are of some use for rough identification purposes, the reader should bear in mind four main qualifications. First, as is evidenced by reference to the Prize citations (see column 8 of Table 1), it is possible to divide certain broad fields of study into various subfields. In the case of micro-economics, for example, one can identify such specialist areas as general equilibrium theory and welfare theory (as evidenced by the Prize citation for Hicks and Arrow: 1972), and industrial organisation (as evidenced by the Prize citation for Stigler: 1982). Second, some of the fields of study we have identified could be subsumed within broader categories, thus significantly reducing our eleven-fold classification. Examples include grouping 'economic growth' and 'international economics' as part of 'macroeconomics', and treating 'econometrics' as part of 'methods of economic investigation'. Third, in line with our second qualification, there is inevitably a degree of overlap between certain of the broad fields we have identified. For example, as reflected in the 1999 Prize citation, Mundell's award could be classified under macroeconomics or international economics. Fourth, some Laureates' work classified under a particular heading feeds directly into other areas, again illustrating the problem of overlap. For example, much of the work of Akerlof and Stiglitz who (along with Spence) were jointly awarded the 2001 Prize 'for their analyses of markets with asymmetric information' has provided important microfoundations for new Keynesian macro-economics. Having offered these qualifications in respect of our preferred classification, it is evident that roughly 58 per cent of the Prize awards have gone to the broad fields of microeconomics and macroeconomics. Three awards have been made in econometrics; two awards in each of financial economics, international economics, economic growth, methods of economic investigation and macro-econometrics; and a single award in each of public economics, development economics and economic history.

Laureates' Citizenship
Of the 55 economists who have, to date, been awarded the Prize, 36 have been US citizens. Of these, 27 were born in the USA and nine were foreign born. The fact that just under two-thirds of the awards, as of 2004, have been made to US citizens reflects the leading role the United States has played in pioneering economic research since 1969.

Next in terms of ranking by nationality of recipient are eight Laureates with UK citizenship. Of these, six were born in the UK and two were foreign born. The remaining awards under the heading of citizenship have been distributed as follows. Three awards to citizens of Norway. Two awards to citizens of Sweden. Single awards to citizens of: the Netherlands, the Soviet Union, France, Germany, India, Canada and Israel.

Affiliations of Laureates (At Time of Award)

Not surprisingly the Laureates were affiliated, at the time of the award, with some of the most famous universities in the world (see column 6 of Table 1). Only 12 universities have ever been associated with more than one award, namely:

1. University of Chicago, USA: nine awards (Friedman, 1976; Schultz, 1979; Stigler, 1982; Miller, 1990; Coase, 1991; Becker, 1992; Fogel, 1993; Lucas, 1995; Heckman, 2000);
2. Harvard University, USA: four awards (Kuznets, 1971; Arrow, 1972; Leontief, 1973; Merton, 1997);
3. University of Cambridge, UK: four awards (Meade, 1977; Stone, 1984; Mirrlees, 1996; Sen, 1998);
4. University of California, Berkeley, USA: four awards (Debreu, 1983; Harsanyi, 1994; McFadden, 2000; Akerlof, 2001);
5. Columbia University, USA: three awards (Vickrey, 1996; Mundell, 1999; Stiglitz, 2001);
6. Massachusetts Institute of Technology, USA: three awards (Samuelson, 1970; Modigliani, 1985; Solow, 1987);
7. Princeton University, USA: three awards (Lewis, 1979; Nash, 1994; Kahneman, 2002);
8. Stanford University, USA: three awards (Sharpe, 1990; Scholes, 1997; Spence, 2001);
9. George Mason University, USA: two awards (Buchanan, 1986; Smith, 2002);
10. University of Oslo, Norway: two awards (Frisch, 1969; Haavelmo, 1989);
11. Yale University, USA: two awards (Koopmans, 1975; Tobin, 1981); and
12. Carnegie-Mellon University, USA: two awards (Simon, 1978; Kydland, 2004).

With respect to the affiliation of the Laureates, two points are worth noting. First, 41 out of the 55 Prize winners (75 per cent) have at the time of the award been affiliated to American universities, again illustrating the leading role the United States has played in pioneering modern economic research. Second, while acknowledging the rank order of the 12 universities noted above, some economists have made their outstanding contributions while working in universities other than the one where they were in post at the time of the award. For example, Sen held professorial posts at Delhi University (1963–71), the London School of Economics (1971–77), the University of Oxford (1977–87) and Harvard University (1987–98), before joining the University of Cambridge in 1998, the year in which he was awarded the Prize.

Laureates' Doctorates
Again, as one would expect, the Laureates have trained in some of the world's most renowned universities (see column 5 of Table 1). Of the 55 Laureates, 41 received their doctorates from 14 select universities. The 14 universities that have given doctoral training to two or more Laureates are (with names of Laureates and year they were awarded their doctorates in brackets):

1. University of Chicago, USA: seven (Simon, 1943; Stigler, 1938; Buchanan, 1948; Markowitz, 1954; Becker, 1955; Lucas, 1964; Scholes, 1969);
2. Harvard University, USA: five (Samuelson, 1941; Tobin, 1947; Solow, 1951; Spence, 1972; Smith, 1955);
3. Massachusetts Institute of Technology, USA: five (Klein, 1944; Merton, 1970; Mundell, 1956; Akerlof, 1966; Stiglitz, 1966);
4. Columbia University, USA: four (Kuznets, 1926; Arrow, 1951; Friedman, 1946; Vickrey, 1948);
5. Johns Hopkins University, USA: two (Miller, 1952; Fogel, 1963);
6. Princeton University, USA: two (Nash, 1950; Heckman, 1971);
7. University of California, Berkeley, USA: two (North, 1952; Kahneman, 1961);
8. Carnegie-Mellon University, USA: two (Kydland, 1973; Prescott, 1967);
9. University of Cambridge, UK: two (Mirrlees, 1963; Sen, 1959);
10. University of Leiden, The Netherlands: two (Tinbergen, 1929; Koopmans, 1936);
11. University of London, UK: two (Lewis, 1940; Coase, 1951);
12. University of Oslo, Norway: two (Frisch, 1926; Haavelmo, 1946);
13. University of Paris, France: two (Debreu, 1956; Allais, 1949); and
14. University of Stockholm, Sweden: two (Myrdal, 1927; Ohlin, 1924).

Table 1 reveals that 52 of the 55 Laureates have undertaken a doctorate, most of which (34 or 65 per cent) were awarded by American universities.

Forecasting Nobel Memorial Prize Winners in Economics

Anyone trying to forecast a likely future winner of the Nobel Memorial Prize in Economics would be well advised to bear in mind the information contained in Table 1. In summary, of the 55 Prize winners: 65 per cent have been US citizens; 75 per cent have been affiliated to American universities; and 65 per cent have received their PhDs from American universities. As discussed in the case of the Laureates' affiliation, and the place of their doctoral training, there has been a marked concentration on a small number of top American universities.

Additional indicators of potential Nobel Memorial status include high citation counts (for further details, see, for example, Quandt, 1976; Grubel, 1979) and the prior award of prestigious honours. In the latter case, for example, a number of recipients of the John Bates Clark Medal have subsequently been awarded the Nobel Memorial Prize. The Medal – named after the American economist John Bates Clark, 1847–1938 – was instituted in 1947 by the American Economic Association and is awarded every two years to an *American* economist under the age of 40 who is adjudged to have made 'a significant contribution to economic thought and knowledge'. To date, of the 28 economists who have been awarded the John Bates Clark Medal (no award was made in 1953), 11 have subsequently been awarded the Nobel Memorial Prize, namely (with year of Medal award followed by year of Memorial Prize award): Samuelson (1947, 1970); Friedman (1951, 1976); Tobin (1955, 1981); Arrow (1957, 1972); Klein (1959, 1980); Solow (1961, 1987); Becker (1967, 1992); McFadden (1975, 2000); Stiglitz (1979, 2001); Spence (1981, 2001); and Heckman (1983, 2000).[1]

In using the award of the John Bates Clark Medal as an indicator of potential Nobel Memorial status, one has to take into account an

---

[1] Interestingly, the Francis A. Walker Medal (named after the American economist, Francis Walker, 1840–97), which was instituted in 1947 by the American Economic Association and awarded every five years to the living *American* economist who during their career has 'made the greatest contribution to economics', was discontinued in 1981 as the Nobel Memorial Prize had made it superfluous. Unlike the Francis A. Walker Medal, the Nobel Memorial Prize is not restricted to American economists.

average time lag of 22 years between the receipt of the two awards. Given that four winners of the Medal since 1975 have been awarded the Nobel Memorial Prize since 2000, it will be interesting to see which other Medal winners since 1975 (Martin S. Feldstein, 1977; Jerry A. Hausman, 1985; Sandford J. Grossman, 1987; David M. Kreps, 1989; Paul R. Krugman, 1991; Lawrence H. Summers, 1993; David Card, 1995; Kevin M. Murphy, 1997; Andrei Shleifer, 1999; Mathew Rabin, 2001; Steven Levitt, 2003) go on to win the Nobel Memorial Prize. Of course, this does not preclude earlier living winners of the Medal receiving the Nobel Memorial Prize. Here it is interesting to note that the pre-1975 winners are: Kenneth E. Boulding, 1949 (d. 1993); Hendrik S. Houthakker, 1963; Zvi Griliches, 1965 (d. 1999); Marc Leon Nerlove, 1969; Dale W. Jorgensen, 1971; and Franklin M. Fisher, 1973.

For biographical details of many of these major economists, including their principal contributions, the reader is referred to Blaug (1999) and Blaug and Vane (2003).

Controversy Surrounding the Award of a Nobel Memorial Prize in Economics
Ever since the idea of instituting a new award was first put forward, a degree of controversy has surrounded the Nobel Memorial Prize in Economics. At the outset, objections were raised by some members of the Royal Swedish Academy of Sciences that Economics is a 'soft' social science, not sufficiently robust to be awarded a Prize by the Academy on a par with the 'hard' natural sciences of Physics and Chemistry. In addition, there were complaints that Economics does not contribute enough to the 'benefit of mankind' to be given a Prize in memory of Alfred Nobel in line with the views originally expressed in his will. Despite these concerns, the Academy nevertheless agreed to introduce the new Prize.

However, since its inception the award in Economics has been the subject of a number of other controversies. In particular three main criticisms have been made of the Prize. First, concerns have been voiced that the Prize Committee has shown a bias towards, and favoured, the Chicago School of neoclassical economics. As noted, of the 55 awards nine (Friedman, Schultz, Stigler, Miller, Coase, Becker, Fogel, Lucas and Heckman) have been made to faculty members of the University of Chicago and a further four (Simon, Buchanan, Markovitz and Scholes) to economists who received their doctoral training from the University of Chicago, but who were affiliated to other American universities at the time of the award. Taken together, 24 per cent of all Memorial Prizes in Economics have gone to faculty members, and doctoral-trained economists, of the University of Chicago.

Second, concerns have been expressed that some of the more recent awards are less meritorious than earlier ones. Unlike the original five Nobel Prizes which have been awarded since 1901, the Memorial Prize in Economics only started in 1969. In the first two decades following its inception the Academy needed to clear a long backlog of specific achievements by outstanding economists, many of whom made their seminal contributions in the 1940s and 1950s or even earlier. Eventually this accumulated debt to those who had made important breakthroughs in economics was met either by the award of the Prize, or the death of a potential Prize winner (the Prize cannot be given posthumously). In the latter case some outstanding economists were arguably denied the Prize either because they died before it was instigated (for example, John Maynard Keynes, 1883–1946), or before the debt to them could be honoured (for example, Joan Robinson, 1903–1983).[2] Given these circumstances it has become more likely, since the 1990s, that the Prize may be awarded to more contemporary economists (notable exceptions being Coase and Vickrey, the 1991 and 1996 Laureates, who received the Prize when they were in their 80s). Perhaps this makes it inevitable that some recent awards are likely to be more contentious than many in the past. Moreover, as Lindbeck (2001) has noted, because the Prize selection committee has opted for a pluralist view of economic research, there will always be adherents of one perspective or another who adopt a critical stance towards work which they find has little sympathy with their own 'brand' of economics.

One recent award which did attract a degree of controversy was that in 1998 to Amartya Sen. A member of the Prize committee had even predicted that 'Sen will never get the prize' (Nasar, 1998). This statement was apparently based on Sen's interest in ethical matters and his rather broad research agenda; both were seen to be at vari-

---

[2] See Snowdon and Vane (1999, pp. 94, 127, 148–9, 247 and 283) for the views of five Nobel Memorial Laureates – James Tobin, Milton Friedman, Robert Lucas, Franco Modigliani and Robert Solow – on whether Keynes would have been awarded the first Nobel Memorial Prize in Economics if he had still been alive in 1969.

ance with the neoclassical mainstream in economics. Other commentators have suggested that Sen's award was a form of 'Nobel penance', intended to restore the reputation of the Prize after it had arguably been 'tainted' by the business problems of its recipients the previous year: Myron Scholes and Robert Merton. Scholes and Merton were associated with Long-Term Capital Management, a hedge fund now infamous for prompting the near-collapse of the US financial system in the period just before Sen's award (Pressman and Summerfield, 2000). For eloquent explanations of the clear merit in Sen's award, see Arrow (1999) and Atkinson (1999).

Third, concerns have been voiced that the Nobel Memorial Prize has become an object of such desire, given the status and prestige it affords its recipients and the universities to which they are affiliated, that it results in a competitive and unseemly race. Indeed, the Nobel Memorial Prize has become so well known that it is promoted in the media as the economics equivalent of the annual Oscar awards in cinema: a partial reflection of the modern-day cult of celebrity. Franco Modigliani, the 1985 Laureate, once jokingly commented that 'Nobel Prize winners are to the scientific establishment what cardinals are to the church. They are figures who command reverence and benevolence' (Snowdon and Vane, 1999, p. 257).

Our purpose in mentioning these criticisms is not to adjudicate on their validity but merely to highlight the degree of controversy that has surrounded the Nobel Memorial Prize in Economics since its inception.

Concluding Remarks

In conclusion, let us pose a question which we intend to be neither deep nor frivolous, merely interesting. What advice does our analysis offer to Nobel Memorial aspirants? We would suggest that they should try to meet at least some of the following criteria:

- be a US citizen (65 per cent of Laureates are);
- be affiliated to an American university (75 per cent of Laureates are);
- more specifically be an affiliate of a member of an elite group of 12 universities with a track record of employing Laureates at the time of their elevation (ten of the 12 are in the US);
- have doctoral training at one of 14 select universities with a

track record of training Laureates (of these 14, eight are in the US and have trained more than half of all Laureates);
- first win a prestigious award like the John Bates Clark Medal (39 per cent have so far gone on to a Nobel Memorial award);
- be affiliated to the University of Chicago or train there (nine awards to Chicago affiliates – more than twice as many as the next most successful institutions; seven Chicago doctoral students have subsequently won the Nobel Memorial Prize).

Only four (Hicks, Hayek, Kantorovich and Selten) of the 55 Laureates to date have received their award without meeting any of these criteria. A final apparent criterion is that the recipient should be a man.

Table 1   The Nobel 'Memorial' Laureates in Economics: 1969–2004

Year of award	Laureate(s)	Year and country of birth; citizenship	First degree (university and year)	Higher degree (university and year)	Affiliation (at time of award)	Broad field of study	Prize citation (Nobel Foundation, 2004)
1969	**Ragnar A.K. Frisch**	b. 1895, Norway (d. 1973)	BA, University of Oslo, 1919	PhD (Mathematical Statistics), University of Oslo, 1926	University of Oslo, Norway	Macroeconometrics	'for having developed and applied dynamic models for the analysis of economic processes'
	Jan Tinbergen	b. 1903, The Netherlands (d. 1994)		Dr (Physics) University of Leiden, 1929	Netherlands School of Economics, The Netherlands		
1970	**Paul A. Samuelson**	b. 1915, USA	BA, University of Chicago, 1935	PhD, Harvard University, 1941	Massachusetts Institute of Technology, USA	Microeconomics/ Macroeconomics	'for the scientific work through which he has developed static and dynamic economic theory and actively contributed to raising the level of analysis in economic science'
1971	**Simon S. Kuznets**	b. 1901, Russia (d. 1985); US citizen	BA, Columbia University, 1923	PhD, Columbia University, 1926	Harvard University, USA	Economic Growth	'for his empirically founded interpretation of economic growth which has led to new and deepened insight into the economic and social structure and process of development'

Table 1 continued

Year of award	Laureate(s)	Year and country of birth; citizenship	First degree (university and year)	Higher degree (university and year)	Affiliation (at time of award)	Broad field of study	Prize citation (Nobel Foundation, 2004)
1972	**John R. Hicks**	b. 1904, UK (d. 1989)	BA (Philosophy, Politics and Economics), University of Oxford, 1925		University of Oxford, UK	Microeconomics	'for their pioneering contributions to general economic equilibrium theory and welfare theory'
	Kenneth J. Arrow	b. 1921, USA	BSc (Mathematics), City College, New York, 1940	PhD, Columbia University, 1951	Harvard University, USA		
1973	**Wassily Leontief**	b. 1906, Russia (d. 1999); US citizen	MA (Social Science), University of Leningrad, 1925	PhD, University of Berlin, 1928	Harvard University, USA	Methods of Economic Investigation	'for the development of the input–output method and for its application to important economic problems'
1974	**Gunnar Myrdal**	b. 1898, Sweden (d. 1987)	Law Degree, University of Stockholm, 1923	PhD, University of Stockholm, 1927	University of Stockholm, Sweden	Macroeconomics	'for their pioneering work in the theory of money and economic fluctuations and for their penetrating analysis of the interdependence of economic, social and institutional phenomena'
	Friedrich A. von Hayek	b. 1899, Austria (d. 1992); UK citizen	PhD (Law) and PhD (Political Science), University of Vienna, 1921 and 1923		University of Freiburg, West Germany		

Year	Name	Birth/death	Degree	Degree	Institution	Field	Citation
1975	Leonid V. Kantorovich	b. 1912, Russia (d. 1986)	BSc (Mathematics), Leningrad State University, 1930	Dr (Mathematics), Leningrad State University, 1935	Academy of Sciences, Moscow, USSR	Microeconomics	'for their contributions to the theory of optimum allocation of resources'
	Tjalling C. Koopmans	b. 1910, The Netherlands (d. 1985); US citizen	MA (Mathematics and Physics), University of Utrecht, 1933	PhD (Mathematical Statistics), University of Leiden, 1936	Yale University, USA		
1976	Milton Friedman	b. 1912, USA	BA, Rutgers University, 1932	PhD, Columbia University, 1946	University of Chicago, USA	Macroeconomics	'for his achievements in the fields of consumption analysis, monetary history and theory, and for his demonstration of the complexity of stabilization policy'
1977	Bertil G. Ohlin	b. 1899, Sweden (d. 1979)	BA, University of Lund, 1917	PhD, University of Stockholm, 1924	Stockholm School of Economics, Sweden	International Economics	'for their pathbreaking contribution to the theory of international trade and international capital movements'
	James E. Meade	b. 1907, UK (d. 1995)	BA, University of Oxford, 1930	MA, University of Oxford, 1933	University of Cambridge, UK		
1978	Herbert A. Simon	b.1916, USA (d. 2001)	BA, University of Chicago, 1936	PhD, University of Chicago, 1943	Carnegie-Mellon University, USA	Microeconomics	'for his pioneering research into the decision-making process within economic organizations'

Table 1 continued

Year of award	Laureate(s)	Year and country of birth; citizenship	First degree (university and year)	Higher degree (university and year)	Affiliation (at time of award)	Broad field of study	Prize citation (Nobel Foundation, 2004)
1979	**Theodore W. Schultz**	b. 1902, USA (d. 1998)	BA, South Dakota State College, 1926	PhD, University of Wisconsin, 1930	University of Chicago, USA	Development Economics	'for their pioneering research into economic development research with particular consideration of the problems of developing countries'
	W. Arthur Lewis	b. 1915, West Indies (d. 1991); UK citizen	BCom, London School of Economics, 1937	PhD, University of London, 1940	Princeton University, USA		
1980	**Lawrence R. Klein**	b. 1920, USA	BA, University of California, Berkeley, 1942	PhD, Massachusetts Institute of Technology, 1944	University of Pennsylvania, USA	Macroeconometrics	'for the creation of econometric models and their application to the analysis of economic fluctuations and economic policies'
1981	**James Tobin**	b. 1918, USA (d. 2002)	BA, Harvard University, 1939	PhD, Harvard University, 1947	Yale University, USA	Macroeconomics	'for his analysis of financial markets and their relations to expenditure decisions, employment, production and prices'

Year	Name	Birth/citizenship	Degree	Degree	Institution	Field	Citation
1982	George J. Stigler	b. 1911, USA (d. 1991)	BA, University of Washington, 1931	PhD, University of Chicago, 1938	University of Chicago, USA	Microeconomics	'for his seminal studies of industrial structures, functioning of markets and causes and effects of public regulation'
1983	Gerard Debreu	b. 1921, France; US citizen	Degree in Mathematics, University of Paris, 1946	DSc (Mathematics), University of Paris, 1956	University of California, Berkeley, USA	Microeconomics	'for having incorporated new analytical methods into economic theory and for his rigorous reformulation of the theory of general equilibrium'
1984	J. Richard N. Stone	b. 1913, UK (d. 1991)	BA, University of Cambridge, 1935	MA, University of Cambridge, 1938	University of Cambridge, UK	Methods of Economic Investigation	'for having made fundamental contributions to the development of systems of national accounts and hence greatly improved the basis for empirical economic analysis'
1985	Franco Modigliani	b. 1918, Italy (d. 2003); US citizen	Degree in Law, University of Rome, 1939	PhD, New School for Social Research, New York City, 1944	Massachusetts Institute of Technology, USA	Macroeconomics	'for his pioneering analyses of saving and of financial markets'

Table 1 continued

Year of award	Laureate(s)	Year and country of birth; citizenship	First degree (university and year)	Higher degree (university and year)	Affiliation (at time of award)	Broad field of study	Prize citation (Nobel Foundation, 2004)
1986	**James M. Buchanan**	b. 1919, USA	BA, Middle Tennessee State College, 1940	PhD, University of Chicago, 1948	George Mason University, USA	Public Economics	'for his development of the contractual and constitutional bases for the theory of economic and political decision-making'
1987	**Robert M. Solow**	b. 1924, USA	BA, Harvard University, 1947	PhD, Harvard University, 1951	Massachusetts Institute of Technology, USA	Economic Growth	'for his contributions to the theory of economic growth'
1988	**Maurice F.C. Allais**	b. 1911, France	Ancien élève, École Polytechnique, Paris, 1933	PhD (Engineering), University of Paris, 1949	École Nationale Supérieur des Mines de Paris, France	Microeconomics	'for his pioneering contributions to the theory of markets and efficient utilization of resources'
1989	**Trygve Haavelmo**	b. 1911, Norway (d. 1999)	Degree in Political Economy, University of Oslo, 1933	PhD, University of Oslo, 1946	University of Oslo, Norway	Econometrics	'for his clarification of the probability theory foundations of econometrics and his analyses of simultaneous economic structures'

Year	Name	Born	Degree	Degree	Institution	Field	Citation
1990	**Harry M. Markowitz**	b. 1927, USA	BPh (Liberal Arts), University of Chicago, 1947	PhD, University of Chicago, 1954	City University of New York, USA	Financial Economics	'for their pioneering work in the theory of financial economics'
	Merton H. Miller	b. 1923, USA (d. 2000)	BA, Harvard University, 1944	PhD, Johns Hopkins University, 1952	University of Chicago, USA		
	William F. Sharpe	b. 1934, USA	BA, University of California, Los Angeles, 1955	PhD, University of California, Los Angeles, 1961	Stanford University, USA		
1991	**Ronald H. Coase**	b. 1910, UK	B Com, University of London, 1932	PhD, University of London, 1951	University of Chicago, USA	Microeconomics	'for his discovery and clarification of the significance of transaction costs and property rights for the institutional structure and functioning of the economy'
1992	**Gary S. Becker**	b. 1930, USA	BA, Princeton University, 1951	PhD, University of Chicago, 1955	University of Chicago, USA	Microeconomics	'for having extended the domain of microeconomic analysis to a wide range of human behaviour and interaction, including nonmarket behaviour'

Table 1 continued

Year of award	Laureate(s)	Year and country of birth; citizenship	First degree (university and year)	Higher degree (university and year)	Affiliation (at time of award)	Broad field of study	Prize citation (Nobel Foundation, 2004)
1993	Robert W. Fogel	b. 1926, USA	BA, Cornell University, 1948	PhD, Johns Hopkins University, 1963	University of Chicago, USA	Economic History	'for having renewed research in economic history by applying economic theory and quantitative methods in order to explain economic and institutional change'
	Douglass C. North	b. 1920, USA	BA, University of California, Berkeley, 1942	PhD, University of California, Berkeley, 1952	Washington University, St Louis, USA		
1994	John C. Harsanyi	b. 1920, Hungary (d. 2000); US citizen	M Pharmacy, University of Budapest, 1944	PhD (Philosophy and Sociology) University of Budapest, 1947; PhD, Stanford University, 1958	University of California, Berkeley, USA	Microeconomics	'for their pioneering analysis of equilibria in the theory of non-cooperative games'
	John F. Nash Jr	b. 1928, USA	BS (Mathematics) Carnegie-Mellon University, 1948	PhD (Mathematics), Princeton University, 1950	Princeton University, USA		

Year	Name	Born			University	Field	Citation
	Reinhard Selten	b. 1930, Germany	MA (Maths), Johann-Wolfgang-Goethe University, Frankfurt, 1957	PhD (Maths), Johann-Wolfgang-Goethe University, Frankfurt, 1961	Rheinische Friedrich-Wilhelms-University, Bonn, Federal Republic of Germany		
1995	**Robert E. Lucas Jr**	b. 1937, USA	BA (History), University of Chicago, 1959	PhD, University of Chicago, 1964	University of Chicago, USA	Macroeconomics	'for having developed and applied the hypothesis of rational expectations, and thereby transformed macroeconomic analysis and deepened our understanding of economic policy'
1996	**James A. Mirrlees**	b. 1936, UK	MA (Maths), University of Edinburgh, 1957	PhD, University of Cambridge, 1963	University of Cambridge, UK	Microeconomics	'for their fundamental contributions to the economic theory of incentives under asymmetric information'
	William S. Vickrey	b. 1914, Canada (d. 1996); US citizen	BS (Maths), Yale University, 1935	PhD, Columbia University, 1948	Columbia University, USA		
1997	**Robert C. Merton**	b. 1944, USA	BS (Engineering and Maths), Columbia University, 1966	PhD, Massachusetts Institute of Technology, 1970	Harvard University, USA	Financial Economics	'for a new method to determine the value of derivatives'
	Myron S. Scholes	b. 1941, Canada; US citizen	BA, McMaster University, 1961	PhD, University of Chicago, 1969	Stanford University, USA		

Table 1 continued

Year of award	Laureate(s)	Year and country of birth; citizenship	First degree (university and year)	Higher degree (university and year)	Affiliation (at time of award)	Broad field of study	Prize citation (Nobel Foundation, 2004)
1998	**Amartya K. Sen**	b. 1933, India	BA, Calcutta University, 1953	PhD, University of Cambridge, 1959	University of Cambridge, UK	Microeconomics	'for his contributions to welfare economics'
1999	**Robert A. Mundell**	b. 1932, Canada	BA (Economics and Slavonic Studies), University of British Columbia, 1953	PhD (Industrial Economics), Massachusetts Institute of Technology, 1956	Columbia University, USA	Macroeconomics – International Economics	'for his analysis of monetary and fiscal policy under different exchange rate regimes and his analysis of optimum currency areas'
2000	**James J. Heckman**	b. 1944, USA	BA (Maths), Colorado College, 1965	PhD, Princeton University, 1971	University of Chicago, USA	Econometrics	'for his development of theory and methods for analysing selective samples'
	Daniel L. McFadden	b. 1937, USA	BS (Physics), University of Minnesota, 1957	PhD (Behavioural Science), University of Minnesota, 1962	University of California, Berkeley, USA		'for his development of theory and methods for analysing discrete choice'

Year	Name	Birth	BA	PhD	Institution	Field	Citation
2001	George A. Akerlof	b. 1940, USA	BA, Yale University, 1962	PhD, Massachusetts Institute of Technology, 1966	University of California, Berkeley, USA	Microeconomics	'for their analyses of markets with asymmetric information'
	A. Michael Spence	b. 1943, USA	BA (Philosophy), Princeton University, 1966	PhD, Harvard University, 1972	Stanford University, USA		
	Joseph E. Stiglitz	b. 1943, USA	BA, Amherst College, 1964	PhD, Massachusetts Institute of Technology, 1966	Columbia University, USA		
2002	Daniel Kahneman	b. 1934, Israel; US/Israeli citizen	BA (Psychology and Maths), Hebrew University, Jerusalem, 1954	PhD (Psychology), University of California, Berkeley, 1961	Princeton University, USA	Microeconomics	'for having integrated insights from psychological research into economic science, especially concerning human judgment and decision-making under uncertainty'
	Vernon L. Smith	b. 1927, USA	BSEE, California Institute of Technology, 1949	PhD, Harvard University, 1955	George Mason University, USA		'for having established laboratory experiments as a tool in empirical economic analysis, especially in the study of alternative market mechanisms'

Table 1 continued

Year of award	Laureate(s)	Year and country of birth; citizenship	First degree (university and year)	Higher degree (university and year)	Affiliation (at time of award)	Broad field of study	Prize citation (Nobel Foundation, 2004)
2003	Robert F. Engle	b. 1942, USA	BS (Physics), Williams College, 1964	PhD, Cornell University, 1969	New York University, USA	Econometrics	'for methods of analysing economic time series with time-varying volatility (ARCH)'
	Clive W.J. Granger	b. 1934, UK	BA (Maths), University of Nottingham, UK, 1955	PhD (Stats), University of Nottingham, UK, 1959	University of California, San Diego, USA		'for methods of analysing economic time series with common trends (cointegration)'
2004	Finn E. Kydland	b. 1943, Norway	Siviløkonom (Bus. Admin.), Norwegian School of Economics, 1968	PhD, Carnegie-Mellon University, 1973	Carnegie-Mellon University; University of California, Santa Barbara, USA	Macroeconomics	'for their contributions to dynamic macroeconomics: the time consistency of economic policy and the driving forces behind business cycles'
	Edward C. Prescott	b. 1940, USA	BA (Maths), Swarthmore College, 1962	PhD, Carnegie-Mellon University, 1967	Arizona State University, USA		

THE 1969 NOBEL MEMORIAL LAUREATES

RAGNAR FRISCH
AND
JAN TINBERGEN

Ragnar A.K. Frisch
(1895–1973)

© The Nobel Foundation

Ragnar Frisch was born in Oslo, Norway in 1895. Concurrent with an apprenticeship as a goldsmith, he studied economics at the University of Oslo and obtained a BA in 1919. In the early 1920s Frisch undertook studies in France and Great Britain, and after completing his dissertation in mathematical statistics was awarded a doctorate from the University of Oslo in 1926. In receipt of a Rockefeller Foundation Fellowship (1926–28) he travelled in the United States before becoming a lecturer at the University of Oslo (1928–29). He subsequently returned to America as a visiting professor at Yale University from 1930 to 1931.

In 1931 Frisch was appointed to the Chair of Economics at the University of Oslo and in 1932 became director of the newly created Institute for Social Economy at the university, posts he held until his retirement in 1965. During the 1930s, and the early postwar period, he was an adviser to the Norwegian Labour Party, and also periodically acted as an adviser to the governments of a number of developing countries, including India (1954–55) and Egypt (1957–64). In 1969 he was awarded, jointly with the Dutch economist Jan Tinbergen, the first Nobel Memorial Prize in Economics 'for having developed and applied dynamic models for the analysis of economic processes' (Nobel Foundation, 2004).

Ragnar Frisch is best known for his important contributions in three main areas, namely: econometrics, dynamic economic theory and economic planning. In the first area he contributed to the creation and development of econometrics (a term he coined in 1926) by applying mathematical and statistical methods to economic analysis. In 1930 he helped found the Econometric Society (see also entry on Tinbergen) and was president of the Society, and chief editor of the Society's journal *Econometrica* from 1933 to 1955. He focused his work on the problems that arise when statistical methods are applied to economic data, including the development of statistical confluence analysis (Frisch, 1934b) and what are now known as the problems of identification and multicollinearity. This pioneering work paved the way for subsequent research in the field and the development of econometrics as a science.

A second main area of research undertaken by Frisch, and the one for which he is perhaps best known, was his pioneering work in the field of dynamic economic theory, and in particular the development of dynamic models explaining business cycles. He contributed to the concepts in economic dynamics and his article 'On the Notion of Equilibrium and Disequilibrium' (Frisch, 1936b) became a classic. Another of Frisch's most important contributions was 'Propagation Problems and Impulse Problems in Dynamic Economics' (Frisch, 1933). In this paper he constructed the first macrodynamic model which simulated business cycles through the solution of an equation. His analysis included an explanation of how random shocks to the economy (both exogenously and endogenously generated) can be transformed into oscillations characteristic of business cycles.

The third main area of Frisch's research entailed the development of models for economic planning. In an early article, 'Circulation Planning' (Frisch, 1934a), he discussed the problem of reviving production and circulation in an economy experiencing a depression due to insufficient demand. From the 1950s onwards he developed 'decision models' which were based on input–output analysis and the use of linear and non-linear programming. His work in this field of study, which made an important contribution both to the literature on economic planning, and subsequent research, is reflected in publications such as *Planning for India: Selected Explorations in Methodology* (Frisch, 1960) and *Economic Planning Studies: A Collection of Essays* (Frisch, 1976).

In addition to his influential contributions to these three fields of study, Frisch also made important contributions to a number of other areas including: the theory of consumer behaviour (see, for example, Frisch, 1932); the theory of cost of living index numbers (Frisch, 1936a); production theory (see, for example, Frisch, 1965 – a book first published in Norwegian in 1962); and the development of the theory of national income accounting. His lasting impact on economics is even more remarkable when one considers that much of his wide-ranging work has never been published in English.

Main Published Works

(1932), *New Methods of Measuring Marginal Utility*, Tübingen: Mohr.

(1933), 'Propagation Problems and Impulse Problems in Dynamic Economics', in *Economic Essays in Honor of Gustav Cassel*, London: Allen & Unwin, pp. 171–205; reprinted in R.A. Gordon and L.R. Klein (eds) (1965), *Readings in Business Cycles*, Homewood, IL: R.D. Irwin, pp. 155–85 and in O. Bjerkholt (ed.) (1995), *Foundations of Modern Econometrics: The Selected Essays of Ragnar Frisch*, vol. 2, Aldershot: Edward Elgar, pp. 311–45.

(1934a), 'Circulation Planning', *Econometrica*, 2, July, pp. 258–336 and October, pp. 422–35; pp. 258–336 of the July issue of *Econometrica* are reprinted in O. Bjerkholt (ed.) (1995), *Foundations of Modern Econometrics: The Selected Essays of Ragnar Frisch*, vol. 1, Aldershot: Edward Elgar, pp. 360–438.

(1934b), *Statistical Confluence Analysis by Means of Complete Regression Systems*, Oslo: University Institute of Economics.

(1936a), 'Annual Survey of General Economic Theory: The Problem of Index Numbers', *Econometrica*, 4, January, pp. 1–38; reprinted in O. Bjerkholt (ed.) (1995), *Foundations of Modern Econometrics: The Selected Essays of Ragnar Frisch*, vol. 1, Aldershot: Edward Elgar, pp. 51–88.

(1936b), 'On the Notion of Equilibrium and Disequilibrium', *Review of Economic Studies*, 3, February, pp. 100–105; reprinted in O. Bjerkholt (ed.) (1995), *Foundations of Modern Econometrics: The Selected Essays of Ragnar Frisch*, vol. 1, Aldershot: Edward Elgar, pp. 454–9.

(1960), *Planning for India: Selected Explorations in Methodology*, Calcutta: Indian Statistical Institute.

(1965), *Theory of Production*, Dordrecht: D. Reidel.

(1966), *Maxima and Minima: Theory and Economic Applications*, Dordrecht: D. Reidel.

(1976), *Economic Planning Studies: A Collection of Essays* (ed. F. Long), Dordrecht: D. Reidel.

(1995), *Foundations of Modern Econometrics: The Selected Essays of Ragnar Frisch* (ed. O. Bjerkholt), 2 vols, Aldershot: Edward Elgar.

Secondary Literature

Arrow, K.J. (1960), 'The Work of Ragnar Frisch, Econometrician', *Econometrica*, **28**, April, pp. 175–92.

Johansen, L. (1969), 'Ragnar Frisch's Contributions to Economics', *Swedish Journal of Economics*, **71**, December, pp. 302–24.

See also Beaud and Dostaler (1997, pp. 238–41); Blaug (1998, pp. 73–4; 1999, p. 401); Cate (1997, pp. 195–7); Nobel Foundation (2004).

Jan Tinbergen
(1903–94)

© The Nobel Foundation

Jan Tinbergen was born in The Hague, Netherlands in 1903. He studied physics at the University of Leiden from 1922 to 1926 and obtained his doctorate in 1929 from the university with his thesis, 'Minimum Problems in Physics and Economics'. From 1929 to 1945 he worked as a statistician, studying business cycles, at the Dutch Central Bureau of Statistics, apart from a short spell from 1936 to 1938 working as an economist at the League of Nations in Geneva. As a part-time lecturer he taught statistics at the University of Amsterdam from 1931 and was a part-time Professor of Economic Science at the Netherlands School of Economics in Rotterdam (now the Erasmus University) from 1933 to 1955. In 1945 he was appointed director of the newly established Central Planning Bureau of the Dutch government in The Hague where he served until 1955. After a one-year teaching position as a visiting professor at Harvard University (1956–57), he held the post of Professor of Development Planning at the Netherlands School of Economics from 1957 to 1973 and subsequently became Professor of International Cooperation at the University of Leiden from 1973 to his retirement in 1975.

Tinbergen's many offices and honours included acting as a consultant and adviser to numerous governments of developing countries, the Organisation for Economic Cooperation and Development

(OECD), the World Bank and various United Nations agencies. From 1966 to 1975 he chaired the United Nations Committee for Development Planning. In 1969 he was awarded, jointly with the Norwegian economist Ragnar Frisch, the first Nobel Memorial Prize in Economics 'for having developed and applied dynamic models for the analysis of economic processes' (Nobel Foundation, 2004).

Tinbergen's principal contributions to economics roughly coincide with the focus of his work in the three main phases of his career. While working at the Dutch Central Bureau of Statistics and the League of Nations (1929–45), he contributed to the creation and development of econometrics as a science. In 1930 he participated with Irving Fisher and Ragnar Frisch in the creation of the Econometric Society (and served as its president in 1947), the main purpose of which is 'to promote studies that aim at a unification of the theoretical–quantitative and empirical–quantitative approach to economic problems and that are penetrated by constructive and rigorous thinking similar to that which has come to dominate in the natural sciences'. He constructed the first macroeconometric model of the Dutch economy, a model which contained 24 equations describing such key macroeconomic relationships as consumption and investment spending. This pioneering work on macroeconometric model building, initially published in Dutch in 1936, was subsequently translated into English (see Tinbergen, 1959, pp. 37–84). Tinbergen's approach to business cycle problems (Tinbergen, 1937) involved dynamic economic theory based on the cobweb theorem, which he discovered in 1930. In the latter case, Tinbergen was able to explain why prices and quantities often move in opposite directions in agricultural markets if output responds to prices with a time lag. While at the League of Nations, Tinbergen was asked to test the prevailing theories of the business cycle reviewed in Gottfried Haberler's (1937) book, *Prosperity and Depression*. His pioneering work resulted in the publication of a two-volume book (Tinbergen, 1939). The first volume was *A Method and Its Applications to Investment Activity*. In the second volume, *Business Cycles in the United States of America, 1919–1932*, he developed a 48-equation model of the US economy. Undaunted by criticism of his methods (see, for example, Keynes, 1939 and Tinbergen, 1940) and widespread scepticism of such model building at the time, he went on to build a similar model for the UK economy (Tinbergen, 1951).

On his appointment as director of the Central Planning Bureau at the end of the Second World War the main focus of Tinbergen's work shifted to the problem of economic policy making. At the Bureau he helped develop a model of the Dutch economy which provided the basis for economic forecasting and advice to the government as to how policy instruments should be set to achieve the chosen targets of economic policy in the Netherlands. In addition, his work on the theoretical problems of policy making resulted in the publication of three important books (Tinbergen, 1952; 1954; 1956), the most influential of which is his 1952 work *On the Theory of Economic Policy*. The central message of Tinbergen's approach to the formulation of macroeconomic policy is that to simultaneously achieve a given number of independent policy objectives (such as full employment and a stable price level) policy makers need at least the same number of independent (effective) policy instruments (such as government expenditure and the money supply). This insight is popularly known as 'Tinbergen's rule'. Overall, this work undertaken in the second phase (1945–55) of his career provided the foundation for what became the conventional approach to economic policy in the 1950s and 1960s.

In the final phase of his career, from the mid-1950s to his retirement in 1975, he once again shifted the focus of his work, this time to the problems of development planning, particularly in underdeveloped countries and international economic cooperation. Tinbergen's work on planning for long-term development is documented in a series of books which include *The Design of Development* (1958) and *Development Planning* (1967). He sought to find solutions to the policy problems of poor countries and called for a reshaping of the international order (Tinbergen, 1962a; Tinbergen et al. 1976). His retirement coincided with the publication of a book (Tinbergen, 1975) seeking to analyse the causes of changes in the distribution of income over time and policies to reduce income inequality.

In addition to his pioneering work on econometric modelling, in particular the macroeconomic modelling of business cycles, the theory of economic policy and development planning, Tinbergen also made important contributions to a number of other fields of economics including economic growth (Tinbergen and Bos, 1962b) and education (Tinbergen and Bos, 1965), to name but two. He continued to write long after his retirement and had books published when he was in his 80s (see for example, Tinbergen, 1985; 1990).

Main Published Works

(1937), *An Econometric Approach to Business Cycle Problems*, Paris: Hermann & Compagnie.

(1939), *Statistical Testing of Business Cycle Theories*, 2 vols, Geneva: League of Nations.

(1940), 'On a Method of Statistical Business Cycle Research: A Reply', *Economic Journal*, **50**, March, pp. 141–54.

(1951), *Business Cycles in the United Kingdom, 1870–1914*, Amsterdam: North-Holland.

(1952), *On the Theory of Economic Policy*, Amsterdam: North-Holland.

(1954), *Centralization and Decentralization in Economic Policy*, Amsterdam: North-Holland.

(1956), *Economic Policy: Principles and Design*, Amsterdam: North-Holland.

(1958), *The Design of Development*, Baltimore, MD: Johns Hopkins University Press.

(1959), *Selected Papers* (eds L.H. Klaassen, L.M. Koyck and H.J. Witteveen), Amsterdam: North-Holland.

(1962a), *Shaping the World Economy: Suggestions for an International Economic Policy*, New York: Twentieth Century Fund.

(1962b), *Mathematical Models of Economic Growth* (with H.C. Bos), New York: McGraw-Hill.

(1965), *Econometric Models of Education* (with H.C. Bos), Paris: OECD.

(1967), *Development Planning*, New York: McGraw-Hill.

(1975), *Income Distribution: Analysis and Policies*, Amsterdam: North-Holland.

(1976), *Reshaping the International Order: A Report to the Club of Rome* (ed. with A.J. Dolman and J.V. Ettinger), New York: E.P. Dutton.

(1985), *Production, Income and Welfare: The Search for an Optimal Social Order*, Lincoln, NB: University of Nebraska Press.

(1990), *World Security and Equity*, Aldershot: Edward Elgar.

Secondary Literature

Haberler, G. (1937), *Prosperity and Depression*, Cambridge, MA: Harvard University Press.

Hansen, B. (1969), 'Jan Tinbergen: An Appraisal of His Contributions to Economics', *Swedish Journal of Economics*, **71**, December, pp. 325–36.

Keynes, J.M. (1939), 'Professor Tinbergen's Method', *Economic Journal*, **49**, September, pp. 306–18.

See also Beaud and Dostaler (1997, pp. 428–31); Blaug (1998, pp. 281–4; 1999, p. 1103); Nobel Foundation (2004); Pressman (1999, pp. 132–6).

THE 1970 NOBEL MEMORIAL LAUREATE
PAUL SAMUELSON

Paul A. Samuelson
(b. 1915)

© The Nobel Foundation

Paul Samuelson was born in Gary, Indiana, USA in 1915. As an undergraduate he studied under such leading economists of the time as Frank Knight (1885–1972) and Jacob Viner (1892–1970) at the University of Chicago, from where he received his BA in 1935. He moved to Harvard University to undertake graduate work and was awarded an MA in 1936 and a PhD in 1941. Samuelson's doctoral dissertation won Harvard's prestigious David A. Wells Prize. In 1940 he joined Massachusetts Institute of Technology (MIT) as an Assistant Professor of Economics and was subsequently promoted to Associate Professor in 1944 and Professor of Economics in 1947, at the age of 32. In 1966 he became an institute professor and, following his retirement in 1986, he is currently Institute Professor of Economics, Emeritus, at MIT. In addition to his academic career, Samuelson has also served as an adviser to the National Resources Planning Board (1941–43), the United States Treasury (1945–52, 1961–74), the Council of Economic Advisers (1960–68) and, since 1965, the Federal Reserve Board.

Samuelson's many offices and honours include: the award of the first John Bates Clark Medal of the American Economic Association in 1947; presidencies of the Econometric Society in 1952, the American Economic Association in 1961 and the International Economic

Association from 1965 to 1968; and the award of the National Medal of Science in 1996. In 1970, Samuelson was the first American to be awarded the Nobel Memorial Prize in Economics 'for the scientific work through which he has developed static and dynamic economic theory and actively contributed to raising the level of analysis in economic science' (Nobel Foundation, 2004).

Samuelson is widely acknowledged as being one of the greatest economic theorists of the twentieth century. His contributions to the discipline span, quite remarkably, nearly every branch within economics, as exemplified by the contents of the five volumes of his *Collected Scientific Papers* (Samuelson, 1966; 1972; 1977; 1986), which contain 388 publications. Rather than attempt the almost impossible task of surveying the depth and breadth of his scientific work, in what follows we merely sketch *some* of his main contributions to the fields of consumer theory, international trade theory and macroeconomics.

In one of his earliest published papers, which he wrote when he was a graduate student at Harvard University, Samuelson (1938) demonstrated that the demand curve could be derived from observing actual purchases in markets. As such, the household 'revealed' its preferences on the basis of its observable market behaviour. In the field of consumer theory, Samuelson's notion of 'revealed preferences' (see also Samuelson, 1948b) has allowed empirical studies of observable market behaviour to become much more closely integrated with theoretical designs, such as utility maximisation.

In international trade theory, Samuelson has made a number of important contributions, including an analysis of the gains from international trade between two countries (Samuelson, 1939b), and the effects of tariffs on the distribution of income (Stolper and Samuelson, 1941) whereby, according to the so-called 'Stolper–Samuelson theorem', protectionist trade policies raise the real wages of a country's scarce factor of production. Using the framework developed by Heckscher and Ohlin (see entry for Ohlin in this volume), Samuelson has also demonstrated the conditions under which international trade results in the equalisation of factor prices between trading countries – an analysis which has come to be known as the 'factor price equalization theorem'.

The third area we have chosen to illustrate some of Samuelson's central contributions to economics concerns the field of macroeconomics. Here three examples will suffice. First, in an article published in the *Review of Economic Statistics* in 1939, he analysed the 'Interactions Between the Multiplier Analysis and the Principle of Acceleration' (Samuelson, 1939a) and was thereby able to explain the nature of short-term fluctuations associated with the Keynesian approach to the business cycle – an approach subsequently developed further by Hicks (see entry in this volume). Second, in another article on this topic published in the *Journal of Political Economy* later in the same year (Samuelson, 1939c), he introduced the Keynesian cross-diagram, or what has also come to be known as the Keynesian 45-degree line model. The cross-diagram has come to be the standard tool used for teaching first-year undergraduates the Keynesian theory of income determination. Third, in a paper published in the *American Economic Review* in 1960, which was co-authored with Robert Solow (see entry in this volume), he introduced the Phillips curve to the United States by considering the relationship between the rate of wage increase and unemployment for American data.

In addition to making significant contributions to these three fields of study, Samuelson has also offered important insights into other areas including: public economics (for example, his 1954 *Review of Economics and Statistics* paper, 'The Pure Theory of Public Expenditure', in which he analysed the optimal allocation of resources given the presence of private and public goods, rigorously defining the characteristics of public goods); capital theory (for example, Samuelson, 1958a, in which he presented an overlapping generations model); and the theory of economic growth (for example, his article with Robert Solow, 'Balanced Growth under Constant Returns to Scale', Solow and Samuelson, 1953).

Samuelson's fame derives not only from the publication of numerous scientific papers in top-ranked journals but also from the publication of three highly influential books. His magnum opus, *Foundations of Economic Analysis*, was published in 1947. In this path-breaking book, which was based on his 1941 Harvard PhD dissertation, Samuelson, using mathematical analysis, demonstrated how economic behaviour could be understood as maximisation or minimisation under constraints. This book further revolutionised the study of economics by integrating comparative statics and dynamics and by developing dynamic stability analysis. His seminal 1939 article on the interaction between the multiplier and the accelerator provides a good example of such analysis. In 1958, Samuelson produced *Linear Programming and Economic Analysis*, co-authored with Robert Dorfman and Robert Solow (1958b). This classic book utilised optimisation techniques to integrate price theory and growth theory, and also christened the 'turnpike theorem', which defines conditions for providing an optimal growth path with the highest rate of growth. One indicator of the influence of these two books has been the subsequent increased use of mathematical analysis across the economics profession and the manner in which instructors at the graduate level have increasingly come to employ linear algebra and the mathematics of differential and integral calculus.

The third highly influential book is Samuelson's introductory textbook *Economics* (Samuelson, 1948c), which was first published in 1948. The book, which has been revised approximately every three years and which, since the twelfth edition in 1985, has been co-authored with William D. Nordhaus, reached its eighteenth edition in 2004, and has been translated into more than 40 languages. Among the then-notable features of earlier editions of the book, its first edition included the Keynesian cross-diagram, while the concepts of the 'neoclassical synthesis' and the Phillips curve were introduced in the third and fifth editions published in 1955 and 1961, respectively.

Samuelson's place as one of the greatest theorists who has ever lived is steadfastly assured. He has contributed fundamental insights in nearly every major area of economic theory and has raised the level of scientific and mathematical analysis in economics. Having written what is almost certainly the world's most famous introductory textbook and contributed a regular column in *Newsweek* over the period from 1966 to 1981, Samuelson has done more than most to raise public awareness of his discipline.

Main Published Works

(1938), 'A Note on the Pure Theory of Consumer Behaviour', *Economica*, 5, February, pp. 61–71.

(1939a), 'Interactions Between the Multiplier Analysis and the Principle of Acceleration', *Review of Economic Statistics*, 21, May, pp. 75–8.

(1939b), 'The Gains from International Trade', *Canadian Journal of Economics and Political Sciences*, 5, May, pp. 195–205.

(1939c), 'A Synthesis of the Principle of Acceleration and the Multiplier', *Journal of Political Economy*, 47, December, pp. 786–97.

(1941), 'Protection and Real Wages' (with W.F. Stolper), *Review of Economic Studies*, 9, November, pp. 58–73.

(1947), *Foundations of Economic Analysis*, Cambridge, MA: Harvard University Press; enlarged edition published by Harvard University Press in 1983.

(1948a), 'International Trade and the Equalisation of Factor Prices', *Economic Journal*, **58**, June, pp. 163–84.

(1948b), 'Consumer Theory in Terms of Revealed Preferences', *Economica*, **15**, November, pp. 243–53.

(1948c), *Economics: An Introductory Analysis*, New York: McGraw-Hill.

(1953), 'Balanced Growth under Constant Returns to Scale' (with R.M. Solow), *Econometrica*, **21**, July, pp. 412–24.

(1954), 'The Pure Theory of Public Expenditure', *Review of Economics and Statistics*, **36**, November, pp. 387–9.

(1958a), 'An Exact Consumption-Loan Model of Interest With or Without the Social Contrivance of Money', *Journal of Political Economy*, **66**, December, pp. 467–82.

(1958b), *Linear Programming and Economic Analysis* (with R. Dorfman and R.M. Solow), New York: McGraw-Hill.

(1960), 'Analytical Aspects of Anti-Inflation Policy' (with R.M. Solow), *American Economic Review*, **50**, May, pp. 177–94.

(1966), *The Collected Scientific Papers of Paul A. Samuelson*, vols 1 and 2 (ed. J.E. Stiglitz), Cambridge, MA: MIT Press.

(1972), *The Collected Scientific Papers of Paul A. Samuelson*, vol. 3 (ed. R.C. Merton), Cambridge, MA: MIT Press.

(1977), *The Collected Scientific Papers of Paul A. Samuelson*, vol. 4 (ed. H. Nagatani and K. Crowley), Cambridge, MA: MIT Press.

(1986), *The Collected Scientific Papers of Paul A. Samuelson*, vol. 5 (ed. K. Crowley), Cambridge, MA: MIT Press.

Secondary Literature

Lindbeck, A. (1970), 'Paul Anthony Samuelson's Contributions to Economics', *Swedish Journal of Economics*, **72**, December, pp. 342–54.

Skousen, M. (1997), 'The Perseverance of Paul Samuelson's *Economics*', *Journal of Economic Perspectives*, **11**, Spring, pp. 137–52.

See also Beaud and Dostaler (1997, pp. 393–6); Blaug (1998, pp. 247–50; 1999, pp. 976–7); Cate (1997, pp. 560–62); Nobel Foundation (2004); Pressman (1999, pp. 162–6); Snowdon and Vane (2002, pp. 644–9).

THE 1971 NOBEL MEMORIAL LAUREATE

SIMON KUZNETS

© The Nobel Foundation

Simon S. Kuznets
(1901–85)

Simon Kuznets was born in Pinsk, Russia in 1901. After emigrating to the United States in 1922 (later becoming a US citizen), he studied economics at Columbia University where he obtained his BA (1923), MA (1924) and PhD (1926). In 1927 he joined the National Bureau of Economic Research (NBER) where he was a member of the research staff until 1961. During his career Kuznets held chairs at three universities. In 1930 he joined the teaching staff at the University of Pennsylvania and was subsequently appointed Professor of Economics and Statistics at the university, a position he held from 1936 to 1954. His period at the University of Pennsylvania was temporarily interrupted during the Second World War, when he became associate director of the Bureau of Planning and Statistics of the US War Production Board from 1942 to 1944. In 1954 he moved from the University of Pennsylvania to Johns Hopkins University, where he held the post of Professor of Political Economy from 1954 to 1960. Moving again, this time to Harvard University in 1960, he held the position of Professor of Economics until his retirement in 1971.

Among his many offices and honours, Kuznets was elected president of the American Statistical Association in 1949 and the American Economic Association in 1954. In 1971, he was awarded the

Nobel Memorial Prize in Economics 'for his empirically founded interpretation of economic growth which has led to new and deepened insight into the economic and social structure and process of development' (Nobel Foundation, 2004).

Kuznets's main contributions to economics roughly coincide with the focus of his work in the three main periods of his life. In the prewar period, working at the NBER, he became best known for his pioneering work measuring the size of, and changes in, national income and its principal components (such as consumption, saving and investment) in the United States over extended periods. Founded in 1920, the NBER is a private, non-profit, non-partisan research organisation whose aim is 'to promote a greater understanding of how the economy works' by 'understanding and disseminating unbiased economic research among policymakers, business professionals, and the academic community' (National Bureau of Economic Research, 2004). At the time Kuznets joined the Bureau in 1927, its director was Wesley Mitchell, who had supervised Kuznets's doctoral dissertation on cyclical fluctuations in retail and wholesale trade (Kuznets, 1926). At the Bureau, Kuznets was responsible for producing estimates of national income in the United States, initially dating back to 1929, then 1919 and eventually back to 1869. His research results, published in a series of influential books (Kuznets, 1934; 1937; 1938; 1946a; Kuznets et al., 1941; 1946b), provided a wealth of time-series and cross-section data for economists and econometricians to test various elements of the Keynesian revolution in macroeconomic thought. Interestingly, Kuznets's (Kuznets et al., 1946b) findings that in the long run the average propensity to consume in the United States had not changed significantly since 1869 contradicted Keynes's view, embodied in the absolute income hypothesis, that the relationship between consumption and income is non-proportional. This led to subsequent attempts to reconcile seemingly conflicting evidence from various types of study in terms of a unified theory, including the relative income, permanent income and life-cycle hypotheses associated with, respectively, James Duesenberry, Milton Friedman and Franco Modigliani.

In the postwar period, Kuznets switched the main focus of his research to the study of modern economic growth. In a series of books (Kuznets, 1959; 1961; 1964; 1965; 1966; 1968; 1971; Kuznets and Thomas, 1957) he examined the characteristics and determinants of economic growth both in the United States and in a number of other major industrial countries. Part of this work involved an interpretation of the relationship between cycles and trends, which he had already examined in earlier research (Kuznets, 1930; 1933). Kuznets (1930) identified 15–20 year-long cycles of economic fluctuations, which subsequently came to be referred to in the literature as the 'Kuznets cycle', a term coined by Arthur Lewis. Kuznets identified a number of contributory factors to the process of economic growth including: population change, structural change, technological advance, the role of capital formation, changes in the quality of the labour force and changes in the political and social fabric. In particular, he emphasised the significance of technological advance as a major contributory factor to increased productivity and economic growth. His books, *Modern Economic Growth* (Kuznets, 1966) and the *Economic Growth of Nations* (Kuznets, 1971) – a comparative study of economic growth of different countries – together provide a survey of his main research findings in this area.

Following his retirement in 1971, Kuznets again redirected the main focus of his research, this time to the fields of population and income distribution (Kuznets, 1973; 1979). In the former case he focused much of his writing on the relationship between population growth and economic development. In the latter he concentrated his analysis on the relationship between income inequalities and economic development. This involved an extension of earlier work undertaken in the 1950s (Kuznets, 1955 – his presidential address to the American Economic Association; Kuznets and Jenks, 1953) which examined the connection between changes in the distribution of income and business cycles and economic growth. His finding that income inequality increases in the early stages of economic development as income per capita levels rise, then levels off, before it decreases in the later stages of economic development has become popularly known as the 'Kuznets inverse-U relationship'. His final book, *Economic Development, the Family and Income Distribution*, (Kuznets, 1989), was published after his death in 1985.

Above all else, Kuznets will be remembered for the approach which informed all his research: the detailed and careful gathering, measurement and interpretation of statistical data relevant to understanding the process of social and economic change.

Main Published Works

(1926), *Cyclical Fluctuations: Retail and Wholesale Trade, United States, 1919–1925*, New York: Adelphi.

(1930), *Secular Movements in Production and Prices: Their Nature and their Bearing upon Cyclical Fluctuations*, Boston, MA: Houghton Mifflin.

(1933), *Seasonal Variations in Industry and Trade*, New York: National Bureau of Economic Research.

(1934), *National Income, 1929–1932*, New York: National Bureau of Economic Research.

(1937), *National Income and Capital Formation, 1919–1935*, New York: National Bureau of Economic Research.

(1938), *Commodity Flow and Capital Formation*, New York: National Bureau of Economic Research.

(1941), *National Income and its Composition, 1919–1938* (with E. Jenks and L. Epstein), New York: National Bureau of Economic Research.

(1946a), *National Income: A Summary of Findings*, New York: National Bureau of Economic Research.

(1946b), *National Product since 1869* (with E. Jenks and L. Epstein), New York: National Bureau of Economic Research.

(1953), *Shares of Upper Income Groups in Income and Savings* (with E. Jenks), New York: National Bureau of Economic Research.

(1955), 'Economic Growth and Income Inequality', *American Economic Review*, **45**, March, pp. 1–28.

(1957), *Population Redistribution and Economic Growth: United States, 1870–1950* (ed. with D.S. Thomas), Philadelphia, PA: American Philosophical Society.

(1959), *Six Lectures on Economic Growth*, Glencoe, IL: Free Press.

(1961), *Capital in the American Economy: Its Formation and Financing*, Princeton, NJ: Princeton University Press.

(1964), *Postwar Economic Growth: Four Lectures*, Cambridge, MA: Harvard University Press.

(1965), *Economic Growth and Structure: Selected Essays*, New York: W.W. Norton.

(1966), *Modern Economic Growth: Rate, Structure and Spread*, New Haven, CT: Yale University Press.

(1968), *Toward a Theory of Economic Growth: With Reflections on the Economic Growth of Modern Nations*, New York: W.W. Norton.

(1971), *Economic Growth of Nations: Total Output and Production Structure*, Cambridge, MA: Harvard University Press.

(1973), *Population, Capital and Growth: Selected Essays*, New York: W.W. Norton.

(1979), *Growth, Population and Income Distribution: Selected Essays*, New York: W.W. Norton.

(1989), *Economic Development, the Family and Income Distribution: Selected Essays*, Cambridge: Cambridge University Press.

Secondary Literature

Kapuria-Foreman, V. and M. Perlman (1995), 'An Economic Historian's Economist: Remembering Simon Kuznets', *Economic Journal*, **105**, November, pp. 1524–47.

Lundberg, E. (1971), 'Simon Kuznets' Contribution to Economics', *Swedish Journal of Economics*, **73**, December, pp. 444–61.

See also   Beaud and Dostaler (1997, pp. 307–9); Blaug (1998, pp. 146–8; 1999, p. 643); Cate (1997, pp. 358–60); Nobel Foundation (2004); Pressman (1999, pp. 120–24).

THE 1972 NOBEL MEMORIAL LAUREATES

JOHN HICKS
AND
KENNETH ARROW

John R. Hicks
(1904–89)

John Hicks was born in Warwick, England in 1904. As an undergraduate he attended Balliol College, Oxford where he first studied mathematics before switching to study philosophy, politics and economics. He graduated with a BA in 1925. After a year of graduate work at Balliol College, Hicks joined the London School of Economics (LSE) in 1926 as a Lecturer in Economics. In 1935 he moved to a lectureship at Cambridge University and a fellowship of Gonville and Caius College. After three years at Cambridge he left in 1938 to take up the Stanley Jevons professorship at the University of Manchester, where he remained until 1946. Hicks returned to Oxford in 1946 where he was a research fellow of Nuffield College, and then Drummond Professor of Political Economy and fellow of All Souls College from 1952 until he retired in 1965.

Among his many offices and honours, Hicks became a fellow of the British Academy in 1942, was president of the Royal Economic Society from 1960 to 1962, and was knighted in 1964. In 1972 he was awarded, jointly with the American economist Kenneth Arrow, the Nobel Memorial Prize in Economics 'for their pioneering contributions to general economic equilibrium theory and welfare theory' (Nobel Foundation, 2004).

Over the course of his distinguished academic career, Hicks made numerous influential contributions to the broad fields of both microeconomics and macroeconomics. In his first book *The Theory of Wages*, published in 1932, he presented a marginal productivity theory of distribution and introduced the concept of the elasticity of substitution to show that labour-saving technical progress will not necessarily reduce labour's relative share of the national income. If the elasticity of substitution between the two inputs of labour and capital is large then, following labour-saving technical progress, labour will increase its relative income share. Two years later in a brace of articles published in *Economica*, which he co-authored with the mathematician Roy Allen, Hicks (1934) used indifference curve analysis, rather than the then-dominant marginal utility theory, to explain consumer behaviour. Furthermore, using indifference curves and a budget line, he and Allen were able to separate the substitution and income effects of a price change. Their analysis is now used as a standard diagrammatic tool in the teaching of intermediate undergraduate microeconomics.

Hicks's most acclaimed work is undoubtedly his 1939 book *Value and Capital* (Hicks, 1939a), which he divided into four parts: 'The Theory of Subjective Value' (Chapters 1–3); 'General Equilibrium' (Chapters 4–8); 'The Foundations of Dynamic Economics' (Chapters 9–14); and 'The Working of the Dynamic System' (Chapters 15–24). In this book, Hicks constructed a complete economic equilibrium model and in doing so he became one of the first to introduce Walrasian general equilibrium analysis, an approach which has come to rival and, in some areas, displace the once-dominant Marshallian partial equilibrium analysis in economic theory. In addition to his pioneering contributions to general equilibrium theory, Hicks's Nobel Memorial citation includes specific reference to his pioneering contributions to welfare theory. This work is reflected in a series of papers, which followed the publication of 'Foundations of Welfare Economics' in the *Economic Journal* in 1939 (Hicks, 1939c) and its application to social accounting (for example, in his 1942 textbook, *The Social Framework*). Among his most influential contributions to welfare theory are the so-called 'Hicks–Kaldor compensation test', and his refinement of the concept of consumer surplus (see Hicks, 1956). In the former case, Hicks and Nicholas Kaldor (1908–86) devised a compensation criterion for welfare change. The test is positive if, following some particular economic change, those who gain can compensate the losers and still be better off than they were before the change. In the latter case, the concept of consumer surplus can be defined as the difference between the highest price a consumer would be willing to pay for a good and the price he/she would pay for the good. Both the compensation test and Hicks's definition of the concept of consumer surplus have come to be important tools in cost–benefit analysis.

Although Hicks first gained international recognition for his work in the field of microeconomics, he also made a number of important contributions to macroeconomics. Foremost among these is his celebrated 1937 *Econometrica* article entitled 'Mr. Keynes and the "Classics": A Suggested Interpretation', one of the most cited and reprinted papers in macroeconomics. In the article he introduced the IS–LL diagram, subsequently labelled the now famous IS–LM diagram by Alvin Hansen (1887–1975). The IS and LM curves trace out a locus of combinations of the interest rate and income associated with equilibrium in the goods and money markets, respectively. Equilibrium in both markets is simultaneously attained where the two curves intersect. In this article, Hicks used the diagram to explain the conflict between Keynes's *General Theory* (published in 1936) and what Keynes referred to as 'classical economics' in terms of different beliefs about the slopes of the two curves. The IS–LM diagram came to dominate the teaching of Keynesian economics above the introductory level and still occupies a space, more than 65 years after its invention, in most intermediate macroeconomics textbooks.

While the IS–LL diagram is Hicks's most famous innovation in macroeconomics, he also made a number of other important contributions. Three examples will suffice. First, in a 1935 article in *Economica*, 'A Suggestion for Simplifying the Theory of Money', he applied portfolio theory to the demand for money involving a choice-theoretic approach. Second, his discussion of the theory of interest in much of his work (see, for example, Chapters 11–13 of *Value and Capital*) acted as a catalyst to subsequent research on the term structure of interest rates. Third, in his 1950 book, *A Contribution to the Theory of the Trade Cycle*, Hicks developed the ideas of the British economist Roy Harrod (1900–1978) on growth and cycle theory, and the interaction of the multiplier and accelerator, by introducing a ceiling and floor which constrained the problem of instability in the form of explosiveness and accounted for turning points in the cycle.

In addition to his work in microeconomics and macroeconomics, Hicks also contributed to other fields of study including: growth theory (for example, Hicks, 1965, in which he developed the concepts of and distinction between 'fix-price' and 'flex-price' markets – see also Hicks, 1974) and capital theory (for example, Hicks, 1973, in which he considered a neo-Austrian approach to capital theory); as well as co-authoring works on public finance with his wife Ursula (for example, Hicks and Hicks, 1939b), who was also an economist.

Hicks will be remembered as one of the most influential and outstanding economic theorists of the twentieth century. His work has had a profound influence on the content and direction of contemporary economic theory and the concepts and diagrams he developed have become an integral part of the toolkit used by economists today. His *Collected Essays on Economic Theory* have been gathered together in three volumes: 'Wealth and Welfare'; 'Money, Interest and Wages'; and 'Classics and Moderns' (Hicks, 1981; 1982; 1983).

Main Published Works

(1932), *The Theory of Wages*, London: Macmillan; expanded edition published in 1963.

(1934), 'A Reconsideration of the Theory of Value' (with R.D.G. Allen), *Economica*, **1**, February and May, pp. 52–76 and 196–219.

(1935), 'A Suggestion for Simplifying the Theory of Money', *Economica*, **2**, February, pp. 1–19.

(1937), 'Mr. Keynes and the "Classics": A Suggested Interpretation', *Econometrica*, **5**, April, pp. 147–59.

(1939a), *Value and Capital: An Inquiry into Some Fundamental Principles of Economic Theory*, Oxford: Clarendon Press; 2nd edn 1946.

(1939b), 'Public Finance in the National Income' (with U.K. Hicks), *Review of Economic Studies*, **6**, February, pp. 147–55.

(1939c), 'The Foundations of Welfare Economics', *Economic Journal*, **49**, December, pp. 696–712.

(1942), *The Social Framework: An Introduction to Economics*, Oxford: Clarendon Press.

(1950), *A Contribution to the Theory of the Trade Cycle*, Oxford: Clarendon Press.

(1956), *A Revision of Demand Theory*, Oxford: Clarendon Press.

(1965), *Capital and Growth*, Oxford: Oxford University Press.

(1973), *Capital and Time: A Neo-Austrian Theory*, Oxford: Clarendon Press.

(1974), *The Crisis in Keynesian Economics*, Oxford: Basil Blackwell.

(1981), *Collected Essays on Economic Theory*, vol. 1, Oxford: Basil Blackwell.

(1982), *Collected Essays on Economic Theory*, vol. 2, Oxford: Basil Blackwell.

(1983), *Collected Essays on Economic Theory*, vol. 3, Oxford: Basil Blackwell.

Secondary Literature

Baumol, W.J. (1972), 'John R. Hicks' Contribution to Economics', *Swedish Journal of Economics*, **74**, December, pp. 503–27.

Hagemann, H. and O.F. Hamouda (eds) (1994), *The Legacy of Hicks: His Contributions to Economic Analysis*, London: Routledge.

Hamouda, O.F. (1993), *John R. Hicks: The Economist's Economist*, Oxford: Basil Blackwell.

Klamer, A. (1989), 'An Accountant Among Economists: Conversations with Sir John R. Hicks', *Journal of Economic Perspectives*, **3**, Fall, pp. 167–80.

See also   Beaud and Dostaler (1997, pp. 273–6); Blaug (1998, pp. 105–8; 1999, pp. 530–31); Cate (1997, pp. 241–4); Nobel Foundation (2004); Pressman (1999, pp. 136–41); Snowdon and Vane (2002, pp. 322–6).

Kenneth J. Arrow
(b. 1921)

© The Nobel Foundation

Kenneth Arrow was born in New York City, USA in 1921. As an undergraduate he studied mathematics at the City College of New York, from where he graduated with a BSc in 1940. Arrow undertook graduate work at Columbia University where he was awarded an MA in mathematics in 1941 and a PhD in 1951. His graduate schooling was, however, interrupted by wartime service in the US Army Air Corps from 1942 to 1946. After the Second World War Arrow worked, from 1946 to 1949, as a research associate at the Cowles Commission for Research in Economics at the University of Chicago, and was appointed Assistant Professor of Economics at Chicago in 1948. In 1949 he moved to Stanford University where he was promoted, in 1953, from Assistant Professor of Economics and Statistics, to Professor of Economics, Statistics and Operations Research. In 1968 he accepted an appointment as Professor of Economics at Harvard University, where he remained before returning to Stanford in 1979 as Joan Kenney Professor of Economics and Professor of Operations Research. Arrow retired in 1991, since when he has been Professor, Emeritus, at Stanford University.

Among his many offices and honours Arrow was awarded the John Bates Clark Medal of the American Economic Association in 1957 and the John von Neumann Theory Prize of ORSA/TIMS in

1986; served as president of the Econometric Society in 1956, the Institute of Management Sciences in 1963, the American Economic Association in 1973, and the International Economic Association from 1983 to 1986; and was a member of the US Council of Economic Advisers in 1962. In 1972 Arrow was awarded, jointly with the British economist John Hicks, the Nobel Memorial Prize in Economics 'for their pioneering contributions to general economic equilibrium theory and welfare theory' (Nobel Foundation, 2004).

Arrow is best known for his contributions to the fields of social choice and general equilibrium theory. His most famous and frequently cited work is his 1951 book *Social Choice and Individual Values* (Arrow, 1951a), which is based on his doctoral thesis. In this work, Arrow generalised Condorcet's voting paradox (named after the eighteenth-century French politician) to show that it is impossible to derive a voting rule that allows rational individual preferences to be translated into rational social preferences or choices.

Table 2   Voting paradox

Voter	Preference		
	1	2	3
A	X	Y	Z
B	Y	Z	X
C	Z	X	Y

Arrow's so-called 'impossibility theorem' can be illustrated as follows. Suppose there are three individuals A, B and C whose preferences between three options are summarised in Table 2. Reference to the table reveals that A prefers X to Y and Y to Z; B prefers Y to Z and Z to X; while C prefers Z to X and X to Y. In this situation a majority (two out of three voters, namely A and C) prefer X to Y. A majority (two out of three voters, namely A and B) prefer Y to Z. Unfortunately a majority do not prefer X to Z, as voters B and C prefer Z to X. What emerges under the democratic method of majority choice is a stalemate. In other words, Arrow demonstrated that it is impossible to aggregate an individual's rational choices to produce an unambiguous, consistent social choice. Studying the consequences of Arrow's impossibility theorem has resulted in much subsequent work both in political theory and in welfare economics. In the latter case the reader should refer to the entry on Amartya Sen, the 1998 Nobel Memorial Laureate, in this volume.

Arrow's other main contribution to economics concerns his pioneering work on the existence, stability and optimality of general equilibrium systems. In his 1951 Berkeley Symposium paper, 'An Extension of the Basic Theorems of Classical Welfare Economics' (Arrow, 1951b), he showed that general (market) equilibrium states are Pareto optimal and that Pareto-optimal states can be obtained by achieving general (market) equilibrium. More importantly, in his seminal 1954 *Econometrica* paper, co-written with Gerard Debreu (see entry in this volume), on the 'Existence of an Equilibrium for a Competitive Economy', Arrow produced a rigorous and definitive mathematical proof of the existence of general equilibrium in a model of a market economy. Arrow and Debreu established that the proof of the existence of general equilibrium requires forward markets in all goods and services (that is, markets where one can pay today in order to obtain forward or future delivery, or accept delivery today against the promise of a forward or future payment). While this requirement led some economists to cast doubt on the usefulness of the Arrow–Debreu proof, in subsequent work with Frank Hahn, Arrow (1971a) demonstrated the relevance of general equilibrium analysis even to economies where forward markets are missing. In other work Arrow has extended the analysis to consider the stability of competitive equilibria – see, for example, his 1977 book co-edited with Leonid Hurwicz, *Studies in Resource Allocation Processes*.

In addition to his pioneering work on welfare theory and general equilibrium theory, Arrow has made a number of important contributions to other areas of study. Four examples will suffice. First, he has undertaken work on the theory of inventory and production (for example, Arrow et al., 1958), including the problems of optimal capital investment and optimal production scheduling for private firms. Second, in a famous 1961 paper published in the *Review of Economics and Statistics*, co-written with Hollis Chenery, Bagicha Minhas and Robert Solow, Arrow introduced a production function that has a constant elasticity of substitution (CES) between labour and capital. Third, in a frequently cited paper published in 1962 in the *Review of Economic Studies*, 'The Economic Implications of Learning by Doing', he constructed a model in which ideas are a byproduct of production or investment that contribute to productivity. Other leading economists (such as Paul Romer) have subsequently built upon this work as part of what has come to be known as the new endogenous growth theory. Fourth, some of Arrow's most important contributions to the economics of uncertainty can be found in his book *Essays in the Theory of Risk-Bearing* (Arrow, 1971b), which include work on adverse selection, moral hazard, measures of risk aversion and optimal insurance.

Arrow is a highly respected economist who has made important contributions to a wide range of areas, most notably in economic theory, but also in applied economics. The breadth (and depth) of his work is reflected in the six volumes of his *Collected Papers* (Arrow, 1983–85) published by Harvard University Press: *Social Choice and Justice; General Equilibrium; Individual Choice under Certainty and Uncertainty; The Economics of Information; Production and Capital;* and *Applied Economics.*

Main Published Works

(1951a), *Social Choice and Individual Values*, New York: John Wiley & Sons; 2nd edn 1963.
(1951b), 'An Extension of the Basic Theorems of Classical Welfare Economics', in J. Neyman (ed.), *Proceedings of the Second Berkeley Symposium of Mathematical Statistics and Probability*, Berkeley, CA: University of California Press, pp. 507–32.
(1954), 'Existence of an Equilibrium for a Competitive Economy' (with G. Debreu), *Econometrica*, **22**, July, pp. 265–90.
(1958), *Studies in the Mathematical Theory of Inventory and Production* (ed. with S. Karlin and H. Scarf), Stanford, CA: Stanford University Press.
(1961), 'Capital–Labour Substitution and Economic Efficiency' (with H.B. Chenery, B.S. Minhas and R.M. Solow), *Review of Economics and Statistics*, **43**, August, pp. 225–50.
(1962), 'The Economic Implications of Learning by Doing', *Review of Economic Studies*, **29**, June, pp. 155–73.
(1971a), *General Competitive Analysis* (with F.H. Hahn), San Francisco: Holden-Day.
(1971b), *Essays in the Theory of Risk Bearing*, Amsterdam: North-Holland.
(1977), *Studies in Resource Allocation Processes* (ed. with L. Hurwicz), Cambridge: Cambridge University Press.
(1983), *Collected Papers of Kenneth J. Arrow*, vol. 1, *Social Choice and Justice;* vol. 2, *General Equilibrium*, Cambridge, MA: Harvard University Press.
(1984), *Collected Papers of Kenneth J. Arrow*, vol. 3, *Individual Choice under Certainty and Uncertainty;* vol. 4, *The Economics of Information*, Cambridge, MA: Harvard University Press.
(1985), *Collected Papers of Kenneth J. Arrow*, vol. 5, *Production and Capital;* vol. 6, *Applied Economics*, Cambridge, MA: Harvard University Press.

Secondary Literature

Feiwel, G.R. (ed.) (1987a), *Arrow and the Foundations of the Theory of Economic Policy*, London: Macmillan.

Feiwel, G.R. (ed.) (1987b), *Arrow and the Ascent of Modern Economic Theory*, London: Macmillan.
von Weizsäcker, C.C. (1972), 'Kenneth Arrow's Contribution to Economics', *Swedish Journal of Economics*, **74**, December, pp. 488–502.

See also Beaud and Dostaler (1997, pp. 169–71); Blaug (1998, pp. 7–10; 1999, p. 38); Cate (1997, pp. 21–4); Nobel Foundation (2004); Pressman (1999, pp. 177–81).

THE 1973 NOBEL MEMORIAL LAUREATE

WASSILY LEONTIEF

© The Nobel Foundation

Wassily W. Leontief
(1906–99)

Wassily Leontief was born in Saint Petersburg, Russia in 1906. At the age of 15 he entered the University of Saint Petersburg (renamed Leningrad in 1924) where he studied philosophy, sociology and economics and from where he obtained his MA in social science as a 'learned economist' in 1925. Leaving Russia, Leontief went to Germany where he worked at the Institute for World Economics at the University of Kiel. In 1928 he obtained a PhD from the University of Berlin. After a year spent in China, as an economic adviser to the Chinese government on the railway network, he went to the United States in 1931 (later becoming a US citizen) where he worked for a brief period as a research associate at the National Bureau of Economic Research. In 1932 Leontief joined the faculty at Harvard University where over a period of four decades he was promoted from instructor (1932–33) to assistant professor (1933–39), associate professor (1939–46) and Professor of Economics (1946–53), before finally holding the Henry Lee Chair of Political Economy from 1953 to 1975. While at Harvard he founded the Harvard Economic Research Project, devoted to input–output analysis, and served as its director from 1948 to 1973. In 1975 he left Harvard to join New York University, where he founded the Institute of Economic Analysis.

Leontief's many offices and honours included the presidencies of the Econometric Society in 1954 and the American Economic Association in 1970. In 1973 he was awarded the Nobel Memorial Prize in Economics 'for the development of the input–output method and for its application to important economic problems' (Nobel Foundation, 2004).

Over the course of a long and distinguished career, the main focus of Leontief's research was directed to the development and practical applications of input–output analysis. Input–output analysis describes the interrelationships between the sectors or industries in an economy in terms of the inputs required per unit of each sector's output. In doing so it gives a crucial insight into the overall structure and operation of the economy. The approach allows analysts to calculate (via the derivation of technical coefficients from the input–output table) how a change in production in any one sector or industry will affect other sectors and industries in the economy. In consequence, input–output analysis has proved to be particularly useful to policy makers for forecasting and planning (for example, avoiding bottlenecks in key sectors of the economy following a planned change in final demand for consumption, investment, government expenditure and exports) in both developed and developing countries.

Leontief's first article on input–output analysis, entitled 'Quantitative Input and Output Relations in the Economic System of the United States', was published in the *Review of Economics and Statistics* in 1936. Five years later the numerical results of two ten-sector tables (consolidated from a matrix of relations between 44 sectors), which were calculated for the United States for 1919 and 1929, were published in his first book, *The Structure of the American Economy* (Leontief, 1941). Over the years he refined and extended his first basic model to produce increasingly sophisticated and complex models (for example, by increasing the numbers of sectors covered, a task aided by the development of computers) and applied the approach to study a wide variety of important economic problems. His 1941 monograph was followed by the publication of a number of other important books based on input–output analysis (see, for example, Leontief, 1951 – the second edition of his 1941 book; 1966b; Leontief et al., 1953b; 1977b) and numerous articles in which he explored the practical applications of the approach.

Three examples will suffice to illustrate the practical applications of the analysis Leontief developed in his published work. First, in an early article entitled 'Wages, Profits and Prices' (Leontief, 1946), he showed how inflationary pressures, which originate in different sectors, are diffused throughout the economy. Second, he applied input–output analysis to the study of US foreign trade (Leontief, 1953a; 1956) and surprisingly found that US exports were less capital intensive and more labour intensive than US imports. Leontief's findings seemingly contradicted the Heckscher–Ohlin approach which explains the composition of international trade in terms of the relative factor endowments of different countries. According to Heckscher and Ohlin, given its relative abundance of capital, the United States should export capital-intensive goods and import labour-intensive goods. Leontief's result – now known as the 'Leontief paradox' – has provided fertile ground for much subsequent research in the field of international trade. Third, he used input–output analysis to study the environmental repercussions of increasing economic activity (see, for example, Leontief, 1970).

While Leontief will be remembered first and foremost for the development of input–output analysis and its practical applications, he also undertook work in other areas of economics including demand and supply curve analysis, composite commodities and the problem of index numbers, the theory of international trade and the significance of Marxian economics for current economic theory. Some of his classic contributions to economics have been gathered together in two collections of essays (Leontief, 1966a; 1977a). Underlying nearly all of his work is the recurrent theme that economics is an empirical and applied science which above all else should be directed to analysing real-world problems rather than developing formal mathematical models at the expense of their practical relevance (see, for example, Leontief, 1971 – his presidential address to the American Economic Association).

Main Published Works

(1936), 'Quantitative Input and Output Relations in the Economic System of the United States', *Review of Economics and Statistics*, **18**, August, pp. 105–25.

(1941), *The Structure of the American Economy, 1919–1929: An Empirical Application of Equilibrium Analysis*, Cambridge, MA: Harvard University Press; 2nd edn 1951, New York: Oxford University Press.

(1946), 'Wages, Profits and Prices', *Quarterly Journal of Economics*, **61**, November, pp. 26–39.

(1953a), 'Domestic Production and Foreign Trade: The American Capital Position Re-examined', *Proceedings of the American Philosophical Society*, **97**, September, pp. 332–49.

(1953b), *Studies in the Structure of the American Economy: Theoretical and Empirical Explorations in Input-Output Analysis* (with H.B. Chenery and others), New York: Oxford University Press.

(1956), 'Factor Proportions and the Structure of American Trade: Further Theoretical and Empirical Analysis', *Review of Economics and Statistics*, **38**, November, pp. 386–407.

(1966a), *Essays in Economics: Theories and Theorizing*, New York: Oxford University Press.

(1966b), *Input–Output Economics*, New York: Oxford University Press; 2nd edn 1986.

(1970), 'Environmental Repercussions and the Economic Structure: An Input–Output Approach', *Review of Economics and Statistics*, **52**, August, pp. 262–71.

(1971), 'Theoretical Assumptions and Nonobserved Facts', *American Economic Review*, **61**, March, pp. 1–7.

(1977a), *Essays in Economics: Theories, Facts and Policies*, Oxford: Basil Blackwell.

(1977b), *The Future of the World Economy* (with A.P. Carter and P. Petri), New York: Oxford University Press.

Secondary Literature

Dorfman, R. (1973), 'Wassily Leontief's Contribution to Economics', *Swedish Journal of Economics*, **75**, December, pp. 430–49.

See also Beaud and Dostaler (1997, pp. 316–18); Blaug (1998, pp. 157–60; 1999, pp. 673–4); Cate (1997, pp. 368–70); Nobel Foundation (2004); Pressman (1999, pp. 145–9).

THE 1974 NOBEL MEMORIAL LAUREATES

GUNNAR MYRDAL
AND
FRIEDRICH VON HAYEK

Gunnar Myrdal
(1898–1987)

© The Nobel Foundation

Gunnar Myrdal was born in a rural farming community in central Sweden in 1898. He studied law at the University of Stockholm and was awarded his degree in 1923. Switching from law to economics he obtained a doctorate in economics from the University of Stockholm in 1927. After a year spent studying in the United States as a Rockefeller Foundation Scholar, Myrdal embarked on careers in politics and academia. In the former case he became an adviser to the new Social Democrat government of Sweden in 1932, served as a member of the Swedish Parliament on two occasions: from 1934 to 1936 and 1942 to 1946; he was also chairman of the Swedish Post-War Planning Commission and Minister for Trade and Commerce from 1945 to 1947. As an academic at the University of Stockholm, Myrdal held the Lars Hierta Chair in Political Economy from 1933 to 1939, and was Professor of International Economics from 1961 until he retired from the university in 1965, thereafter holding the title of Professor Emeritus until his death in 1987. While Professor of International Economics he founded the Institute of International Economic Research in Stockholm to undertake work on trade and development. Myrdal also served as Executive Secretary of the United Nations Economic Commission for Europe in Geneva between 1947 and 1957.

Myrdal's many offices and honours included the award of over 30 honorary degrees from universities around the world. In 1974 Myrdal[3] was awarded, jointly with Friedrich von Hayek, the Nobel Memorial Prize in Economics 'for their pioneering work in the theory of money and economic fluctuations and for their penetrating analysis of the interdependence of economic, social and institutional phenomena' (Nobel Foundation, 2004).

Myrdal's academic career can be traced back to the 1927 publication (in Swedish) of his doctoral thesis, 'The Problem of Price Formation under Economic Change', in which he emphasised the role of expectations. Many of the ideas included in his PhD were subsequently incorporated into his first book published in English: *Monetary Equilibrium* (Myrdal, 1939). Originally published in Sweden in 1931, then published in translation in Germany in 1933, the book deals with dynamic analysis of cumulative processes, introducing and incorporating the concepts of *ex ante* (what is planned or intended) and *ex post* (what is realised or actually happens) in relation to savings and investment. In Myrdal's analysis, a gap between *ex ante* savings and investment (monetary disequilibrium) results in *ex post* balance due to unexpected gains and losses following price changes. Along with fellow Swedish economists Bertil Ohlin and Erik Lindahl, Myrdal became a leading member of the 'Stockholm School of Economics', famous for the development of the dynamic method and many concepts later identified as being central to Keynesian ideas.

During the 1930s, Myrdal also made his mark in Sweden in his parallel career both as an adviser to politicians and as a politician, proposing various policy measures to reduce the adverse effects of unemployment, and was highly influential in helping shape the Swedish welfare state. In a report to the Unemployment Committee in 1934, he developed a theoretical framework for analysing the economic effects of fiscal policy, and demonstrated the possibility of using expansionary policy to reduce unemployment.

In 1938, the Carnegie Corporation invited Myrdal to investigate the problems of the black population in the United States. Under their sponsorship his four-year multi-disciplinary study led to the publication of *An American Dilemma: The Negro Problem and Modern*

---

[3]   His wife Alva, a sociologist, whom he married in 1924, was awarded the Nobel Peace Prize in 1982 for her work on disarmament.

Democracy (Myrdal et al., 1944). The 'dilemma' in the book's title being the divide between the ideal of equal opportunity embodied in the constitution and the actual treatment of blacks in America. The pioneering book (1500 pages in length), which combines insights from economics, sociology, politics, history, anthropology, psychology and law, soon became a classic. In his study, Myrdal utilised the Wicksellian concept of cumulative causation to explain the socio-economic problems experienced by black Americans. Identifying a 'bundle of interdependent causative factors' he demonstrated how a cumulative process of deterioration or improvement will arise following a change in one of the interrelated factors such as low income, poor health and education, and racial discrimination by whites. A deterioration or improvement in one causative factor will lead to mutually reinforcing changes in other factors resulting in either a 'vicious circle' or 'virtuous circle'.

In the postwar period, Myrdal switched the main focus of his research to the problems of less-developed countries and world poverty. This research led to the publication of a series of books (Myrdal, 1957; 1960; 1963; 1968; 1970), of which particular mention should be made of the 1968 three-volume *Asian Drama: An Inquiry into the Poverty of Nations*. This monumental classic (over 2250 pages in length) was the culmination of a ten-year study of eight countries (India, Pakistan, Burma, Thailand, Malaya, Indonesia, the Philippines and Ceylon) in which he analysed their social, political and economic structures, as well as their historical backgrounds. He again used the concept of cumulative causation, this time to explain the vicious circle of poverty, poor health, lack of education and underutilisation of the labour force in less-developed countries in South Asia. To break the vicious circle of poverty and start a virtuous circle of development through the process of cumulative causation, he advocated government development planning involving a number of measures including institutional reform.

Even from this brief overview of his career and main published works it should be apparent that Myrdal was an exceptionally talented individual. After making a number of important contributions to economic theory in his early work, he adopted a multidisciplinary approach to explain and put forward solutions to the real-world problems of black Americans and less-developed countries. In adopting this approach he stressed the importance of a number of interdependent causative factors. He rejected many of the concepts used within, and solutions provided by, orthodox economic analysis. For example, he thought it inappropriate to use Western concepts of underemployment and unemployment when studying the problems of less-developed countries. He argued that the solution to underutilisation of the labour force (in terms of low participation rates, duration of work and low productivity) in South Asia cannot rely simply on expanding aggregate demand.

Myrdal was also highly critical of the view that positive economics can be separated from normative economics. In an early book entitled *The Political Element in the Development of Economic Theory* (first published in Swedish in 1930, and subsequently published in German in 1932, and English in 1953) he highlighted the political or valuation element underlying the economic theories put forward by classical and neoclassical economists. He argued that economics always involves implicit value judgements (for example, in the choice of problems studied) and that economists must explicitly state their value judgements and also acknowledge institutional conditions. He pursued this theme in later books, presenting a critical appraisal of objectivity in social science research (Myrdal, 1969) and stressing the importance of taking interdependent political, social and institutional factors into account in economic research (Myrdal, 1973). As such he will be remembered as a radical or dissenting economist, outside of the mainstream, who adopted a multi-disciplinary approach to explain and find solutions to real-world problems.

Main Published Works

(1939), *Monetary Equilibrium*, London: W. Hodge & Co.

(1944), *An American Dilemma: The Negro Problem and Modern Democracy* (with the assistance of R. Sterner and A. Rose), New York: Harper & Brothers.

(1953), *The Political Element in the Development of Economic Theory*, London: Routledge & Kegan Paul.

(1957), *Rich Lands and Poor: The Road to World Prosperity*, New York: Harper & Brothers; UK edn *Economic Theory and Underdeveloped Regions*, London: Duckworth.

(1960), *Beyond the Welfare State: Economic Planning and Its International Implications*, New Haven, CT: Yale University Press.

(1963), *Challenge to Affluence*, New York: Pantheon Books.

(1968), *Asian Drama: An Inquiry into the Poverty of Nations*, vols 1–3, New York: Pantheon Books and Twentieth Century Fund.

(1969), *Objectivity in Social Research*, New York: Pantheon Books.

(1970), *The Challenge of World Poverty: A World Anti-Poverty Program in Outline*, New York: Pantheon Books.

(1973), *Against the Stream: Critical Essays on Economics*, New York: Pantheon Books.

GUNNAR MYRDAL

Secondary Literature

Dostaler, G., D. Ethier and L. Lepage (eds) (1992), *Gunnar Myrdal and his Works*, Montreal: Harvest House.
Kindleberger, C.F. (1987), 'Gunnar Myrdal, 1898–1987', *Scandinavian Journal of Economics*, **89** (4), pp. 393–403.
Lundberg, E. (1974), 'Gunnar Myrdal's Contribution to Economic Theory: A Short Survey', *Swedish Journal of Economics*, **76**, December, pp. 472–8.
Reynolds, L.G. (1974), 'Gunnar Myrdal's Contribution to Economics, 1940–1970', *Swedish Journal of Economics*, **76**, December, pp. 479–97.

See also Arestis and Sawyer (2000, pp. 424–32); Beaud and Dostaler (1997, pp. 355–8); Blaug (1998, pp. 210–13; 1999, pp. 814–15); Cate (1997, pp. 459–62); Nobel Foundation (2004); Pressman (1999, pp. 112–16).

Friedrich A. von Hayek

(1899–1992)

© The Nobel Foundation

Friedrich August von Hayek was born in Vienna, the then capital of the Austro-Hungarian Empire, in 1899. He studied at the University of Vienna where he obtained a doctorate in law in 1921 and a doctorate in political science in 1923. After a short spell of study in America, Hayek returned to Vienna to join a private seminar group led by Ludwig von Mises. Together with Mises he founded the Austrian Institute for Business Cycle Research in 1927 and served as its director until 1931. In 1931 he emigrated to England (later becoming a UK citizen) where he accepted the post of Tooke Professor of Economic Science and Statistics at the London School of Economics, a position he held until 1950. In 1950 Hayek moved to the United States, where he was appointed Professor of Social and Moral Sciences at the University of Chicago. In 1962 he left Chicago, and returned to Europe as Professor of Economics at the University of Freiburg in West Germany. He retired from Freiburg in 1967 (thereafter holding the title of Professor Emeritus) and then moved to the University of Salzburg in Austria in 1969 to accept a position as honorary professor. In 1977 he returned to Freiburg, remaining there until his death in 1992. In 1974 Hayek was awarded, jointly with Gunnar Myrdal, the Nobel Memorial Prize in Economics 'for their pioneering work in the theory of money and economic fluctuations and for their penetrating analysis of the interdependence of economic, social and institutional phenomena' (Nobel Foundation, 2004).

In the early phase of his career the main focus of Hayek's research was in the field of economics, in particular publications which significantly contributed to the development of the Austrian theory of business cycles (for example, Hayek, 1931; 1933; 1939) and the theory of capital (Hayek, 1941). In *Monetary Theory and the Trade Cycle* (a book first published in German in 1929 and subsequently translated and published in English in 1933) he analysed the causal role played by monetary factors in the trade cycle. Hayek showed how a boom financed by credit expansion, which exceeds the rate of voluntary saving, will end in crisis and unemployment. Credit expansion allows the market rate of interest (cost of borrowing) to fall below the natural rate (return on capital) and results in increased investment which cannot be sustained. After a period of time the price of consumer goods relative to producer goods will start to rise, as will the market rate of interest. When this occurs a crisis ensues as some investments cannot be profitably completed, resulting in a period of liquidation and higher unemployment. He criticised Keynesian policies which sought to expand consumer demand in order to reduce unemployment, believing that a depression must run its course.

From the 1940s onwards, Hayek redirected the main focus of his research away from economic theory to the fields of political and legal philosophy. This research included a study of comparative economic systems embracing socialism, capitalism, planning and the market system. In a famous and compelling book, *The Road to Serfdom*, published in 1944, he attacked socialism and economic planning, warning that the curtailing of individual freedom these implied would lead ultimately to the triumph of totalitarianism. Central to this argument was the role played by the 'division of knowledge' in society (see, for example, Hayek, 1945) and the importance of 'spontaneous order'. Hayek argued that knowledge is fragmented and dispersed among individuals in society. In consequence it is impossible for a single central authority to acquire the total knowledge of all individuals and coordinate economic decisions efficiently. In contrast, the market system (a spontaneous order), which developed as the result of the byproduct of human actions rather than by conscious design, coordinates economic decisions made by millions of individuals far more effectively. In viewing the market as a process he emphasised the role the price system plays as a communication network, providing incentives to put information to its best uses, and he was strongly opposed to government interference in economic affairs. He also drew attention to the harmful effects of inflation, which he argued distorts the reliability of price signals.

In analysing how efficiently knowledge is used in different economic systems, Hayek studied the institutional and legal frameworks (for example, governing property rights) that exist in society. In doing so he demonstrated the 'interdependence of economic, social and institutional phenomena'. In the 1960s and 1970s he focused his studies on philosophy, politics and economics (Hayek, 1967; 1978), and also published *The Constitution of Liberty* (Hayek, 1960), and *Law, Legislation and Liberty* (Hayek, 1973; 1976; 1979). A 'libertarian', he argued that laws that treat all citizens equally promote prosperity and was opposed to attempts to redistribute income in society.

In the field of economics, Hayek will be remembered for his work on: the theory of business cycles; criticising Keynesian expansionary aggregate demand policies to reduce unemployment; the harmful effects of inflation; and the benefits of free markets. In addition he made important contributions to the history of economic thought (for example, Hayek, 1951) and the philosophy of science (for example, Hayek, 1952a). Quite remarkably, his contributions spanned not just the fields of economic theory, the history of economic thought and the philosophy of science, but also psychology (for example, Hayek, 1952b) and political and legal philosophy. The legacy of Hayek in politics, philosophy and economics is considered in a three-volume collection of papers (Boettke et al., 2000).

Main Published Works

(1931), *Prices and Production*, London: George Routledge & Sons.
(1933), *Monetary Theory and the Trade Cycle*, London: Jonathan Cape.
(1939), *Profits, Interest and Investment*, London: Routledge & Kegan Paul.
(1941), *The Pure Theory of Capital*, London: Routledge & Kegan Paul.
(1944), *The Road to Serfdom*, London: George Routledge; Chicago: University of Chicago Press.
(1945), 'The Use of Knowledge in Society', *American Economic Review*, 35, September, pp. 519–30.
(1948), *Individualism and Economic Order*, London: Routledge & Kegan Paul; Chicago: University of Chicago Press.

(1951), *John Stuart Mill and Harriet Taylor*, London: Routledge & Kegan Paul; Chicago: University of Chicago Press.

(1952a), *The Counter-Revolution of Science*, Glencoe, IL: Free Press.

(1952b), *The Sensory Order: An Inquiry into the Foundations of Theoretical Psychology*, London: Routledge & Kegan Paul; Chicago: University of Chicago Press.

(1960), *The Constitution of Liberty*, London: Routledge & Kegan Paul; Chicago: University of Chicago Press.

(1967), *Studies in Philosophy, Politics and Economics*, London: Routledge & Kegan Paul; Chicago: University of Chicago Press.

(1973), *Law, Legislation and Liberty*, vol. 1, London: Routledge & Kegan Paul; Chicago: University of Chicago Press.

(1976), *Law, Legislation and Liberty*, vol. 2, London: Routledge & Kegan Paul; Chicago: University of Chicago Press.

(1978), *New Studies in Philosophy, Politics and Economics and the History of Ideas*, London: Routledge & Kegan Paul; Chicago: University of Chicago Press.

(1979), *Law, Legislation and Liberty*, vol. 3, London: Routledge & Kegan Paul; Chicago: University of Chicago Press.

Secondary Literature

Barry, N.P. (1979), *Hayek's Social and Economic Philosophy*, London: Macmillan.

Boettke, P.J., A. Farrant, G. Ranson and G.O. Salgado (eds) (2000), *The Legacy of Friedrich von Hayek*, Cheltenham, UK and Northampton, MA, USA: Edward Elgar.

Machlup, F. (1974), 'Friedrich von Hayek's Contribution to Economics', *Swedish Journal of Economics*, **76**, December, pp. 498–531.

See also Beaud and Dostaler (1997, pp. 267–71); Blaug (1998, pp. 100–104; 1999, p. 509); Cate (1997, pp. 615–29); Nobel Foundation (2004); Pressman (1999, pp. 116–20).

THE 1975 NOBEL MEMORIAL LAUREATES

LEONID KANTOROVICH
AND
TJALLING KOOPMANS

Leonid V. Kantorovich (1912–86)

© The Nobel Foundation

Leonid Kantorovich was born in Saint Petersburg, Russia in 1912. His distinguished career can be divided into three main phases. The first involved his university education and subsequent period teaching and his research work in Leningrad[4] until 1960. At the age of only 14 years he entered Leningrad State University to study mathematics and obtained his degree in 1930 and his doctorate in 1935. Kantorovich's doctoral thesis on partially ordered function spaces led to the name 'K-spaces' in his honour. In the 1930s he taught mathematics at the Leningrad Institute of Construction Engineering and Leningrad State University, where he became a professor in 1934. Between 1948 and 1960 he was head of the department of mathematics at the Academy of Sciences in Leningrad. The second phase of Kantorovich's career involved his work in Novosibirsk, where from 1960 to 1971 he was deputy director of the Siberian Institute of Mathematics. The final part of his career was spent working in Moscow. From 1971 to 1976, he was head of the Institute of National Economic Management, and from 1976 to 1986 head of the Institute of Systems Analysis of the Academy of Sciences in Moscow.

[4] St Petersburg was renamed Leningrad following the Soviet revolution; it is now, once again, St Petersburg.

Kantorovich's many offices and honours included: full member-ship of the Academy of Sciences of the USSR in 1964; and the award of the Stalin prize in mathematics in 1949. Together with Nemchinov and Novozhilov, he received the Lenin prize in economics in 1965. Kantorovich was awarded numerous honorary degrees from uni-versities around the world and was a fellow of the Econometric Society from 1973 until his death in 1986. In 1975 he was awarded, jointly with the Dutch-born econometrician–economist Tjalling Koopmans, the Nobel Memorial Prize in Economics 'for their con-tributions to the theory of optimum allocation of resources' (Nobel Foundation, 2004).

Kantorovich was initially trained as a mathematician and during his career as a mathematician–economist made a number of impor-tant contributions to various branches of mathematical analysis, in-cluding functional analysis (see Kantorovich and Akilov, 1982). His outstanding contribution to economics entailed the development of linear programming and its application to a wide range of practical problems. Linear programming is an analytical technique which in-volves the formulation and solution of constrained optimisation prob-lems by maximising or minimising a linear function subject to a number of linear and inequality constraints.

Kantorovich first developed a mathematical method for organis-ing and planning production in a plywood factory in a working paper published in Russian by Leningrad State University Press in 1939. This paper was not, however, published in English until 1960 (Kantorovich, 1960). His 1939 paper, with minor alterations, was republished in English in 1964 (Kantorovich, 1964a). This early mi-cro research paved the way for the application of the technique not only to production planning in individual enterprises, but also to a range of problems including transport optimisation (Kantorovich, 1958). However, his most influential and famous work is his 1965 book *The Best Use of Economic Resources*, which was first published in Russian in 1959. In the book, Kantorovich analysed the problem of the optimum allocation of resources for a socialist economy as a whole. The optimal solution is based on an iterative method of what Kantorovich called 'resolving multipliers', or what are essen-tially shadow prices. His work, which highlighted the importance of a price system, including investment criteria, formed the basis of proposals to decentralise production decisions and improve eco-nomic planning in the Soviet economy. In other published work he developed both static and dynamic models of economic planning (for example, Kantorovich, 1964b; 1976b).

Above all else Kantorovich will be remembered for his contribution to the development of linear programming and the application of the technique to the problem of the optimum allocation of resources. Over the course of his career he applied optimisation methods to a range of problems including, in the last phase of his career, the problem of technical progress (Kantorovich, 1976a). His views on the problems of a planned economy, most notably the Soviet economy, can be found in his Nobel Memorial Lecture (Kantorovich, 1989).

Main Published Works

(1958), 'On the Translocation of Masses', *Management Science*, **5**, October, pp. 1–4; first published in Russian in 1942.

(1960), 'Mathematical Methods of Organizing and Planning Production', *Management Science*, **6**, July, pp. 363–422; first published in Russian in 1939.

(1964a), 'Mathematical Methods of Production Planning and Organization', in A. Nove (ed.), *The Use of Mathematics in Economics*, Edinburgh and London: Oliver & Boyd, pp. 225–80; Kantorovich's 1939 paper (see above), with minor alterations, first published in Russian in 1959.

(1964b), 'Further Development of Mathematical Methods and Prospects of Their Application in Economic Planning', in A. Nove (ed.), *The Use of Mathematics in Economics*, Edinburgh and London: Oliver & Boyd, pp. 281–321; first published in Russian in 1959.

(1965), *The Best Use of Resources*, Oxford: Pergamon Press; first published in Russian in 1959.

(1976a), 'Economic Problems of Scientific and Technical Progress', *Scandinavian Journal of Economics*, **78** (4), pp. 521–41.

(1976b), *Essays in Optimal Planning* (ed. L. Smolinski), White Plains, NY: International Arts and Sciences Press.

(1982), *Functional Analysis* (with G.P. Akilov), 2nd edn, Oxford: Pergamon Press; first published in Russian in 1977.

(1989), 'Mathematics in Economics: Achievements, Difficulties, Perspectives – Nobel Memorial Lecture, December 11, 1975', *American Economic Review*, **79**, December, pp. 18–22.

Secondary Literature

Gardner, R. (1990), 'L.V. Kantorovich: The Price Implications of Optimal Planning', *Journal of Economic Literature*, **28**, June, pp. 638–48.

Johansen, L. (1976), 'L.V. Kantorovich's Contribution to Economics', *Scandinavian Journal of Economics*, **78** (1), pp. 61–80.

See also   Beaud and Dostaler (1997, pp. 292–4); Blaug (1999, pp. 599–600); Nobel Foundation (2004).

Tjalling C. Koopmans

(1910–85)

© The Nobel Foundation

Tjalling Koopmans was born in Graveland, The Netherlands in 1910. He studied mathematics and physics at the University of Utrecht and obtained his MA in 1933, before being awarded a PhD in mathematical statistics from the University of Leiden in 1936. After a period teaching at the Netherlands School of Economics in Rotterdam, and then employed as an economist at the League of Nations in Geneva, Koopmans emigrated in 1940 to the United States (later becoming a US citizen). Following employment in a research post at Princeton University he worked as a statistician at the Combined Shipping Adjustment Board in Washington from 1942 to 1944. In 1944 he moved to the University of Chicago where he was research associate (1944–48); Director of Research of the Cowles Commission (1948–54); associate professor (1944–48); and Professor of Economics (1948–55). In 1955 he moved, as did the Cowles Commission, from the University of Chicago to Yale University in New Haven, Connecticut. Here he served as director of the Cowles Foundation for Research in Economics from 1961 to 1967, and as Professor of Economics from 1955 until he retired from the university in 1981.

Koopmans's many offices and honours included the presidencies of the Econometric Society in 1950, and the American Economic

Association in 1978. In 1975 Koopmans was awarded, jointly with the Russian mathematician–economist Leonid Kantorovich, the Nobel Memorial Prize in Economics 'for their contributions to the theory of optimum allocation of resources' (Nobel Foundation, 2004).

Koopmans will be remembered first and foremost for his pathbreaking work on activity analysis. The development of the technique arose out of his early research on transportation economics (Koopmans, 1939) and his work as a statistician at the Combined Shipping Adjustment Board during the Second World War. In a 1942 memorandum for the Board, 'Exchange Ratios between Cargoes on Various Routes' (first published in Koopmans, 1970), he put forward a scheme for deciding the optimal allocation of cargo ships among routes. He also showed how 'potentials' or shadow prices could aid decisions on the allocation of ships. However, his seminal article on the technique, entitled 'Analysis of Production as an Efficient Combination of Activities', appears in the proceedings of a conference he organised in 1949, published in 1951 (Koopmans, 1951). Rather than study the relationship between inputs and outputs from the standpoint of the existence of a conventional 'production function', he analysed the production choices of a firm operating under constraints. In reality, a firm is unable to adopt all possible combinations of inputs because it has limited amounts of inputs at its disposal. Furthermore, these limited inputs can only be combined in a finite number of ways as they are constrained by existing production techniques. In other words, activity levels or levels of output produced are constrained by the availability of inputs and how such inputs can be combined. Koopmans explored the implications of activity analysis, including optimality and efficiency in production and their relation to the price system. In subsequent work he extended activity analysis and examined its applications (for example, Koopmans,1953a). He applied the technique not only to problems in transportation economics but also to problems of allocating resources over time. His work in the field of activity analysis is intrinsically linked to the development of linear programming (see entry on Leonid Kantorovich).

In addition to his pioneering work on activity analysis, Koopmans also made important contributions to a number of other areas including econometric theory, methodology and the theory of optimal economic growth. His work in the field of econometrics can be traced back to the publication of his doctoral thesis: 'Linear Regression Analysis of Economic Time Series' (Koopmans, 1937). In the 1940s and early 1950s he focused his econometric research efforts on the problem of estimation and identification of structural parameters in economic models (Koopmans, 1945; 1949a). At the Cowles Commission he led a team of econometricians which tackled this problem, resulting in the publication of two important monographs which helped to popularise the use of simultaneous equation models (Koopmans, 1950; Hood and Koopmans, 1953b).

In the field of methodological debate, Koopmans's most influential contribution was his review (Koopmans, 1947) of Arthur Burns and Wesley Mitchell's book *Measuring Business Cycles*, which was published by the National Bureau of Economic Research (NBER) in 1946. He attacked Burns and Mitchell's (NBER) 'inductive–empirical' methodology, where observation and measurement informs or suggests theory, describing it as 'measurement without theory'. In its place he advocated the Cowles Commission's 'theoretical–deductive' approach where theory is used to develop models whose parameters can be estimated and tested using econometric techniques. After Mitchell's death in 1948, one of his colleagues at the NBER, Rudledge Vining, defended the NBER methodology and continued the debate with Koopmans (see Koopmans, 1949b). Finally, brief mention should be made of Koopmans's research in the 1960s which contributed to the field of economic growth theory. In particular he made important contributions to the theory of optimal economic growth, efficiency in growth and preference orderings (see, for example, Koopmans, 1964; 1967).

For the interested reader, many of Koopmans's most important scientific papers have been gathered together in two volumes (Koopmans, 1970; 1985). His views on the state of economic science can be found in his three essays on: allocation of resources and the price system; the construction of economic knowledge; and the interaction of tools and problems in economics (Koopmans, 1957).

Main Published Works

(1937), *Linear Regression Analysis of Economic Time Series*, Haarlem: De Erven Bohn.

(1939), *Tanker Freight Rates and Tankship Building*, Haarlem: De Erven Bohn.

(1945), 'Statistical Estimation of Simultaneous Economic Relations', *Journal of the American Statistical Association*, **40**, December, pp. 448–66.

(1947), 'Measurement without Theory', *Review of Economic Statistics*, **29**, August, pp. 161–72.

(1949a), 'Identification Problems in Economic Model Construction', *Econometrica*, **17**, April, pp. 125–44.

(1949b), 'Koopmans on the Choice of Variables to be Studied and the Methods of Measurement: A Reply', *Review of Economic Statistics*, **31**, May, pp. 86–91.

(1950), *Statistical Inference in Dynamic Economic Models* (ed.), New York: John Wiley.

(1951), *Activity Analysis of Production and Allocation* (ed.), New York: John Wiley.

(1953a), 'Activity Analysis and Its Applications', *American Economic Review*, **43**, May, pp. 406–14.

(1953b), *Studies in Econometric Method* (ed. with W.C. Hood), New York: John Wiley.

(1957), *Three Essays on the State of Economic Science*, New York: McGraw-Hill.

(1964), 'Economic Growth at a Maximal Rate', *Quarterly Journal of Economics*, **78**, August, pp. 355–94.

(1967), 'Objectives, Constraints and Outcomes in Optimal Growth Models', *Econometrica*, **35**, January, pp. 1–15.

(1970), *The Scientific Papers of Tjalling C. Koopmans*, Berlin: Springer-Verlag.

(1985), *The Scientific Papers of Tjalling C. Koopmans*, vol. 2, Cambridge, MA: MIT Press.

Secondary Literature

Jungenfelt, K.G. (1976), 'Tjalling Koopmans' Contribution to Economics – II. Koopmans and the Recent Development of Growth Theory', *Scandinavian Journal of Economics*, **78** (1), pp. 94–102.

Malinvaud, E. (1972), 'The Scientific Papers of Tjalling C. Koopmans: A Review Article', *Journal of Economic Literature*, **10**, September, pp. 798–802.

Werin, L. (1976), 'Tjalling Koopmans' Contribution to Economics – I. Activity Analysis, Methodology and Econometrics', *Scandinavian Journal of Economics*, **78** (1), pp. 81–93 and 99–102.

See also Beaud and Dostaler (1997, pp. 301–3); Blaug (1998, pp. 140–42; 1999, pp. 627–8); Nobel Foundation (2004).

THE 1976 NOBEL MEMORIAL LAUREATE

MILTON FRIEDMAN

© The Nobel Foundation

Milton Friedman
(b. 1912)

Milton Friedman was born in Brooklyn, New York, USA in 1912. The son of working-class Jewish immigrants from Central Europe, he studied mathematics and economics at Rutgers University, from where he graduated with a BA in 1932. Upon receipt of a scholarship, Friedman commenced graduate studies at the University of Chicago where he was awarded an MA in 1933. After a year of further graduate work at Columbia University, he returned to Chicago as a research assistant. From 1935 to 1937 he was employed as an economist at the National Resources Committee in Washington, DC, investigating consumer expenditures in the United States. In 1937 he accepted a post at Columbia University as a part-time lecturer and in the same year joined the research staff at the National Bureau of Economic Research (NBER). At the NBER, Friedman assisted Simon Kuznets (see entry in this volume) in his studies of the incomes of professionals (Kuznets and Friedman, 1945). This work formed the basis of Friedman's doctoral dissertation and he was subsequently awarded a PhD from Columbia University in 1946. During the Second World War, Friedman worked first at the US Treasury Department on wartime tax policy from 1941 to 1943, and then from 1943 to 1945 as associate director of the Statistical Research Group of the Division of War Research at Columbia University. In 1945, following the end of the war, he joined the University of Minnesota as an associate professor. After one year at Minnesota he accepted the post of associate professor at the University of Chicago in 1946, where he was subsequently promoted to a full professorship in 1948. Apart from visiting posts at Cambridge University (1953–54), Columbia University (1964–65), the University of California, Los Angeles (1967) and the University of Hawaii (1972), Friedman remained at Chicago before retiring from active teaching in 1977. Since then he has been a senior research fellow at the Hoover Institution at Stanford University. In addition to his posts at Chicago, Friedman also worked as a member of the research staff at the NBER for a second period from 1948 to 1981.

Friedman's many offices and honours have included: the award of the John Bates Clark Medal of the American Economic Association in 1951 and the National Medal of Science in 1988; serving as president of the American Economic Association in 1967 and the Mont Pelerin Society from 1970 to 1972; and the award of honorary degrees from numerous universities around the world. In 1976 he was awarded the Nobel Memorial Prize in Economics 'for his achievements in the fields of consumption analysis, monetary history and theory, and for his demonstration of the complexity of stabilization policy' (Nobel Foundation, 2004).

Friedman is best known as the founding father and leading exponent of the monetarist school of macroeconomic thought, and for championing the case for the efficacy of free markets in a wide variety of contexts. Over the course of his long and distinguished career he has made contributions to many areas including: methodology; consumer behaviour; international economics; monetary theory, history and policy; and the causes of business cycles and inflation. In attempting to survey his most important works in these areas we begin with what Friedman believes to be his best scientific work, namely his 1957 book, *A Theory of the Consumption Function*. In this work he put forward his permanent income hypothesis, whereby consumption is held to depend upon expected long-run average or lifetime income, rather than current disposable income as in Keynesian analysis. In doing so Friedman was able to reconcile the seemingly conflicting evidence from cross-section and time-series studies of the consumption–income relationship. One implication of the hypothesis is that if individuals believe that a specific income change is only temporary, then it will have only a small effect on their permanent income and, in consequence, a small effect on their consumption. As such, an economist who believes that consumption is a function of permanent income is likely to be more sceptical about the usefulness of a tax change for stabilisation purposes than one who believes that consumption depends on current disposable income. Friedman's permanent income hypothesis, together with the life-cycle hypothesis associated with the work of Franco Modigliani (see entry in this volume) and Richard Brumberg, has had a profound and lasting influence on the direction of research in the area of consumer behaviour.

Friedman's most influential book, *A Monetary History of the United States, 1867–1960* (which he co-authored with Anna Schwartz), was published in 1963 (Friedman and Schwartz, 1963a). In their monumental study, Friedman and Schwartz presented persuasive evidence to support the monetarist belief that changes in the stock of money play a largely independent role in cyclical fluctuations. Particularly controversial is their interpretation that the Great Depression resulted from the failure of the Federal Reserve to prevent the US money stock from falling by about a third between October 1929 and June 1933. Subsequent research with Anna Schwartz at the NBER resulted in the publication of *Monetary Statistics of the United States* (1970) and *Monetary Trends in the United States and the United Kingdom* (1982).

This series of volumes for the NBER can be seen as part of a much wider body of work undertaken by Friedman from the late 1940s/ early 1950s onwards which has sought to re-establish the quantity theory of money approach to macroeconomic analysis. According to adherents of this approach, changes in the money supply are the predominant, though not the only, factor explaining changes in money income. In his famous essay 'The Quantity Theory of Money – A Restatement', Friedman (1956, pp. 3–21) put forward a theory of the demand for money asserting that the demand for money is a stable function of a limited number of variables. If the demand for money function is stable, then velocity will also be stable and will change in a predictable manner if any of the limited number of variables in the demand for money function should change. Friedman's restatement of the quantity theory as, in the first instance, a theory of the demand for money, acted as a catalyst for many subsequent empirical studies on which variables influence the demand for money and whether the relationship between the demand for money and these variables is stable over time.

Another theme of Friedman's research on the importance of money involves his work examining the timing of the relationship between changes in money and money income (for example, Friedman, 1958; 1961; Friedman and Schwartz, 1963a; 1963b). One of the most influential of his findings is that the outside lag associated with monetary policy is both long and variable. In discussing 'The Role of Monetary Policy' in his 1967 presidential address to the American Economic Association, Friedman (1968) introduced the concept of a natural rate of unemployment, which he argued is determined by the structure of the labour and goods markets, including market imperfections. By augmenting the Phillips curve with the expected rate of inflation as an additional variable that determines the rate of change of money wages, he was able to demonstrate that a trade-off between inflation and unemployment only exists in the short run, and that in the long run the Phillips curve is vertical at the natural rate of unemployment. Furthermore, any attempt to maintain unemployment below the natural rate will lead to accelerating inflation. In his Nobel Memorial Lecture, Friedman (1977) offered an explanation of the existence of a positively-sloped Phillips curve for a period of several years, which is compatible with a vertical long-run Phillips curve at the natural rate of unemployment.

This body of interrelated work helped to forge Friedman's views on the role and conduct of stabilisation policy. Given the numerous problems associated with stabilisation policy, including time lags (most notably the length of the inside lag associated with fiscal policy in the United States and the length and variability of the outside lag associated with monetary policy), and the inflationary consequences of reducing unemployment below the natural rate (the precise value of which is uncertain), discretionary policy activism could turn out to be destabilising. Since the late 1940s Friedman has addressed the issue of an appropriate 'Monetary and Fiscal Framework for Economic Stability' (Friedman, 1948). He has been particularly vociferous in advocating that the authorities should follow a stable rate of monetary growth in line with the trend/long-run growth rate of the economy (see, for example, Friedman, 1968); the famous 'k' per cent monetary rule.

While many of these ideas were particularly controversial at the time Friedman first presented them, over the years a number of his key insights have been absorbed into mainstream macroeconomics. Most notably, the views that the long-run Phillips curve is vertical, and that money is neutral in the long run, are now widely accepted and form part of the modern mainstream consensus. Furthermore, Friedman has convinced a majority of economists and policy makers that sustained inflation is not possible without excessive monetary growth and that the potential of activist discretionary fiscal and monetary policy is much more limited than conceived prior to the monetarist counter-revolution.

In addition to his work on the consumption function, the role of money in the business cycle, and the role and conduct of stabilisation policy, Friedman has also made important contributions to methodology and international economics. Two essays, both of which first appeared in his 1953 book, *Essays in Positive Economics*, have been particularly influential in each of these fields of study. In his essay 'The Methodology of Positive Economics', Friedman argued that the appropriate test of a theory is its ability to yield empirically corroborated predictions, not the realism of its assumptions. Here, the stamp of a fruitful economic theory is its capacity to make accurate predictions. This methodological approach, mirrored throughout his work, has led Friedman to favour small-scale empirical models that are simple to test and that can explain a limited set of phenomena under a wide range of circumstances. In another pioneering essay, 'The Case for Flexible Exchange Rates', he argued that such a regime would improve the process of balance of payments adjustment. His anticipation of the breakdown of the Bretton Woods fixed exchange rate system, in an analogous manner to that anticipating accelerating inflation ahead of the events of the 1970s (see Friedman, 1968), lent further weight to his arguments and his favoured methodological approach.

As well as his many scientific contributions, Friedman has sought to communicate his views on a wide range of issues to non-economists. A regular provider of columns for *Newsweek* over the 1966–84 period, he has also written such worldwide best sellers as *Capitalism and Freedom* (Friedman, 1962) and *Free to Choose* (1980, co-written with his wife Rose Friedman). Both books have been translated into more than 15 languages, while *Free to Choose*, which champions the case for the free market, was made into a ten-part television series shown in many countries. His gift for writing about topics in applied economics, accessible to a mass audience, has established Friedman as one of the most famous contemporary economists. However, above all, his formidable output of technical books and learned journal articles, which has helped shape both modern macroeconomic theory and policy making, has made Friedman one of the most influential and outstanding economists in the history of the discipline.

Main Published Works

(1945), *Income from Independent Professional Practice* (with S. Kuznets), New York: National Bureau of Economic Research.

(1948), 'A Monetary and Fiscal Framework for Economic Stability', *American Economic Review*, **38**, June, pp. 245–64; reprinted in *Essays in Positive Economics*, Chicago: University of Chicago Press, 1953.

(1953), *Essays in Positive Economics*, Chicago: University of Chicago Press.

(1956), *Studies in the Quantity Theory of Money* (ed.), Chicago: University of Chicago Press.

(1957), *A Theory of the Consumption Function*, Princeton, NJ: Princeton University Press.

(1958), 'The Supply of Money and Changes in Prices and Output', in *The Relationship of Prices to Economic Stability and Growth*, Washington, DC: Congressional Report, pp. 241–56; reprinted in *The Optimum Quantity of Money and Other Essays*, Chicago: Aldine, 1969.

(1961), 'The Lag in Effect of Monetary Policy', *Journal of Political Economy*, **69**, October, pp. 447–66; reprinted in *The Optimum Quantity of Money and Other Essays*, Chicago: Aldine, 1969.

(1962), *Capitalism and Freedom*, Chicago: University of Chicago Press.

(1963a), *A Monetary History of the United States, 1867–1960* (with A.J. Schwartz), Princeton, NJ: Princeton University Press.

(1963b), 'Money and Business Cycles' (with A.J. Schwartz), *Review of Economics and Statistics*, **45**, February, pp. 32–64; reprinted in *The Optimum Quantity of Money and Other Essays*, Chicago: Aldine, 1969.

(1968), 'The Role of Monetary Policy', *American Economic Review*, **58**, March, pp. 1–17; reprinted in *The Optimum Quantity of Money and Other Essays*, Chicago: Aldine, 1969.

(1969), *The Optimum Quantity of Money and Other Essays*, Chicago: Aldine.

(1970), *Monetary Statistics of the United States* (with A.J. Schwartz), New York: Columbia University Press.

(1977), 'Nobel Lecture: Inflation and Unemployment', *Journal of Political Economy*, **85**, June, pp. 451–72.

(1980), *Free to Choose: A Personal Statement* (with R. Friedman), New York: Harcourt Brace Jovanovich.

(1982), *Monetary Trends in the United States and the United Kingdom: Their Relation to Income, Prices, and Interest Rates, 1867–1975* (with A.J. Schwartz), Chicago: University of Chicago Press.

Secondary Literature

Butler, E. (1985), *Milton Friedman: A Guide to His Economic Thought*, Aldershot: Gower.

Hammond, J.D. (ed.) (1999), *The Legacy of Milton Friedman as Teacher*, Cheltenham, UK and Northampton, MA, USA: Edward Elgar.

Snowdon, B. and H.R. Vane (1997), 'Modern Macroeconomics and Its Evolution from a Monetarist Perspective: An Interview with Professor Milton Friedman', *Journal of Economic Studies*, **24** (4), pp. 192–222.

Thygesen, N. (1977), 'The Scientific Contributions of Milton Friedman', *Scandinavian Journal of Economics*, **79** (1), pp. 56–98.

See also   Beaud and Dostaler (1997, pp. 234–8); Blaug (1998, pp. 68–72); Blaug and Vane (2003, pp. 272–4); Cate (1997, pp. 191–5); Nobel Foundation (2004); Pressman (1999, pp. 156–62); Snowdon and Vane (2002, pp. 271–84).

THE 1977 NOBEL MEMORIAL LAUREATES

BERTIL OHLIN
AND
JAMES MEADE

Bertil G. Ohlin
(1899–1979)

© The Nobel Foundation

Bertil Ohlin was born in Klippan, Sweden in 1899. He studied economics, mathematics and statistics at the University of Lund, obtaining a BA in 1917. He subsequently studied at the Stockholm School of Economics and Business, Harvard University and the University of Cambridge, before being awarded a doctorate from the University of Stockholm in 1924 with his thesis, 'The Theory of Trade'. From 1925 to 1930, Ohlin was Professor of Economics at the University of Copenhagen. In 1930 he returned to the Stockholm School of Economics and Business where he held the post of Professor of Economics until his retirement in 1965.

In addition to his academic career, Ohlin was actively engaged in politics. During his political career he was chairman of the Liberal Youth Federation from 1934 to 1939, a member of the Swedish Parliament from 1938 to 1970, leader of the (opposition) Swedish Liberal Party from 1944 to 1967, and he served in the coalition government as Minister of Trade from 1944 to 1945. In 1977 Ohlin was awarded, jointly with the British economist James Meade, the Nobel Memorial Prize in Economics 'for their pathbreaking contribution to the theory of international trade and international capital movements' (Nobel Foundation, 2004).

Although Ohlin first gained international recognition in the late 1920s following his debate with John Maynard Keynes on the transfer problem in the context of Germany's First World War reparations (see Ohlin, 1929a; 1929b), his international reputation was steadfastly established in 1933 with the publication of his seminal book, *Interregional and International Trade* (Ohlin, 1933b). Building upon, and extending, the work of his teacher Eli Heckscher (most notably Heckscher's article, 'The Effect of Foreign Trade on the Distribution of Income' published in Swedish in 1919), Ohlin explained the pattern of international trade in terms of the relative factor endowments of different countries. According to what became known as the Heckscher–Ohlin theorem, assuming similar demand patterns in trading countries, a country will export those goods that require factors of production with which it is abundantly endowed and import those goods that require, if home produced, its relatively scarce factors. The model quickly became integrated into textbooks on international trade and provided fertile ground for much subsequent research by scholars who sought to theoretically develop the model and empirically test its implications (see, for example, the entries on Paul Samuelson, the 1970 Nobel Memorial Laureate and Wassily Leontief, the 1973 Nobel Memorial Laureate).

In addition to his seminal contribution to the theory of international trade, Ohlin also made important contributions to macroeconomics. In a number of publications (for example, Ohlin, 1927; 1933a) he anticipated some of the ideas (such as the multiplier) which formed the building blocks of the Keynesian revolution in macroeconomic thought. Indeed it can be argued that Ohlin, along with other members of the 'Stockholm School' (see the entry on Gunnar Myrdal, the 1974 Nobel Memorial Laureate), was a precursor of Keynes and that he anticipated some of the key ideas contained in Keynes's *General Theory of Employment, Interest and Money* published in 1936 (see, for example, Ohlin, 1937).

Ohlin's main contribution to economics is undoubtedly his model of international trade. The measure of his insight can be gleaned from the fact that, more than 70 years after it was first put forward, nearly all textbooks on international trade devote space to a discussion of the Heckscher–Ohlin model. His lasting impact on economics is even more remarkable when one considers that, in addition to his distinguished career as an economist, he also pursued a very active career as a politician and journalist. In the latter case he was a prolific writer, contributing economic and political articles on a regular basis to Swedish daily newspapers from the early 1920s until his death in 1979.

Main Published Works

(1927), *Get Production Going*, Stockholm: Aschehaug, published in Swedish.

(1929a), 'The Reparation Problem: A Discussion, I. Transfer Difficulties, Real and Imagined', *Economic Journal*, **39**, June, pp. 172–8.

(1929b), 'Mr. Keynes' Views on the Transfer Problem: A Rejoinder', *Economic Journal*, **39**, September, pp. 400–404.

(1933a), 'To the Question of the Formulation of Monetary Theory', *Ekonomisk Tidskrift*, **35**, March, pp. 45–81, published in Swedish; published in English in 1978 in *History of Political Economy*, **10**, pp. 353–88.

(1933b), *Interregional and International Trade*, Cambridge, MA: Harvard University Press; revised edition published by Harvard University Press in 1967.

(1937), 'Some Notes on the Stockholm Theory of Savings and Investment: I and II', *Economic Journal*, **47**, March, pp. 53–69 and June, pp. 221–40.

Secondary Literature

Caves, R.E. (1978), 'Bertil Ohlin's Contribution to Economics', *Scandinavian Journal of Economics*, **80** (1), pp. 86–93; bibliography (pp. 93–9) compiled by Bertil Ohlin.

Lundberg, E. (1980), 'Bertil Ohlin', *Challenge*, September–October, pp. 54–7.

Samuelson, P.A. (1981), 'Bertil Ohlin (1899–1979)', *Scandinavian Journal of Economics*, **83** (3), pp. 355–71.

Steiger, O. (1976), 'Bertil Ohlin and the Origins of the Keynesian Revolution', *History of Political Economy*, **8**, Fall, pp. 342–67.

Steiger, O. (1981), 'Bertil Ohlin, 1899–1979', *History of Political Economy*, **13**, Summer, pp. 179–88.

See also   Beaud and Dostaler (1997, pp. 368–70); Blaug (1998, pp. 217–19; 1999, pp. 848–9); Cate (1997, pp. 487–90); Nobel Foundation (2004).

James E. Meade
(1907–95)

© The Nobel Foundation

James Meade was born in Swanage, England in 1907. He studied classics and economics at Oriel College, Oxford and obtained his BA in 1930. After graduating he was appointed as a Lecturer in Economics at Hertford College, Oxford but only started teaching there in 1931, after spending a year engaged in graduate work at Trinity College, Cambridge, where he participated in the 'Cambridge Circus' debating Keynes's ideas. In 1937 Meade left Oxford to work as an economist for the League of Nations in Geneva. Returning to Britain in 1940, he served as a member (1940–45) and director (1946–47) of the Economic Section of the British Cabinet Office. In 1947 he returned to academic life, first as Professor of Economics at the London School of Economics from 1947 to 1957, and then as Professor of Political Economy at the University of Cambridge from 1957 until his retirement in 1969. From 1969 until his death in 1995 he was a senior research fellow of Christ's College, Cambridge.

Meade's many offices and honours included the chairmanship of an Economic Survey Mission to Mauritius in 1960, presidency of the Royal Economic Society from 1964 to 1966, and chairmanship of a committee of the Institute of Fiscal Studies from 1975 to 1977. In 1977 Meade was awarded, jointly with the Swedish economist Bertil Ohlin, the Nobel Memorial Prize in Economics 'for their pathbreaking con-tribution to the theory of international trade and international capital movements' (Nobel Foundation, 2004).

Meade's main contribution to economics was in the field of inter-national economics, primarily through his two-volume study, *The Theory of International Economic Policy* (Meade, 1951; 1955a). In the first volume, *The Balance of Payments*, published in 1951, he synthe-sised Keynesian theory with general equilibrium theory and ex-tended the traditional theory of the balance of payments beyond current account transactions to include international capital move-ments. Analysing the relationship between internal balance (full employment) and external balance (overall balance of payments equilibrium), he demonstrated the need to use two instruments (aggregate demand management and the exchange rate) in order to achieve the two policy targets of internal and external balance (see also Meade, 1993 – his Nobel Memorial Lecture). Interestingly, the relationship between policy objectives and instruments was devel-oped independently in the early 1950s by the Dutch economist Jan Tinbergen, the first Nobel Memorial Laureate. In the second volume of his study, *Trade and Welfare*, published in 1955, Meade examined the relationship between controls on international trade and factor movements, and economic welfare. In doing so he discovered the 'theory of second best' which soon became an important addition to the literature on welfare economics. The theory of second best was subsequently developed by Richard Lipsey and Kelvin Lancaster in an article published in the *Review of Economic Studies* in 1956.

Meade also made a number of other influential contributions to the field of international economics, including the development of a geometrical portrayal of international trade using 'offer curves' (Meade, 1952), and an extension of the work of the Canadian economist Jacob Viner on customs unions and the effects of such unions on 'trade creation' and 'trade diversion' (Meade, 1955b). Overall, his work on the theory of international trade and eco-nomic policy provided fertile ground for much subsequent re-search in the field.

While Meade will be remembered first and foremost for his pio-neering work in international economics, he also made important contributions to a number of other areas. These include: (i) the early presentation of Keynesian ideas in his book *An Introduction to Eco-nomic Analysis and Policy* (Meade, 1936), and a simplified algebraic presentation (Meade, 1937) of the main arguments put forward in Keynes's seminal book *The General Theory of Employment, Interest and Money* which was published in 1936; (ii) his co-authored 1944 book with Richard Stone (who was awarded the Nobel Memorial Prize in Economics in 1984 for his 'contributions to the development of systems of national accounts') on 'double-entry' accounts, *National Income and Expenditure*; (iii) the theory of economic growth (Meade, 1961); and (iv) the field of welfare economics. In the last, he expressed his concerns over the distribution of income and capital in a series of books (Meade, 1964; 1971; 1974; 1975; 1976). Besides writing a significant number of influential books, Meade also wrote numerous papers which were published in learned journals. Many of his most important works have been gathered together in four volumes: *Collected Papers* (Meade, 1988; 1989).

Main Published Works

(1936), *An Introduction to Economic Analysis and Policy*, London: Oxford University Press.

(1937), 'A Simplified Model of Mr. Keynes' System', *Review of Economic Studies*, 4, February, pp. 98–107.

(1944), *National Income and Expenditure* (with J.R.N. Stone), London: Oxford University Press.

(1951), *The Theory of International Economic Policy: I. The Balance of Payments*, London: Oxford University Press.

(1952), *A Geometry of International Trade*, London: George Allen & Unwin.

(1955a), *The Theory of International Economic Policy: II. Trade and Welfare*, London: Oxford University Press.

(1955b), *The Theory of Customs Unions*, Amsterdam: North-Holland.

(1961), *A Neo-Classical Theory of Economic Growth*, London: George Allen & Unwin.

(1964), *Efficiency, Equality and the Ownership of Property*, London: George Allen & Unwin.

(1965), *Principles of Political Economy: I. The Stationary Economy*, London: George Allen & Unwin.

(1968), *Principles of Political Economy: II. The Growing Economy*, London: George Allen & Unwin.

(1971), *Principles of Political Economy: III. The Controlled Economy*, London: George Allen & Unwin.

(1974), *The Inheritance of Inequalities*, London: Oxford University Press.

(1975), *The Intelligent Radical's Guide to Economic Policy*, London: George Allen & Unwin.

(1976), *Principles of Political Economy: IV. The Just Economy*, London: George Allen & Unwin.

(1988), *The Collected Papers of James Meade* (eds S. Howson and D. Moggridge), vols 1–3, London: Unwin Hyman.

(1989), *The Collected Papers of James Meade* (eds S. Howson and D. Moggridge), vol. 4, London: Unwin Hyman.

(1993), 'The Meaning of Internal Balance', *American Economic Review*, 83, December, pp. 3–9.

Secondary Literature

Johnson, H. (1978), 'James Meade's Contribution to Economics', *Scandinavian Journal of Economics*, 80 (1), pp. 64–85.

Lipsey, R.G. and K.J. Lancaster (1956), 'The General Theory of Second Best', *Review of Economic Studies*, **24**, October, pp. 11–32.

See also   Beaud and Dostaler (1997, pp. 341–3); Blaug (1998, pp. 189–91; 1999, p. 761); Cate (1997, pp. 414–17); Nobel Foundation (2004).

THE 1978 NOBEL MEMORIAL LAUREATE

HERBERT SIMON

Herbert A. Simon
(1916–2001)

© The Nobel Foundation

Herbert Simon was born in Milwaukee, Wisconsin, USA in 1916. He studied political science at the University of Chicago where he obtained a BA in 1936 and a PhD in 1943. His early posts included a position at the International City Managers' Association in Chicago from 1938 to 1939. Subsequently he became Director of Administrative Measurement Studies at the Bureau of Public Administration of the University of California at Berkeley from 1939 to 1942. In 1942 Simon returned to Chicago, where he was appointed initially as an Assistant Professor of Political Science at Illinois Institute of Technology, before becoming a full professor in 1947. In 1949 he moved to Pittsburgh, where he was Professor of Administration and Psychology at the Carnegie Institute of Technology (later renamed Carnegie-Mellon University) from 1949 to 1955, and Professor of Computer Science and Psychology from 1955 until he retired in 1988.

Simon's many offices and honours included: the Distinguished Scientific Contribution Award of the American Psychological Association in 1969; the A.M. Turing Award of the Association for Computing Machinery (with A. Newell) in 1975; a Distinguished Fellowship of the American Economic Association (1976); the James Madison Award of the American Political Science Association in

1984; the award of the National Medal of Science in 1986; the John von Neumann Theory Prize of ORSA/TIMS in 1988; the Research Excellence Award of the International Joint Conference on Artificial Intelligence in 1995; and the award of numerous honorary degrees from universities around the world. In 1978, Simon was awarded the Nobel Memorial Prize in Economics 'for his pioneering research into the decision-making process within economic organizations' (Nobel Foundation, 2004).

In economics Simon is best known for his important contributions to the field of behavioural decision making, especially in large organisations. His pioneering research in this area can be traced back to his PhD thesis on decision-making processes in administrative organisations, which was published (in revised form) in 1947 in his first major book entitled *Administrative Behaviour*. Central to this work is the idea that human decision making results in satisficing, rather than optimising, behaviour. The traditional theory of the firm is based on the assumption of an omniscient, fully rational, profit-maximising entrepreneur. In Simon's approach, the single entrepreneur is replaced by a constellation of decision makers whose rationality is limited and who cooperate to find satisfactory solutions to the problems they face. In consequence, firms are unable to maximise profits. He argued that, in reality, people in large organisations cannot obtain or process all the information needed to make fully rational decisions. Instead, due to limitations of knowledge (for example, about the uncertain future) and the capacity to process information, people 'satisfice' by making decisions which result in acceptable outcomes. In other words, people make decisions which are 'good enough', settling for certain aspiration levels which they adjust occasionally (either upwards or downwards) when outcomes do not match targets. In his book he rejected the idea of 'economic man' who 'optimises' instead introducing the concept of 'administrative man' who 'satisfices'. This view of human decision making, based on 'limited' rationality, or what he subsequently called 'bounded' rationality, results in 'satisficing', not optimising, behaviour.

A central aim of Simon's research was to investigate human rationality. In another influential book entitled *Models of Man* (Simon, 1957), he presented a collection of essays on rational human behaviour in a social setting. This work combined economic with philosophical and psychological perspectives specifically addressing:

causation and influence relationships; social processes; motivation; and rationality and administrative decision making. In a series of books published with others in the 1950s and 1960s (Simon et al., 1950; 1960a; March and Simon, 1958; Simon, 1960b; 1965) he developed the ideas first put forward in his classic book, *Administrative Behaviour*. His interest in human decision making also led him to undertake research in the disciplines of political science, psychology and computer science. In the last case, for example, from the mid-1950s onwards he undertook research with Allen Newell to program computers to simulate human problem-solving behaviour using heuristics based on bounded rationality. This research led to the pioneering idea that computers can exhibit an 'artificial intelligence' which mirrors human thinking (Simon, 1969; Newell and Simon, 1972) and to the 'information processing revolution' in cognitive psychology. His extensive knowledge of, and research in, political science, economics, psychology and computer science allowed him to make insightful links between the disciplines. This led Simon to make important contributions to a number of fields, most notably human cognition, artificial intelligence and management science. Furthermore he explored the implications of this wide-ranging research for economics (see Earl, 2001). While he will be remembered in economics, first and foremost, for his analysis of decision making and its applications, he also undertook work in other areas of the discipline. For example, he made important contributions to mathematical economics, including a theorem concerned with the existence of a solution to an input–output process (Hawkins and Simon, 1949).

As should be evident from this brief overview, Simon was a truly remarkable and talented individual. Over the course of a long and distinguished career he held professorships in political science, administration, psychology and computer science. Through detailed and wide-ranging research he made lasting contributions to a number of disciplines and fields. The common theme running through all his work is that it is concerned with human decision-making and problem-solving processes. Many of Simon's most important papers have been gathered together in six volumes: *Models of Discovery* (Simon, 1977), a collection of his papers on the philosophy of science; *Models of Thought* (Simon, 1979a), a two-volume collection of his papers in psychology; and *Models of Bounded Rationality* (Simon, 1982; 1997), a three-volume collection, containing more than 80 articles, of his papers in economics. The legacy of Herbert Simon in economic analysis is considered in a two-volume collection of 50 papers (Earl, 2001).

Main Published Works

(1947), *Administrative Behaviour*, New York: Macmillan; 4th edn 1997, New York: Free Press.

(1949), 'Note: Some Conditions of Macroeconomic Stability' (with D. Hawkins), *Econometrica*, **17**, July–October, pp. 245–8.

(1950), *Public Administration* (with V.A. Thompson and D.W. Smithburg), New York: Alfred A. Knopf.

(1957), *Models of Man*, New York: John Wiley.

(1958), *Organizations* (with J.G. March), New York: John Wiley; 2nd edn 1993, Cambridge, MA: Blackwell.

(1960a), *Planning Production, Inventories and Work Forces* (with C.C. Holt, F. Modigliani and J. Muth), Englewood Cliffs, NJ: Prentice-Hall.

(1960b), *The New Science of Management Decision*, New York: Harper & Row; revised edn 1977, Englewood Cliffs, NJ: Prentice-Hall.

(1965), *The Shape of Automation for Men and Management*, New York: Harper & Row.

(1969), *The Sciences of the Artificial*, Cambridge, MA: MIT Press; 3rd edn 1996.

(1972), *Human Problem Solving* (with A. Newell), Englewood Cliffs, NJ: Prentice-Hall.

(1977), *Models of Discovery*, Dordrecht: Reidel.

(1979a), *Models of Thought*, New Haven, CT: Yale University Press.

(1979b), 'Rational Decision Making in Business Organizations', *American Economic Review*, **69**, September, pp. 493–513.

(1982), *Models of Bounded Rationality*, 2 vols, Cambridge, MA: MIT Press.

(1992), *Economics, Bounded Rationality and Cognitive Revolution* (with M. Egidi, R. Marris and R. Viale), (eds M. Egidi and R. Marris), Aldershot: Edward Elgar.

(1997), *Models of Bounded Rationality*, vol. 3, Cambridge, MA: MIT Press.

Secondary Literature

Ando, A. (1979), 'On the Contributions of Herbert A. Simon to Economics', *Scandinavian Journal of Economics*, **81** (1), pp. 83–114.

Baumol, W.J. (1979), 'On the Contributions of Herbert A. Simon to Economics', *Scandinavian Journal of Economics*, **81** (1), pp. 74–82 and 94–114.

Earl, P.E. (ed.) (2001), *The Legacy of Herbert Simon in Economic Analysis*, 2 vols, Cheltenham, UK and Northampton, MA, USA: Edward Elgar.

See also Beaud and Dostaler (1997, pp. 406–9); Blaug (1998, pp. 265–7; 1999, p. 1034); Nobel Foundation (2004).

THE 1979 NOBEL MEMORIAL LAUREATES

LAUREATES

THEODORE SCHULTZ
AND
ARTHUR LEWIS

© The Nobel Foundation

Theodore W. Schultz
(1902–98)

Theodore Schultz was born in Arlington, South Dakota, USA in 1902. He studied agricultural economics at South Dakota State College where he received a bachelor's degree in 1926, before obtaining an MS and PhD from the University of Wisconsin in 1928 and 1930, respectively. In 1930, Schultz began his career as a teacher at Iowa State College (an agricultural college), where he served as head of the Department of Economics and Sociology between 1934 and 1943. In 1943 he moved to the University of Chicago, where he was Professor of Economics from 1943 to 1952, and Charles L. Hutchinson Distinguished Service Professor from 1952 until his retirement in 1972. During his career at the University of Chicago he served as chairman of the Department of Economics from 1946 to 1961.

Schultz's many offices and honours included presidency of the American Economic Association in 1960 and the award of the Francis A. Walker Medal of the American Economic Association in 1972, and the Leonard Elmhirst Medal of the International Agricultural Economic Association in 1976. In 1979 he was awarded jointly with Arthur Lewis the Nobel Memorial Prize in Economics 'for their pioneering research into economic development research with particular consideration of the problems of developing countries' (Nobel Foundation, 2004).

Schultz began his academic career as an agricultural economist. Initially focusing his research on the crises and problems of American agriculture, during the 1930s, 1940s and early 1950s his studies were published in a series of articles and influential books (see, for example, Schultz, 1941; 1943; 1945; 1949; 1953). He later turned his attention to the problems facing agriculture in developing countries (Schultz, 1964; 1965; 1968; 1978) and in doing so contributed to a much greater understanding of the relationship between agriculture, economic development and the economics of being poor. His classic book, *Transforming Traditional Agriculture*, published in 1964 by Yale University Press and subsequently translated into Japanese, Korean, Portuguese and Spanish, earned Schultz worldwide fame. The book brought together his views of the problems of agriculture and economic development in poor nations with his views about investment in human beings (see below).

A number of key themes can be identified in Schultz's studies of the agricultural problems of the United States and developing countries including: the possibility of increasing, rather than Marshallian diminishing, returns in agriculture; the importance of prices in determining the use and allocation of resources, both within agriculture and across other sectors in the economy; the treatment of agriculture as an integral part of the whole economy, instead of studying it in isolation; the idea that farmers are rational and that they develop efficient methods of farming in traditional agriculture given the constraints and uncertainty they face; the importance of economic incentives to decision making and how they can be affected by government policies; a critique of the bias given to industrialisation through development planning in poor nations, with its consequential adverse effects on rural poverty and development in those countries; the key role which education and information can play in transforming traditional agriculture into progressive agriculture with the associated potential to promote dynamic development; and, more generally, the importance of human resources in economic and social development.

In addition to his influential contributions to agricultural economics, Schultz is also known for his pioneering research in the field of human capital. The essential idea underlying the theory of human capital is that investments are made in human resources (for example, through education and training), which increase the productivity of those resources. Given that such investments involve costs, investment criteria need to be applied to ascertain whether or not the future benefits or returns outweigh the costs incurred. In Schultz's (1958) first major publication on human capital, which focused on high-school education, he suggested that increases in national income could be attributed to improvements in the *quality* of both human and non-human resources. In subsequent work he considered investment in human capital (Schultz, 1960; 1961a; 1961b; 1962; 1971) and investment in education (Schultz, 1963; 1972). His presidential address to the American Economic Association, 'Investment in Human Capital', published in the March 1961 issue of the *American Economic Review*, was particularly influential in drawing attention to the field of human capital. Indeed, Schultz's pioneering work in the field, together with that of Jacob Mincer and Gary Becker (the 1992 Nobel Memorial Laureate), helped create what has come to be known as a 'human investment revolution' in economics. This revolution has had implications for research undertaken in a number of areas of study, including agricultural economics, business economics, development economics, the economics of education, labour economics and urban economics. Among the insights provided by Schultz in his research on the economics of human resources are: the importance of human capital investment, compared to non-human capital investment, to economic growth; the importance of forgone earnings from employment as a cost of human capital formation when people invest in education; identification of rates of return on investment in people; the importance of the quality of education in determining economic growth; estimates of the extent to which education contributes to economic growth; and the importance of investment in health and disease control, as well as investment in education, in the concept of human capital formation, with implications for economic development in poor nations.

In summary, Schultz will be remembered for his influential and pioneering contributions to agricultural economics, the study of economic development and the economics of human resources, work that has acted as a catalyst to much subsequent new research in these important fields of study.

Main Published Works

(1941), 'Economic Effects of Agricultural Programs', *American Economic Review*, **30**, February, pp. 127–54.

(1943), *Redirecting Farm Policy*, New York: Macmillan.

(1945), *Agriculture in an Unstable Economy*, New York: McGraw-Hill.

(1949), *Production and Welfare of Agriculture*, New York: Macmillan.

(1953), *The Economic Organization of Agriculture*, New York: McGraw-Hill.

(1958), 'The Emerging Economic Scene and Its Relation to High-School Education', in F.S. Chase and H.A. Anderson (eds), *The High School in a New Era*, Chicago: University of Chicago Press, pp. 97–109.

(1960), 'Capital Formation by Education', *Journal of Political Economy*, **68**, December, pp. 571–83.

(1961a), 'Investment in Human Capital', *American Economic Review*, **51**, March, pp. 1–17.

(1961b), 'Investment in Human Capital: A Reply', *American Economic Review*, **51**, December, pp. 1035–9.

(1962), *Investment in Human Beings* (ed.), Chicago: University of Chicago Press.

(1963), *The Economic Value of Education*, New York: Columbia University Press.

(1964), *Transforming Traditional Agriculture*, New Haven, CT: Yale University Press.

(1965), *Economic Crises in World Agriculture*, Ann Arbor, MI: University of Michigan Press.

(1968), *Economic Growth and Agriculture*, New York: McGraw-Hill.

(1971), *Investment in Human Capital: The Role of Education and Research*, New York: Free Press.

(1972), *Investment in Education: The Equity–Efficiency Quandary* (ed.), Chicago: University of Chicago Press.

(1978), *Distortions of Agricultural Incentives* (ed.), Bloomington, IN: Indiana University Press.

Secondary Literature

Bowman, M.J. (1980), 'On Theodore W. Schultz's Contributions to Economics', *Scandinavian Journal of Economics*, **82** (1), pp. 80–107.

See also Beaud and Dostaler (1997, pp. 397–400); Blaug (1998, pp. 253–5; 1999, pp. 1003–4); Nobel Foundation (2004).

W. Arthur Lewis
(1915–91)

© The Nobel Foundation

Arthur Lewis was born in St Lucia, West Indies in 1915. He started work as a clerk at the age of 14 years before winning, at 17, a scholarship which allowed him to study abroad. In 1933 he began his undergraduate studies at the London School of Economics (LSE), where he obtained a BCom in 1937, and a PhD in 1940. Lewis began his academic career at the LSE where he taught from 1938 to 1948, except for attachments to the Board of Trade and the Colonial Office during the Second World War. In 1948 he moved to the University of Manchester, where he held the Stanley Jevons Chair of Political Economy until 1958, a period when some of his most influential work was published. In 1958 he left Manchester to return to the West Indies, where he was principal of University College, West Indies until 1962. Subsequently, when University College was enlarged and renamed, he became the first vice-chancellor of the University of the West Indies. Lewis moved to Princeton University in 1963 as Professor of Economic and Political Affairs, and later occupied the James Madison Chair of Political Economy. In 1970, Lewis left Princeton to become president of the newly created Caribbean Development Bank, but returned to Princeton in 1973 where he remained until he retired in 1983.

During the course of his distinguished career Lewis acted as a consultant and adviser to a number of African countries, including the Gold Coast, Western Nigeria and Ghana, as well as to the United Nations. Lewis's many offices and honours include a knighthood in 1963, and the award of 20 honorary degrees from universities around the world. He was elected president of the American Economic Association in 1983. In 1979, Lewis was awarded jointly with Theodore Schultz the Nobel Memorial Prize in Economics 'for their pioneering research into economic development research with particular consideration of the problems of developing countries' (Nobel Foundation, 2004).

During the first phase of his academic career, while teaching at the LSE, Lewis wrote three main books on international economic history, industrial economics and development economics. In *Economic Survey, 1919–1939*, published in 1949, he analysed the events and policies of the interwar years in the context of 'world economic history' (Lewis, 1949a). His research interest in the economic history of the world economy persisted throughout his career and was manifested almost 30 years later in the publication of his 1978 book, *Growth and Fluctuations* – see below. *Overhead Costs*, also published in 1949, is a collection of his essays on industrial economics and includes chapters on 'fixed costs', 'the two-part tariff' for the pricing of electricity and telephone services, 'competition in retail trade' and 'monopoly and the law' (Lewis, 1949b). In his third main book, *The Principles of Economic Planning* (1950), written while at the LSE, he advocated 'planning through the market' as opposed to 'planning by direction'.

When Lewis moved to the University of Manchester, the focus of his work switched to the study of development economics. During this period of his career his worldwide reputation as a development economist was firmly established, most notably through the publication of his two most famous and influential works, namely, his seminal article, 'Economic Development with Unlimited Supplies of Labour', published in the May 1954 issue of the *Manchester School*, and his 1955 book, *The Theory of Economic Growth*. The remit of the book is far wider than the title suggests as he not only synthesised the state of knowledge on the subject but also considered the development problems of poor nations in the Third World. In his 1954 article, Lewis analysed the 'dual economy' of less-developed countries (LDCs). The 'traditional sector", which includes traditional peasant agriculture, is essentially one of self-support and employment. In contrast in the 'capitalist sector', which includes industrial production such as manufacturing and mining, employment is motivated by the desire to earn profit. In the early stages of development from a traditional economy to a mature modern industrial economy, the large stationary 'traditional sector' is able to supply an unlimited supply of labour to the small dynamic 'capitalist sector' at a given real wage rate. The exogenously given real wage rate for unskilled labour is socially determined by minimum standards of living in traditional agriculture, and remains low as a result of rural underemployment and urban unemployment. Profits earned in the capitalist sector provide the source of funds for reinvestment and expansion of output and employment in the dynamic sector. Only in the later stages of development when the surplus or excess supply of labour from the traditional sector is exhausted will wages begin to rise above the exogenously given low levels, by which time expansion in the capitalist sector will have fostered economic development.

The other main idea Lewis put forward in his 1954 article, and which he subsequently developed in his 1969 Wicksell Lectures (Lewis, 1969), was an explanation of what determines the terms of trade between developed and developing countries. In his model he considered two regions, or groups of countries, which each produce two types of goods. The rich North produces steel and food, while the poor South produces coffee and food; the production of food being common to both regions. The South exports coffee to the North, in exchange for steel. Assuming linear transformation between the two goods produced in each region, the terms of trade are determined by relative labour productivity in food between the two groups of developed and developing countries. Higher agricultural productivity in the rich developed countries of the North compared to that in the poor developing countries of the South explains the adverse effect on the South's terms of trade. Lewis also demonstrated how the South's terms of trade with the North will deteriorate over time due to faster productivity growth in food than in steel in the North and slower productivity growth in food than in coffee in the South (see Lewis, 1969). The implication of his analysis is that measures are required which increase agricultural productivity in developing countries (such as investment in human and physical capital) in order to redress the unfavourable terms of trade they face with developed countries and to help reduce poverty.

In addition to this highly influential work, which acted as a catalyst to much subsequent research in the field of development economics, Lewis also had research published on the problems of development planning (Lewis, 1965; 1966) and, as mentioned earlier, the history of the world economy. In the latter case in his 1978 book, *Growth and Fluctuations*, he considered the evolution of the world economy in the period from 1870 to 1913. In his analysis, expansion of manufacturing provided the 'engine of growth' in a nucleus of four 'core' industrialised countries (Britain, France, Germany and the United States), which served to send out 'growth pulsations' to the rest of the world economy through international trade. Lewis considered how growth and fluctuations in the 'core' countries affected two groups of 'periphery' countries, both of whom exported primary goods to, and imported manufactured goods from, the core. Favourable effects on growth were experienced in the temperate zone of countries of 'recent settlement' such as Argentina, Australia, Canada and New Zealand. These countries were largely populated by migrant labour from Europe, and in the temperate zone unskilled labour earned wages which provided a comparable standard of living to that achieved in the core countries. In contrast, unfavourable growth effects were experienced in the tropical zone, consisting of most of today's LDCs, where subsistence wages resulted from 'unlimited supplies of labour'. In Lewis's analysis, differences in wage levels for unskilled labour reflecting differences in labour productivity in food, had serious implications for the size of the domestic markets in the two peripheries, their terms of trade with the core and their respective potential for economic development through industrialisation. In considering the problems of LDCs within the context of the world economy, Lewis was able to demonstrate important links between the core of developed industrialised countries and the peripheries over the period from 1870 to 1913.

Lewis will be remembered first and foremost for his model of economic development with 'unlimited supplies of labour' and his contributions to development economics. In particular, his pioneering work has led to much subsequent research into the problems of poverty and underdevelopment experienced by people in Third World countries. Many of his most important papers on industrial economics, developing countries, economic development and international economic relations have been gathered together in a 1983 collection entitled *Selected Economic Writings of W. Arthur Lewis*, edited by Mark Gersovitz.

Main Published Works

(1949a), *Economic Survey, 1919–1939*, London: George Allen & Unwin.

(1949b), *Overhead Costs*, London: George Allen & Unwin.

(1950), *The Principles of Economic Planning*, London: George Allen & Unwin.

(1954), 'Economic Development with Unlimited Supplies of Labour', *Manchester School of Economic and Social Studies*, **22**, May, pp. 139–91.

(1955), *The Theory of Economic Growth*, London: George Allen & Unwin.

(1965), *Politics in West Africa*, Oxford: Oxford University Press.

(1966), *Development Planning: The Essentials of Economic Policy*, London: George Allen & Unwin.

(1969), *Aspects of Tropical Trade, 1883–1965*, Stockholm: Almquist & Wicksell.

(1978), *Growth and Fluctuations: 1870–1913*, London: George Allen & Unwin.

(1983), *Selected Economic Writings of W. Arthur Lewis* (ed. M. Gersovitz), New York: New York University Press.

Secondary Literature

Findlay, R. (1980), 'On W. Arthur Lewis' Contributions to Economics', *Scandinavian Journal of Economics*, **82** (1), pp. 62–79.

See also Beaud and Dostaler (1997, pp. 320–22); Blaug (1998, pp. 164–6; 1999, p. 686); Nobel Foundation (2004).

THE 1980 NOBEL MEMORIAL LAUREATE

LAWRENCE KLEIN

Lawrence R. Klein
(b. 1920)

© The Nobel Foundation

Lawrence Klein was born in Omaha, Nebraska, USA in 1920. He obtained a BA from the University of California, Berkeley in 1942 and a PhD from the Massachusetts Institute of Technology in 1944. Klein was a graduate student under Paul Samuelson (the 1970 Nobel Memorial Laureate), and *The Keynesian Revolution*, his revised doctoral thesis, was subsequently published in 1947 (Klein, 1947b). In 1944, he joined the Cowles Commission at the University of Chicago as a research associate, and subsequently worked in the same capacity at the National Bureau of Economic Research from 1948 to 1950, and the Survey Research Center at the University of Michigan from 1949 to 1954. In 1954, in response to Senator Eugene McCarthy's anti-communist witch-hunt, Klein left the United States for Great Britain where he joined the staff at the Oxford University Institute of Statistics, first as a senior research officer and then as reader. After four years at the Institute, Klein left Oxford in 1958 and returned to America as professor at the University of Pennsylvania, where he remained until he retired from teaching in 1991. He is currently the Benjamin Franklin Professor of Economics, Emeritus, at the University of Pennsylvania.

Klein's many offices and honours have included the award of the John Bates Clark Medal of the American Economic Association in

1959, and election to the presidencies of the Econometric Society in 1960 and the American Economic Association in 1977. In 1980, Klein was awarded the Nobel Memorial Prize in Economics 'for the creation of econometric models and their application to the analysis of economic fluctuations and economic policies' (Nobel Foundation, 2004).

Klein's published work covers three main areas, namely economic theory, econometrics and econometric model building. He has made a number of important contributions to economic theory, most notably to the specification and development of Keynesian economics (see, for example, Klein, 1947a; 1947b). His 1947 book *The Keynesian Revolution* established his international reputation as a leading scholar on Keynesian economics. In writing the book he helped to formalise, clarify and extend the central arguments Keynes had put forward in *The General Theory of Employment, Interest and Money* and forcefully demonstrated the nature of the revolution in economic thought that Keynes had instigated. Klein's published work in the field of econometrics has largely been concerned with the teaching of the subject through the publication of a series of books (Klein, 1953; 1962; 1983; Klein and Young, 1980). In addition to writing expository textbooks on econometrics and its practical applications, he has also made contributions to the analysis of such problems as the estimation of distributed lags (Klein, 1958) and simultaneous estimation in econometrics (Klein, 1960). However, above all else, he is primarily known for his pioneering work in the field of econometric model building. Over the course of a long and distinguished career he has constructed a series of models which have been used to provide forecasts of key macroeconomic variables, including GNP, consumption, investment, exports and imports, and the effects of alternative policies on these variables.

Klein's interest in econometric model building began when, in 1944, he joined the Cowles Commission for Research in Economics, at that time located at the University of Chicago. Reinvigorating the early attempts of the Dutch economist Jan Tinbergen (see entry on Tinbergen in this volume) at macroeconometric model building in the 1930s, he began by constructing an interwar model of the United States (Klein, 1950). Next, during his time at the Survey Research Center at the University of Michigan, he designed and constructed, in collaboration with his then-graduate student Arthur Goldberger, a macroeconometric model of the US economy which became popularly known as the Klein–Goldberger model (Klein and Goldberger, 1955). Subsequently, in the mid-1950s while working at the Oxford University Institute of Statistics, he collaborated in building the first econometric model of the United Kingdom (Klein et al., 1961).

The construction of this first series of models was followed by three major research projects while working at the University of Pennsylvania. First, along with James Duesenberry, Klein played a major role in the construction of the Brookings quarterly econometric model of the United States which was used to forecast short-term developments in the US economy (see, 1965 with Duesenberry et al.; Fromm and Klein, 1975). Interested readers should consult his 1976 co-edited book with Edwin Burmeister, *Econometric Model Performance*, and their comparative simulations of the US economy at that time (see also Klein, 1991a). Second, he initiated and oversaw the development of successive generations of what has come to be known as the Wharton Model (Evans and Klein, 1967). The model was the result of the combined work of Lawrence Klein and Michael Evans, who joined the faculty of the University of Pennsylvania having developed a model of the US economy for his doctoral thesis at Brown University. Klein's entrepreneurial talent was reflected by the sale of econometric forecasts generated by the model to buyers both in the public and private sectors. The funds raised were then used to support students and further research at the University of Pennsylvania. This income-generating enterprise evolved into Wharton Econometric Forecasting Associates (WEFA), an organisation he founded, and was later sold as a profit-making company (since October 2002 renamed as Global Insight). Klein's third research project at Pennsylvania was to act as a principal investigator in project LINK. Created in 1968, the project combines national economic models of countries from around the world into a linked model in order to increase understanding of international relationships and improve forecasts of world trade and economic activity.

Although Klein has made important contributions to both economic theory and econometrics, he is best known for his pioneering work in econometric modelling. His efforts in this field have inspired and influenced model building worldwide. For an authoritative discussion of the history of macroeconometric model building, including comparative experience from a number of countries, the reader is referred to Klein's 1991 book on the subject, co-authored with Ronald Bodkin and Kanta Marwah (1991b).

Main Published Works

(1947a), 'Theories of Effective Demand and Employment', *Journal of Political Economy*, **55**, April, pp. 108–31.

(1947b), *The Keynesian Revolution*, New York: Macmillan; 2nd edn 1966.

(1950), *Economic Fluctuations in the United States: 1921–1941*, New York: John Wiley.

(1953), *A Textbook of Econometrics*, Evanston, IL: Row, Peterson & Co; 2nd edn 1974, Englewood Cliffs, NJ: Prentice-Hall.

(1955), *An Econometric Model of the United States: 1929–1952* (with A.S. Goldberger), New York: John Wiley.

(1958), 'The Estimation of Distributed Lags', *Econometrica*, **26**, October, pp. 553–65.

(1960), 'Single Equation vs. Equation System Methods of Estimation in Econometrics', *Econometrica*, **28**, October, pp. 866–71.

(1961), *An Econometric Model of the United Kingdom* (with R.J. Ball, A. Hazelwood and P. Vandome), Oxford: Basil Blackwell.

(1962), *An Introduction to Econometrics*, Englewood Cliffs, NJ: Prentice-Hall.

(1965), *The Brookings Quarterly Econometric Model of the United States* (ed. with J. Duesenberry, G. Fromm and E. Kuh), Chicago: Rand-McNally.

(1967), *The Wharton Econometric Forecasting Model* (with M.K. Evans), Philadelphia, PA: Wharton School of Finance and Commerce.

(1975), *The Brookings Model: Perspective and Recent Developments* (ed. with G. Fromm), New York: John Wiley.

(1976), *Econometric Model Performance* (ed. with E. Burmeister), Philadelphia, PA: University of Pennsylvania Press.

(1980), *An Introduction to Econometric Forecasting and Forecasting Models*, (with R.M. Young), Lexington, MA: Lexington Books.

(1983), *Lectures in Econometrics*, Amsterdam: North-Holland.

(1991a), *Comparative Performance of US Econometric Models* (ed.), New York: Oxford University Press.

(1991b), *A History of Macroeconometric Model-Building* (with R.G. Bodkin and K. Marwah), Aldershot, UK and Brookfield, US: Edward Elgar.

Secondary Literature

Ball, R.J. (1981), 'On Lawrence R. Klein's Contributions to Economics', *Scandinavian Journal of Economics*, **83** (1), pp. 81–103.

See also Beaud and Dostaler (1997, pp. 298–301); Blaug (1998, pp. 133–5; 1999, pp. 620–21); Cate (1997, pp. 352–4); Nobel Foundation (2004).

THE 1981 NOBEL MEMORIAL LAUREATE ·

JAMES TOBIN

James Tobin
(1918–2002)

© The Nobel Foundation

James Tobin was born in Champaign, Illinois, USA in 1918. In receipt of a scholarship, he studied at Harvard University earning a BA in 1939 and an MA in 1940. His graduate studies at Harvard were interrupted by his wartime service, first as a junior economist in the US Office of Price Administration and Civilian Supply and War Production from 1941 to 1942, and then from 1942 to 1946 when he served in the US Navy. In 1946 Tobin returned to Harvard to complete his doctoral thesis on the theory and statistics of the consumption function, and was awarded a PhD in 1947. Tobin then taught at Harvard for three years as a junior fellow during which time he spent a year in England as a visitor to the Department of Applied Economics at Cambridge University from 1949 to 1950. In 1950 he joined the economics department at Yale University as an associate professor, later holding the posts of Professor of Economics (1955–57), Sterling Professor of Economics (1957–88), and chairman of the Economics Department (1968–69 and 1974–78). At Yale he also served as director of the Cowles Foundation for Research in Economics from 1955 to 1961 and from 1964 to 1965. From 1988, until his death in 2002, he was Sterling Professor, Emeritus, at Yale University.

As is evident from this brief biographical overview, Tobin spent almost his entire career at Yale, with the notable exceptions of a year as each of: a member of President Kennedy's Council of Economic Advisers in Washington, DC in 1961–62; a Rockefeller Foundation Visiting Professor at the University of Nairobi's Institute for Development Studies in 1972–73; visiting professor at the University of Minnesota in 1978; and Ford Visiting Research Professor at the University of California, Berkeley in 1983.

Tobin's many offices and honours included the award of the John Bates Clark Medal of the American Economic Association in 1955, and presidencies of the Econometric Society (1958), the American Economic Association (1971) and the Eastern Economic Association (1977). In 1981, Tobin was awarded the Nobel Memorial Prize in Economics 'for his analysis of financial markets and their relations to expenditure decisions, employment, production and prices' (Nobel Foundation, 2004).

James Tobin is widely known as having been one, if not the most eminent, of the world's Keynesian economists and has been described by Buiter (2003) as 'the greatest macroeconomist of his generation'. A self-confessed 'old-style' Keynesian (Tobin, 1993), over the course of his long and distinguished career, Tobin modified, refined and extended many basic Keynesian ideas on how the economy works. While his most important contributions to economics are to be found in the interrelated fields of monetary and macroeconomic theory, he also contributed to the continuing debate over the role and conduct of stabilisation policy. Although he was a lifelong vigorous defender of orthodox Keynesian ideas, especially against the counter-revolutionary attacks posed by monetarism and new classical economics in the 1960s, 1970s and 1980s, he was none the less aware of shortcomings and inadequacies in some of the work of Keynes. Indeed, in his first published paper (Tobin, 1941), he criticised Keynes's treatment of the relation of the money wage and aggregate employment. In much of his subsequent work he sought to clarify and develop Keynes's analysis of a number of key relationships.

In his early work, Tobin concentrated on the monetary side of macroeconomics, in particular focusing his research on Keynesian liquidity preference. His 1947 paper, 'Liquidity Preference and Monetary Policy', was one of the first empirical studies to test for the interest elasticity of the demand for money in the United States. In two subsequent articles, Tobin refined and developed Keynes's liquidity preference theory, thereby providing a much more rigorous and sophisticated analysis of the demand for money. In his 1956 paper, 'The Interest Elasticity of Transactions Demand for Cash', he used an inventory-theoretic approach to explain why the demand for transactions balances would be interest elastic. More significantly, in his seminal 1958 paper, 'Liquidity Preference as Behaviour Towards Risk' (Tobin, 1958b), he put forward a choice-theoretic model to explain why individual agents hold diversified portfolios, rather than holding only cash or only bonds as is implied in Keynes's analysis. In his model, risk-averse individuals will diversify their portfolios between money (a safe asset with a zero yield) and risky assets (with an expected positive return). Agents will trade off the mean return against the variance of return expected on a portfolio of risky assets. Tobin's 1958 paper famously introduced the 'separation' or 'mutual fund' theorem. According to the theorem, while differences in risk aversion affect the proportion in which individual investors divide their wealth between a 'mutual fund' of risky assets and the one safe asset, money, the composition of the fund is independent of individuals' degree of risk aversion. His analysis of portfolio selection by individual households and firms between money and a range of assets, and his separation theorem, laid the foundations for the subsequent development of the theory of finance (see entries on Markowitz and Sharpe in this volume).

In another seminal paper published in 1969 entitled 'A General Equilibrium Approach to Monetary Theory', Tobin presented a summary of his theoretical framework in which he spelt out a complete model of asset equilibrium. In the paper he investigated the channels through which financial disturbances are transmitted to the real sector of the economy. Within the model, q, the ratio of the market value of a firm's capital to the replacement cost of its capital – often referred to as Tobin's q – is a key variable determining the flow of investment. *Ceteris paribus*, the higher the value of q, the higher investment will be. In the concluding remarks to his paper, Tobin suggested that 'the principal way in which financial policies and events affect aggregate demand is by changing the valuation of physical assets relative to their replacement costs' (Tobin, 1969, p. 29). While monetary policy can bring about such changes, so too can changes in asset preferences. Central to this and earlier analysis is the role of portfolio diversification and preferences towards risk within a general equilibrium setting.

Tobin also made important contributions to the theory of macro-economic growth by analysing the links between short-run cyclical fluctuations and long-run economic growth. In a paper published in 1955 in the *Journal of Political Economy*, he constructed a dynamic model which allowed for the interaction of monetary and real factors in explaining both growth and cycles. In another important paper published in 1965 in *Econometrica*, 'Money and Economic Growth', he concluded that monetary policy can affect the degree of capital intensity in an economy. In his analysis, an increase in the rate of money growth leads to an increase in the rate of inflation which in turn causes portfolio substitution by individuals away from money towards capital.

Throughout his career Tobin remained faithful to his vision that Keynesian theory provides a foundation for activist stabilisation policy involving both monetary and fiscal policy. In the early 1970s, he participated in an, at times heated, exchange with Milton Friedman (see entry in this volume). In his 1970 *Quarterly Journal of Economics* paper he accused Friedman of falling foul of the *post hoc ergo propter hoc* fallacy of accepting the empirically observed tendency for monetary changes to precede changes in business activity as strong empirical support of propositions about causation. In his 1972 *Journal of Political Economy* paper (Tobin, 1972b) he criticised Friedman's theoretical framework, while in his *American Economic Review* paper of the same year (Tobin, 1972a) he used the occasion of his presidential address to the American Economic Association to attack Friedman's natural rate hypothesis and defend the existence of a trade-off between inflation and unemployment which could be exploited for stabilisation purposes. For more than four decades Tobin steadfastly and consistently defended the use of activist demand management against the attacks of monetarism and new classical economics and questioned, in the latter case, whether new classical models are plausible enough to guide policy (Tobin, 1980).

In addition to his contributions to the fields of monetary and macroeconomic theory, and the theory and practice of stabilisation policy outlined above, Tobin also made a number of wide-ranging contributions to economic analysis including: contributions to the theory and empirics of the life-cycle model of consumption and saving (see entry on Modigliani in this volume, and Tobin, 1975); the development of new statistical techniques such as the Tobit method for estimating relationships with limited dependent variables (Tobin, 1958a); the development of what has come to be known as the 'Tobin tax', a proposed uniform tax on foreign exchange transactions aimed at deterring short-term currency speculation (see, for example, Tobin, 1978 – his presidential address to the Eastern Economic Association); and papers on poverty and social policy and international economic relations.

A significant proportion of Tobin's published work has taken the form of articles in learned journals. Many of his most important technical papers on macroeconomics, consumption and econometrics, theory and policy, and national and international issues, have been brought together in four volumes: *Essays in Economics* (Tobin, 1971; 1975; 1982; 1996b). A number of his less technical papers can be found in two collections containing policy-orientated essays he wrote from 1973 to 1986 (Tobin, 1987) and 1987 to 1994 (Tobin, 1996a). In addition to their style and clarity, which make them highly accessible to a wide audience, these collections also provide a clear statement of Tobin's defence of Keynesian ideas and his pragmatic liberal activist philosophy.

Main Published Works

(1941), 'A Note on the Money Wage Problem', *Quarterly Journal of Economics*, **50**, May, pp. 508–16.

(1947), 'Liquidity Preference and Monetary Policy', *Review of Economics and Statistics*, **29**, May, pp. 124–31.

(1955), 'A Dynamic Aggregative Model', *Journal of Political Economy*, **63**, April, pp. 103–15.

(1956), 'The Interest Elasticity of Transactions Demand for Cash', *Review of Economics and Statistics*, **38**, August, pp. 241–7.

(1958a), 'Estimation of Relationships for Limited Dependent Variables', *Econometrica*, **26**, January, pp. 24–36.

(1958b), 'Liquidity Preference as Behaviour Towards Risk', *Review of Economic Studies*, **25**, February, pp. 65–86.

(1965), 'Money and Economic Growth', *Econometrica*, **33**, October, pp. 671–84.

(1969), 'A General Equilibrium Approach to Monetary Theory', *Journal of Money, Credit and Banking*, **1**, February, pp. 15–29.

(1970), 'Money and Income: *Post Hoc Ergo Propter Hoc?*', *Quarterly Journal of Economics*, **84**, May, pp. 301–17.

(1971), *Essays in Economics, Vol. 1: Macroeconomics*, Chicago: Markham Publishing Co.

(1972a), 'Inflation and Unemployment', *American Economic Review*, **62**, March, pp. 1–18.

(1972b), 'Friedman's Theoretical Framework', *Journal of Political Economy*, **80**, September–October, pp. 319–37.

(1975), *Essays in Economics, Vol. 2: Consumption and Econometrics*, Amsterdam: North-Holland.

(1978), 'A Proposal for International Monetary Reform', *Eastern Economic Journal*, **4**, July–October, pp. 153–9.

(1980), 'Are New Classical Models Plausible Enough to Guide Policy?', *Journal of Money, Credit and Banking*, **12**, November, pp. 788–99.

(1982), *Essays in Economics, Vol. 3: Theory and Policy*, Cambridge, MA: MIT Press.

(1987), *Policies for Prosperity: Essays in a Keynesian Mode* (ed. P.M. Jackson), Brighton: Wheatsheaf Books.

(1993), 'Price Flexibility and Output Stability: An Old Keynesian View', *Journal of Economic Perspectives*, **7**, Winter, pp. 45–65.

(1996a), *Full Employment and Growth: Further Keynesian Essays on Policy*, Cheltenham, UK and Brookfield, USA: Edward Elgar.

(1996b), *Essays in Economics, Vol. 4: National and International*, Cambridge, MA: MIT Press.

Secondary Literature

Buiter, W.H. (2003), 'James Tobin: An Appreciation of his Contribution to Economics', *Economic Journal*, **113**, November, pp. F585–631.

Myhrman, J. (1982), 'James Tobin's Contributions to Economics', *Scandinavian Journal of Economics*, **84** (1), pp. 89–99.

Purvis, D.D. (1982), 'James Tobin's Contributions to Economics', *Scandinavian Journal of Economics*, **84** (1), pp. 61–88.

Snowdon, B. and H.R. Vane (2002), 'James Tobin, 1918–2002: An Unreconstructed Old Keynesian Who Wouldn't Quit', *World Economics*, **3**, July–September, pp. 121–60.

See also Beaud and Dostaler (1997, pp. 432–4); Blaug (1998, pp. 285–8; 1999, pp. 1105–6); Cate (1997, pp. 605–6); Nobel Foundation (2004); Snowdon and Vane (2002, pp. 704–8).

THE 1982 NOBEL MEMORIAL LAUREATE

GEORGE STIGLER

George J. Stigler
(1911–91)

© The Nobel Foundation

George Stigler was born in Renton (a suburb of Seattle), Washington, USA in 1911. He obtained a BA from the University of Washington in 1931, an MBA from Northwestern University in 1932, and a PhD from the University of Chicago in 1938. A graduate student under Frank Knight at Chicago, his doctoral thesis on the history of production and distribution theories was subsequently published by Macmillan (Stigler, 1941). He was appointed assistant professor at Iowa State College in 1936, a post he held before moving to the University of Minnesota in 1938. Working in the faculty at Minnesota he was promoted from assistant and associate to full professor over the period from 1938 to 1946. In 1942 Stigler went on leave, first to work at the National Bureau of Economic Research (NBER) (where he was a research staff member until 1976), and then to the Statistical Research Group at Columbia University before returning to Minnesota in 1945. In 1946 he accepted the offer of a professorship at Brown University but after a year moved to Columbia University where he was professor from 1947 to 1958. In 1958 Stigler returned to the University of Chicago where he remained until he retired in 1981. From 1981 to 1991 he was the Charles R. Walgreen Distinguished Service Professor, Emeritus, at the University of Chicago. At Chicago he established the Industrial Organization Workshop, founded the Center for the Study of the Economy and the State in 1977, and was an editor of the *Journal of Political Economy* from 1974 until his death in 1991.

Among his many offices and honours, Stigler was president of each of the American Economic Association in 1964, the History of Economics Society in 1977 and the Mont Pelerin Society from 1976 to 1978, and was awarded the National Medal of Science in 1987. In 1982 he was awarded the Nobel Memorial Prize in Economics 'for his seminal studies of industrial structures, functioning of markets and causes and effects of public regulation' (Nobel Foundation, 2004).

Stigler's published work covers four main areas: the history of economic thought, microeconomic theory, industrial organisation and economic regulation. In the field of the history of economic thought the publication of his doctoral thesis, *Production and Distribution Theories*, in 1941, marked the first major attempt to survey the neoclassical theories of production and distribution over the period from 1870 to 1895. This landmark book covers the work of such influential economists as Eugen von Böhm-Bawerk (1851–1914), John Bates Clark (1847–1938), Francis Ysidro Edgeworth (1845–1926), William Stanley Jevons (1835–82), Alfred Marshall (1842–1924), Carl Menger (1840–1921), Léon Walras (1834–1910) and Knut Wicksell (1851–1926). In addition to this definitive study he also wrote numerous articles on the history of economic ideas and the contributions of a number of great economists of the past. Some of his most important articles – including 'The Development of Utility Theory', 'Perfect Competition, Historically Contemplated', 'The Nature and Role of Originality in Scientific Progress', 'The Influence of Events and Politics on Economic Theory' and 'Ricardo and the 93 Per Cent Labour Theory of Value' – have been gathered together in *Essays in the History of Economics* (Stigler, 1965).

Stigler made a number of important contributions both to microeconomic theory (including contributions to the theory of costs and production) and industrial organisation. Rather than attempt to survey the entire breadth of these contributions, in what follows we merely highlight, in approximate chronological order, some of his most important and influential published works. His paper on the diet problem entitled 'The Cost of Subsistence' (Stigler, 1945) played an important role in the subsequent development of the technique of linear programming. The year 1946 marked the publication of the first edition of his intermediate textbook, *The Theory of Price* – an earlier version of the book had been published by Macmillan in 1942 entitled *The Theory of Competitive Price*. One important feature of this influential textbook, which characterised his approach to economics, is the way theory is illustrated with real-world phenomena. Much of his subsequent published work involved the use of empirical evidence to test theories of industrial organisation. In a paper published in 1947 in the *Journal of Political Economy* (Stigler, 1947c), he uncovered the theoretical inadequacy and predictive failures of the kinked demand curve in oligopoly. On the basis of empirical tests he emphasised the frequency of price changes in oligopolistic industries against the traditional prediction that industries containing only a few firms rarely engage in price changes (see also Stigler and Kindahl, 1970).

His 1961 article, 'The Economics of Information', acknowledges that information is imperfect and can only be acquired at a cost. Furthermore, rational economic agents will only have an incentive to search for and acquire information up to the point where the benefit from additional information is equal to the costs incurred. In other words, Stigler recognised that the same considerations, involving a comparison between benefits and costs, apply to the acquisition of information as they do to the consumption and production of other goods and services. This seminal article, together with 'Information in the Labour Market' (Stigler, 1962a), inspired much subsequent work in such fields of study as macroeconomics and labour economics, most notably on search models of unemployment. In another very influential paper published in the *Journal of Political Economy* in 1964 on the theory of oligopoly (Stigler, 1964a) he argued that the stability of collusive behaviour in oligopolistic markets depends on the costs of detecting and enforcing significant movements away from price agreements. Those industries that are more successful than others at price collusion have lower costs of policing the price agreement. Many of his most important papers, which have had such a marked impact on the development of industrial economics since the 1970s, can be found in *The Organization of Industry* (Stigler, 1968).

In addition to these main published works mention should also be made to some of Stigler's important empirical work, which he undertook over the period from 1947 to 1976 as a senior research staff member of the NBER. This work includes NBER monographs on domestic servants, trends in output and employment, employment trends in the service industries, scientific personnel, capital and rates of return in manufacturing industries and the behaviour of industrial prices (Stigler, 1947a; 1947b; 1956; 1963; Blank and Stigler, 1957; Stigler and Kindahl, 1970).

In the early 1960s, Stigler started detailed research into the practice and theory of economic regulation. A 1962 article, co-authored with Claire Friedland (Stigler and Friedland, 1962b), challenged the then-traditional view that public regulation achieves its stated objectives. In examining the case of electricity, Stigler and Friedland concluded that regulation had no significant effect on electricity prices in the United States. In a subsequent study, 'Public Regulation of the Securities Market', Stigler (1964b) concluded that regulation had not benefited investors buying new stock issues. These studies acted as a catalyst for economists in other countries to undertake research into the actual effects of economic regulation. In a seminal article, 'The Theory of Economic Regulation', published in 1971, he argued that 'as a rule, regulation is acquired by the industry and is designed and operated primarily for its benefit' rather than 'for the protection and benefit of the public' (Stigler, 1971, p. 3). Stigler's studies of the 'causes and effects of public regulation' led to a new area of study known as the economics of regulation. One important aspect of his work is the way he integrated the economics of regulation with the economics of politics. For Stigler, participants in the political market, as in the economic market, display self-interested rational behaviour and should therefore be subject to the same tools of analysis. His studies also helped open up another new area of research between economics and law. Some of his most important essays on regulation, including the three papers noted above, have been gathered together in *The Citizen and the State* (Stigler, 1975).

George Stigler will be remembered first and foremost for his pioneering work in industrial organisation and economic regulation. His groundbreaking contributions (most notably Stigler, 1961; 1971) gave birth to two new areas of research on the 'economics of information' and the 'economics of regulation'. He has also been credited by the 1991 Nobel Memorial Laureate, Ronald Coase, with naming and formulating the Coase theorem (see entry on Coase in this volume and Stigler, 1989). A much-admired economist known for his clear, creative and insightful style of writing, Stigler's work is also often laced with humour (see, for example, Stigler, 1982).

Main Published Works

(1941), *Production and Distribution Theories*, New York: Macmillan.

(1945), 'The Cost of Subsistence', *Journal of Farm Economics*, **27**, May, pp. 303–14.

(1946), *The Theory of Price*, New York: Macmillan; 2nd edn 1952, 3rd edn 1966; 4th edn 1987.

(1947a), *Domestic Servants in the United States*, New York: National Bureau of Economic Research.

(1947b), *Trends in Output and Employment*, New York: National Bureau of Economic Research.

(1947c), 'The Kinky Oligopoly Demand Curve and Rigid Prices', *Journal of Political Economy*, **55**, October, pp. 432–9; reprinted in *The Organization of Industry*, Homewood, IL: Richard D. Irwin, 1968.

(1956), *Trends in Employment in the Service Industries*, New York: National Bureau of Economic Research.

(1957), *The Demand and Supply of Scientific Personnel* (with D.M. Blank), New York: National Bureau of Economic Research.

(1961), 'The Economics of Information', *Journal of Political Economy*, **69**, June, pp. 213–25; reprinted in *The Organization of Industry*, Homewood, IL: Richard D. Irwin, 1968.

(1962a), 'Information in the Labour Market', *Journal of Political Economy*, **70**, October, pp. 94–105; reprinted in *The Organization of Industry*, Homewood, IL: Richard D. Irwin, 1968.

(1962b), 'What Can Regulators Regulate? The Case of Electricity' (with C. Friedland), *Journal of Law and Economics*, **5**, October, pp. 1–16; reprinted in *The Citizen and the State: Essays on Regulation*, Chicago: University of Chicago Press, 1975.

(1963), *Capital and Rates of Return in Manufacturing Industries*, Princeton, NJ: Princeton University Press.

(1964a), 'A Theory of Oligopoly', *Journal of Political Economy*, **72**, February, pp. 44–61; reprinted in *The Organization of Industry*, Homewood, IL: Richard D. Irwin, 1968.

(1964b), 'Public Regulation of the Securities Markets', *Journal of Business*, **37**, April, pp. 117–42; reprinted in *The Citizen and the State: Essays on Regulation*, Chicago: University of Chicago Press, 1975.

(1965), *Essays in the History of Economics*, Chicago: University of Chicago Press.

(1968), *The Organization of Industry*, Homewood, IL: Richard D. Irwin.

(1970), *The Behaviour of Industrial Prices* (with J.K. Kindahl), New York: National Bureau of Economic Research.

(1971), 'The Theory of Economic Regulation', *Bell Journal of Economics and Management Science*, **2**, Spring, pp. 3–21; reprinted in *The Citizen and the State: Essays on Regulation*, Chicago: University of Chicago Press, 1975.

(1975), *The Citizen and the State: Essays on Regulation*, Chicago: University of Chicago Press.

(1982), *The Economist as Preacher and Other Essays*, Chicago: University of Chicago Press; Oxford: Basil Blackwell.

(1989), 'Two Notes on the Coase Theorem', *Yale Law Journal*, **99**, December, pp. 631–3.

Secondary Literature

Mincer, J. (1983), 'George Stigler's Contributions to Economics', *Scandinavian Journal of Economics*, **85** (1), pp. 65–75.

Schmalensee, R. (1983), 'George Stigler's Contributions to Economics', *Scandinavian Journal of Economics*, **85** (1), pp. 77–86.

See also   Beaud and Dostaler (1997, pp. 418–21); Blaug (1998, pp. 276–8; 1999, pp. 1067–8); Nobel Foundation (2004).

THE 1983 NOBEL MEMORIAL LAUREATE

GERARD DEBREU

Gerard Debreu
(b. 1921)

© The Nobel Foundation

Gerard Debreu was born in Calais, France in 1921. He studied at the École Normal Supérieure, Paris in the early 1940s and obtained his degree in mathematics from the University of Paris in 1946. From 1946 to 1948 he was a research associate at the Centre National de la Recherche Scientifique in Paris. In receipt of a Rockefeller Foundation Scholarship (1948–50), he spent time in the United States (where he visited Harvard University, the University of California, Berkeley, the University of Chicago and Columbia University), Sweden (where he visited the University of Uppsala) and Norway (where he visited the University of Oslo). From 1950 to 1955, he was a research associate at the Cowles Commission for Research in Economics at the University of Chicago. In 1956 he obtained his doctorate in mathematics from the University of Paris. He moved from Chicago to New Haven, Connecticut in 1955 when the Cowles Commission moved from the University of Chicago to Yale University. He was associate professor at the renamed Cowles Foundation until 1961. In 1962 he joined the faculty of the University of California, Berkeley as Professor of Economics, and in 1975 was appointed Professor of Mathematics, the same year he became a US citizen. Since 1986, Debreu has been Professor of Economics and Mathematics, Emeritus, at Berkeley.

Debreu's many offices and honours include the presidencies of the Econometric Society in 1971 and the American Economic Association in 1990; in 1976 was made a Chevalier of the French Legion of Honour. In 1983, Debreu was awarded the Nobel Memorial Prize in Economics 'for having incorporated new analytical methods into economic theory and for his rigorous reformulation of the theory of general equilibrium' (Nobel Foundation, 2004).

Debreu is best known for his pioneering contributions in two main areas: the theory of general equilibrium and mathematical economics. In order to place his work in perspective we need to mention some insights of two eminent past economists. Writing in the eighteenth century, the Scottish economist and philosopher Adam Smith (1723–90) argued that, in a market economy, the decisions of 'self-interested' agents are coordinated through the 'invisible hand' of the price system. Later in the nineteenth century, the French economist Léon Walras (1834–1910) presented a mathematical formulation of Smith's ideas in which equilibrium in all markets in an economy is simultaneously determined. Although this work was important to the development of the theory of general equilibrium, without the necessary mathematical tools Walras was not able to prove that there exists a set of prices that equilibrates all markets simultaneously. It was not until the mid-1950s that Debreu, working in collaboration with Kenneth Arrow (the 1972 Nobel Memorial Laureate), provided a rigorous and definitive mathematical proof of the existence of general equilibrium in a model of a market economy (Arrow and Debreu, 1954). Their seminal article, 'Existence of an Equilibrium for a Competitive Economy', has come to be known as the Arrow–Debreu model. Given certain assumptions, Arrow and Debreu were able to prove the existence of equilibrium prices using complex mathematical techniques (set theory and topology) not previously used in economics.

Equally famous is Debreu's classic book, *Theory of Value* (Debreu, 1959), in which he put forward what he termed 'an axiomatic analysis of economic equilibrium'. The book, which presents a rigorous yet succinct exposition of the theory of general economic equilibrium, follows a logical and structured direction. Having outlined in the opening chapter the mathematical concepts and results used in the rest of the book, Debreu then discusses the concepts of a commodity and prices, producer behaviour, consumer behaviour, equilibrium, the relationship between equilibrium and Pareto optimality, and uncertainty. Much of Debreu's later work, which is highly technical in nature, has been devoted to an analysis of the uniqueness of an equilibrium (for example, Debreu, 1970), the stability of equilibrium (for example, Debreu and Scarf, 1963), the rate of convergence to a set of equilibria (for example, Debreu, 1975), and an examination of the conditions which ensure that the price system brings about an efficient allocation of resources. For those readers not trained in mathematical economics, more accessible discussions of 'economic theory in a mathematical mode' and the 'mathematization of economic theory' can be found in Debreu (1984 – his Nobel Memorial Lecture); and Debreu (1991 – his presidential address to the American Economic Association).

Compared to the large number of books and articles written by many of the Nobel Memorial Laureates outlined in this volume, Debreu's published works are relatively few in number. His main contributions to economics can be found in his short book *Theory of Value* (Debreu, 1959), which is just over 100 pages in length, and the 20 papers he selected for inclusion in his book *Mathematical Economics* (Debreu, 1983) – a volume which contains an introduction by Werner Hildenbrand assessing Debreu's contributions and the part played by the selected papers in the development of mathematical economics. Despite the relative paucity of his published works Debreu's influence on the form and direction that economic theory has taken since the mid-1950s, most notably the mathematisation of economic theory, has been profound. His pioneering research in the field of general equilibrium theory has made a lasting impression on the (axiomatic) methods and techniques used in numerous fields of study, including the theory of international trade, capital theory and macroeconomic theory. Those readers interested in general equilibrium theory should consult the three-volume set (Debreu, 1996) which gathers together many of the most important articles that have played an influential role in the development of this central field of study.

Main Published Works

(1954), 'Existence of an Equilibrium for a Competitive Economy' (with K.J. Arrow), *Econometrica*, **22**, July, pp. 265–90.

(1959), *Theory of Value: An Axiomatic Analysis of Economic Equilibrium*, New York: John Wiley & Sons; New Haven, CT: Yale University Press, 1971.

(1963), 'A Limit Theorem on the Core of an Economy' (with H. Scarf), *International Economic Review*, **4**, September, pp. 235–46.

(1970), 'Economies with a Finite Set of Equilibria', *Econometrica*, **38**, May, pp. 387–92.

(1975), 'The Rate of Convergence of the Core of an Economy', *Journal of Mathematical Economics*, **2**, pp. 1–7.

(1983), *Mathematical Economics: Twenty Papers of Gerard Debreu*, Cambridge: Cambridge University Press.

(1984), 'Economic Theory in the Mathematical Mode', *American Economic Review*, **74**, June, pp. 267–78.

(1991), 'The Mathematization of Economic Theory', *American Economic Review*, **81**, March, pp. 1–7.

(1996), *General Equilibrium Theory*, 3 vols (ed.), Cheltenham, UK and Brookfield, USA: Edward Elgar.

Secondary Literature

Varian, H.R. (1984), 'Gerard Debreu's Contributions to Economics', *Scandinavian Journal of Economics*, **86** (1), pp. 4–14.

See also   Beaud and Dostaler (1997, pp. 213–16); Blaug (1998, pp. 43–5; 1999, pp. 289–90); Nobel Foundation (2004).

THE 1984 NOBEL MEMORIAL LAUREATE
LAUREATE
RICHARD STONE

© The Nobel Foundation

J. Richard N. Stone
(1913–91)

Richard Stone was born in London, UK in 1913. An undergraduate at Gonville and Caius College, Cambridge from 1931 to 1935 he studied law for two years before switching to economics and graduating with a BA in 1935 and an MA in 1938. Among his teachers at Cambridge were Richard Kahn (1905–89), John Maynard Keynes (1883–1946) and Colin Clark (1905–89), who was a lecturer in statistics and an early pioneer of national income measurement. After graduating he initially worked as an insurance clerk for a brokerage firm in the City of London before joining the staff of the Ministry of Economic Welfare in 1939. In 1940 he was transferred to the Central Economic Information Service (CEIS) of the War Cabinet Office where, with James Meade (the 1977 Nobel Memorial Laureate), he worked on a set of estimates of the UK's economic and financial position. Their estimates were published in 1941 as part of a Government White Paper (Cmd. 6261), *An Analysis of the Sources of War Finance and an Estimate of the National Income and Expenditure in 1938 and 1940.* Following the division of the CEIS into an Economic Section and a Central Statistical Office (CSO) he worked at the CSO from 1941 to 1945 where, as Keynes's assistant, he produced annual estimates of national income and expenditure (a precursor to today's Blue Books: *National Income and Expenditure*).

At the end of the Second World War Stone left the CSO and returned to Cambridge where, with Keynes's support, he was appointed the first director of the then newly-established Department of Applied Economics (DAE). In 1955 he gave up this position to become P.D. Leake Professor of Finance and Accounting at Cambridge University, a post he held until he retired in 1980.

Stone's many offices and honours included the presidencies of the Econometric Society in 1955 and the Royal Economic Society from 1978 to 1980; he was knighted in 1978. In 1984, Stone was awarded the Nobel Memorial Prize in Economics 'for having made fundamental contributions to the development of systems of national accounts and hence greatly improved the basis for empirical economic analysis' (Nobel Foundation, 2004).

Stone is best known for his pioneering contributions to national income accounting. His work on the measurement of national income began in the early 1940s and resulted in two notable early publications with James Meade (Meade and Stone, 1941; 1944). However it was after the Second World War that he truly established his international reputation as a pioneer in the development of national accounts. His report, 'Definition and Measurement of the National Income and Related Tools' (Stone, 1947), provided the foundation for subsequent work on national accounts. From 1949 to 1951 he directed the National Accounts Research Unit of the Organization for European Economic Cooperation (OEEC). The unit, based in Cambridge, produced a number of reports on international standardised systems of national accounts which were published by the OEEC. In 1952 he chaired a committee of experts drawn together by the United Nations Statistical Office to establish a standard system of national accounts. Their report, *A System of National Accounts and Supporting Tables* (SNA), was published in 1953 by the United Nations. In 1968, following revisions to the 1953 SNA, the United Nations published *A System of National Accounts*, the first four chapters of which were written by Stone. Today the SNA forms the basis on which national accounts are compiled worldwide and international comparisons are made.

As should be clear from this brief overview, Stone's contributions to the development of national income accounting have been profound. While he was not the first economist to produce estimates of national income (see, for example, the entry on Simon Kuznets in this volume), he was a pioneer in developing a system of national and social accounts. Viewing the national income as a system of interlocking accounts, his double-entry bookkeeping method – where every income item on one side of an account has to be matched by an opposite expenditure item on another account – provided an important means to check the consistency and reliability of the data and has become the universally accepted way of organising national income statistics among both developed and developing countries.

In addition to his work on national income accounting, Stone also made important contributions to consumer behaviour and the Cambridge Growth Project. Before commenting on this work, mention should be made of one of his earliest publications (Stone and Stone, 1938) in which, with his first wife Winifred Mary Stone, he sought to estimate the marginal propensity to consume and the multiplier – two key concepts introduced by Keynes in his groundbreaking 1936 book *The General Theory of Employment, Interest and Money*. His first major contribution to the empirical analysis of consumer behaviour was his Royal Statistical Society paper on 'The Analysis of Market Demand' (Stone, 1945). However, of much greater significance were his monumental empirical studies, written in collaboration with Deryck Rowe and others, which appeared in two volumes: *The Measurement of Consumers' Expenditure and Behaviour in the United Kingdom, 1920–1938* (Stone et al., 1954; Stone and Rowe, 1966). Again working largely in collaboration with Rowe, he also undertook work on the consumption of durable goods (for example, Stone and Rowe, 1957) and aggregate private savings (for example, Stone and Rowe, 1962a; Stone, 1964).

In the early 1960s Stone, together with Alan Brown (a colleague from the DAE), started the Cambridge Growth Project to look at the ways in which economic policy affected the British rate of economic growth. The main impetus for the project was the widespread concern over the relatively poor international growth experience of the UK economy in the postwar period. Over the period from 1962 to 1974, 12 books were published in the series *A Programme for Growth*. The first of these written by Stone and Brown, *A Computable Model of Economic Growth* (Stone and Brown, 1962b), described the first version of the disaggregated model and its uses. The model made an important contribution to the development of large-scale disaggregated macroeconometric models and acted as a catalyst for much subsequent research in this area.

In the later part of his career Stone also had work published on demographic and social accounting (for example, Stone, 1971; 1985 – his 1984 Nobel Memorial Lecture). However, it is not this work or that on consumer behaviour or the Cambridge Growth Project for which he will be most remembered, rather it is for his 'pioneering work in the development of systems of national accounts' (Nobel Foundation, 2004).

Main Published Works

(1938), 'The Marginal Propensity to Consume and the Multiplier' (with W.M. Stone), *Review of Economic Studies*, **6**, October, pp. 1–24.

(1941), 'The Construction of Tables of National Income, Expenditure, Savings and Investment' (with J.E. Meade), *Economic Journal*, **51**, June–September, pp. 216–31.

(1944), *National Income and Expenditure* (with J.E. Meade), London: Oxford University Press.

(1945), 'The Analysis of Market Demand', *Journal of the Royal Statistical Society*, **108** (3 and 4), pp. 1–98.

(1947), 'Definition and Measurement of the National Income and Related Tools', appendix to *Measurement of National Income and Construction of Social Accounts*, Geneva: United Nations.

(1954), *The Measurement of Consumers' Expenditure and Behaviour in the United Kingdom, 1920–1938*, vol. 1 (with D.A. Rowe, W.J. Corlett, R. Hurstfield and M. Potter), Cambridge: Cambridge University Press.

(1957), 'The Market Demand for Durable Goods' (with D.A. Rowe), *Econometrica*, **25** (3), pp. 423–43.

(1962a), 'A Post-War Expenditure Function' (with D.A. Rowe), *Manchester School of Economic and Social Studies*, **30** (2), pp. 187–201.

(1962b), *A Computable Model of Economic Growth* (with A. Brown), London: Chapman & Hall.

(1964), 'Private Saving in Britain, Past, Present and Future', *Manchester School of Economic and Social Studies*, **32** (2), pp. 79–112.

(1966), *The Measurement of Consumers' Expenditure and Behaviour in the United Kingdom, 1920–1938*, vol. 2 (with D.A. Rowe), Cambridge: Cambridge University Press.

(1971), *Demographic Accounting and Model Building*, Paris: OECD.

(1985), 'The Accounts of Society', in *Les Prix Nobel 1984*, Stockholm: Almquist & Wicksell; reprinted in *Journal of Applied Econometrics*, **1**, January, pp. 5–28, 1986.

Secondary Literature

Johansen, L. (1985), 'Richard Stone's Contributions to Economics', *Scandinavian Journal of Economics*, **87** (1), pp. 4–32.

Pesaran, M.H. and G.C. Harcourt (2000), 'Life and Work of John Richard Nicholas Stone 1913–1991', *Economic Journal*, **110**, February, pp. F146–F165.

See also Beaud and Dostaler (1997, pp. 422–4); Blaug (1999, pp. 1072–3); Cate (1997, pp. 591–4); Nobel Foundation (2004).

THE 1985 NOBEL MEMORIAL LAUREATE

FRANCO MODIGLIANI

Franco Modigliani
(1918–2003)

© The Nobel Foundation

Franco Modigliani was born in Rome, Italy in 1918. At the age of 17 he entered the University of Rome to study law and obtained his degree in law in 1939. At the start of the Second World War he emigrated to the United States (later becoming a US citizen) where he obtained a scholarship to study economics at the New School for Social Research, New York City in the autumn of 1939. Between 1942 and 1944 he was an Instructor in Economics and Statistics at Bard College, Columbia University. In 1943 he returned to the New School for Social Research (where he received his doctoral degree in 1944), first as a lecturer (1943–44) and then as Assistant Professor of Mathematical Economics and Econometrics (1946–48), before leaving New York to join the Cowles Commission as a research consultant (1949–54). In 1949 he joined the University of Illinois as an associate professor and subsequently became Professor of Economics (1950–52). Between 1952 and 1960, Modigliani was Professor of Economics and Industrial Administration at Carnegie Institute of Technology (now Carnegie-Mellon University) and, after a brief spell at Northwestern University (1960–62) as Professor of Economics, he moved to Massachusetts Institute of Technology (MIT) as Professor of Economics and Finance in 1962 where he taught until his retirement in 1988. Between 1964 and 1972, Modigliani was a consultant to the Secretary to the US Treasury and from the mid-1960s a consultant to the Board of Governors of the Federal Reserve System. From 1971 he was a senior adviser to the Brookings Panel on Economic Activity.

Modigliani's many offices and honours included: presidencies of the Econometric Society (1962), the American Economic Association (1976), the American Finance Association (1981), and honorary presidency of the International Economic Association (1983). In 1985 he was awarded the Nobel Memorial Prize in Economics 'for his pioneering analyses of saving and of financial markets' (Nobel Foundation, 2004).

Modigliani is best known for his seminal contributions to three main areas: macroeconomic and monetary theory; the theory of saving; and the theory of finance. His published research output in macroeconomics and monetary theory began with his highly influential 1944 *Econometrica* article, 'Liquidity Preference and the Theory of Interest and Money', which was largely based on his doctoral dissertation. In the article, Modigliani argued that wage rigidity is the crucial hypothesis for explaining underemployment equilibrium in the Keynesian system and that, apart from the special case of the liquidity trap, the main weapon for stabilisation policy is monetary policy, not fiscal policy. In a subsequent article, Modigliani (1963a) refined his analysis, returning to address the issue in 'The Monetarist Controversy or, Should We Forsake Stabilization Policies?', his 1976 Presidential Address to the American Economic Association (Modigliani, 1977). In addition to his theoretical contributions in this area he also sought to test the effects of policy changes on the economy. Working in collaboration with Albert Ando (University of Pennsylvania) in the mid-1960s, he designed and constructed an econometric model of the US economy for the Federal Reserve known as the FMP model (Federal Reserve–MIT–University of Pennsylvania model) to be used for forecasting and stabilisation purposes. In helping to extend Keynesian economics, Modigliani consistently argued that a market economy *'needs* to be stabilized, *can* be stabilized, and therefore *should* be stabilized by appropriate monetary and fiscal policies' (Modigliani, 1977, p. 1; see also Modigliani, 1986).

His research into the theory of saving began in the early 1950s, while at the University of Illinois, in collaboration with Richard Brumberg, then a graduate student at the university. Their work, which has come to be referred to as the 'life-cycle hypothesis' of saving and consumption, was developed in two seminal papers which were published after both had left the University of Illinois (Modigliani and Brumberg, 1954; 1980a). Although the second paper was completed before Brumberg died prematurely in 1955, Modigliani, upset by the death of his friend, did not look at the paper for a long time afterwards and it was not published until 1980. According to the life-cycle hypothesis, an individual's current consumption depends on, and is some fraction of (depending on tastes and preferences), the present value of his or her lifetime resources, which are composed of the person's wealth and lifetime earnings (both current income and expected future income from employment). The theory assumes that an individual will maximise his or her utility by maintaining a stable or smooth pattern of consumption over their entire lifetime. A joint article with Albert Ando (1963b), published in the *American Economic Review*, sought to test the hypothesis and examine its implications. One of the main macroeconomic implications of the hypothesis is that aggregate saving depends primarily on the rate of growth of income, not on income per capita.

The third area of research for which Modigliani is best known is his work in the field of the theory of finance. In two articles written with Merton Miller (who subsequently was awarded the Nobel Memorial Prize in Economics, jointly with Harry Markowitz and William Sharpe, in 1990) they produced what have come to be known as the 'Modigliani–Miller theorems'. In the first of these papers Modigliani and Miller (1958) showed that in a competitive market with rational investors, ignoring the effects of taxes, the financial structure (debt–equity ratio) of a firm has no effect on its market value. In the second paper, Modigliani and Miller (1961) argued that dividend policy has no effect on the market value of a firm's shares. In other words, the market value of a firm's shares will be independent of its policy choice between paying dividends to shareholders or retaining earnings. The Modigliani–Miller theorems have a number of important implications, most notably for investment decisions. This pioneering work paved the way for subsequent research in the field and the development of the modern theory of finance.

In addition to his path-breaking contributions to these three areas, Modigliani also made an influential contribution to the field of management science through his co-authored book, with Charles Holt, John Muth and Herbert Simon (the 1978 Nobel Memorial Laureate), *Planning, Production and Work Forces*, published in 1960. Many of Modigliani's most important papers have been gathered together in five volumes (see Modigliani, 1980b; 1989).

Main Published Works

(1944), 'Liquidity Preference and the Theory of Interest and Money', *Econometrica*, **12**, January, pp. 45–88.

(1954), 'Utility Analysis and the Consumption Function: An Interpretation of Cross-Section Data' (with R. Brumberg) in K.K. Kurihara (ed.) (1954), *Post-Keynesian Economics*, New Brunswick, NJ: Rutgers University Press, pp. 388–436; reprinted in A. Abel (ed.) (1980), *The Collected Papers of Franco Modigliani*, vol. 2, *The Life Cycle Hypothesis of Saving*, Cambridge, MA: MIT Press.

(1958), 'The Cost of Capital, Corporation Finance and the Theory of Investment' (with M.H. Miller), *American Economic Review*, **48**, June, pp. 261–97; reprinted in A. Abel (ed.) (1980), *The Collected Papers of Franco Modigliani*, vol. 3, *The Theory of Finance and Other Essays*, Cambridge, MA: MIT Press.

(1960), *Planning Production, Inventories and Work Forces* (with C.C. Holt, J. Muth and H.A. Simon), Englewood Cliffs, NJ: Prentice-Hall.

(1961), 'Dividend Policy, Growth and the Valuation of Shares' (with M.H. Miller), *Journal of Business*, **34**, October, pp. 411–33; reprinted in A. Abel (ed.) (1980), *The Collected Papers of Franco Modigliani*, vol. 3, *The Theory of Finance and Other Essays*, Cambridge, MA: MIT Press.

(1963a), 'The Monetary Mechanism and its Interaction with Real Phenomena', *Review of Economics and Statistics*, **45**, February, pp. 79–107; reprinted in A. Abel (ed.) (1980), *The Collected Papers of Franco Modigliani*, vol. 1, *Essays in Macroeconomics*, Cambridge, MA: MIT Press.

(1963b), 'The "Life Cycle" Hypothesis of Saving: Aggregate Implications and Tests' (with A. Ando), *American Economic Review*, **53**, March, pp. 55–84; reprinted in A. Abel (ed.) (1980), *The Collected Papers of Franco Modigliani*, vol. 2, *The Life Cycle Hypothesis of Saving*, Cambridge, MA: MIT Press.

(1977), 'The Monetarist Controversy or, Should We Forsake Stabilization Policies?', *American Economic Review*, **67**, March, pp. 1–19; reprinted in A. Abel (ed.) (1980), *The Collected Papers of Franco Modigliani*, vol. 1, *Essays in Macroeconomics*, Cambridge, MA: MIT Press.

(1980a), 'Utility Analysis and Aggregate Consumption Functions: An Attempt at Integration' (with R. Brumberg) in A. Abel (ed.) (1980), *The Collected Papers of Franco Modigliani*, vol. 2, *The Life Cycle Hypothesis of Saving*, Cambridge, MA: MIT Press.

(1980b), *The Collected Papers of Franco Modigliani*: vol. 1, *Essays in Macroeconomics*; vol. 2, *The Life Cycle Hypothesis of Saving*; vol. 3, *The Theory of Finance and Other Essays* (ed. A. Abel), Cambridge, MA: MIT Press.

(1986), *The Debate Over Stabilization Policy*, Cambridge: Cambridge University Press.

(1989), *The Collected Papers of Franco Modigliani*: vol. 4, *Monetary and Stabilisation Policies*; vol. 5, *Savings, Deficits, Inflation and Financial Theory* (ed. S. Johnson), Cambridge, MA: MIT Press.

Secondary Literature

Kouri, P.J.K. (1986), 'Franco Modigliani's Contributions to Economics', *Scandinavian Journal of Economics*, **88** (2), pp. 311–34 and 335–53.

Merton, R.C. (1987), 'In Honour of Nobel Laureate, Franco Modigliani', *Journal of Economic Perspectives*, **1**, Fall, pp. 145–55.

See also Beaud and Dostaler (1997, pp. 348–50); Blaug (1998, pp. 198–200; 1999, pp. 789–90); Cate (1997, pp. 430–33); Nobel Foundation (2004); Pressman (1999, pp. 167–70); Snowdon and Vane (1999, pp. 241–57).

Acknowledgement

Adapted from the entry on Franco Modigliani in B. Snowdon and H.R. Vane (eds) (2002), *An Encyclopedia of Macroeconomics*, Cheltenham, UK and Northampton, MA, USA: Edward Elgar.

THE 1986 NOBEL MEMORIAL LAUREATE

LAUREATE

JAMES BUCHANAN

James M. Buchanan
(b. 1919)

© The Nobel Foundation

James Buchanan was born in Murfreeboro, Tennessee, USA in 1919. He studied at Middle Tennessee State College where he received his BA in 1940, before obtaining an MS from the University of Tennessee in 1941 and a PhD in economics from the University of Chicago in 1948. In the early part of his career, Buchanan taught at the University of Tennessee (1948–51) and then Florida State University (1951–55). In 1956, following a research year in Italy as a Fulbright Scholar, Buchanan became Professor of Economics, and director of the Thomas Jefferson Center of Political Economy and Social Philosophy, at the University of Virginia. While at Virginia in the early 1960s he co-founded, with his colleague Gordon Tullock, the Public Choice Society and the academic journal *Public Choice*. In 1968 Buchanan moved from the University of Virginia to the University of California, Los Angeles (UCLA). After a year at UCLA, he became in 1969 Professor of Economics and general director of the Center for Study of Public Choice at Virginia Polytechnic Institute in Blacksburg. In 1983 he moved the Center to George Mason University, Fairfax, Virginia where he took up a post as professor and has remained ever since. Buchanan is currently advisory general director of the Center for Study of Public Choice and Distinguished Professor Emeritus of Economics at George Mason University, and

University Distinguished Professor Emeritus of Economics and Philosophy at Virginia Polytechnic and State University.

Buchanan was made a distinguished fellow of the American Economic Association in 1983, served as president of the Mont Pelerin Society from 1984 to 1986 and received the Frank Seidman Distinguished Award in Political Economy in 1984. In 1986 he was awarded the Nobel Memorial Prize in Economics 'for his development of the contractual and constitutional bases for the theory of economic and political decision-making' (Nobel Foundation, 2004).

Buchanan's main contribution to economics involves his work as one of the leading pioneers and founders of public choice theory, a research programme concerned with the application of economics to the analysis of 'non-market decision-making'. Also sometimes referred to as the 'new political economy', the programme, which lies at the interface of economics and political science, has changed the way political decision making is analysed and had a marked influence on the development of public economics. Although Buchanan has had many frequently cited articles published in top-ranked journals (for example, Buchanan, 1949; 1954a; 1954b; 1959), he is best known for a series of influential books he has written or co-written since the late 1950s, many of which have been published in translation.

Throughout his long and distinguished career, Buchanan has acknowledged that the three constitutive elements that provide the foundations of modern public choice theory – methodological individualism, *homo economicus*, and politics-as-exchange – can be found in the 1896 dissertation, 'A New Principle of Just Taxation', written by the Swedish economist Knut Wicksell (1851–1926) which he translated in the early 1950s. These elements were developed by Buchanan and his colleague Gordon Tullock in their landmark book published in 1962 entitled *The Calculus of Consent: Logical Foundations of Constitutional Democracy*. In their seminal study, Buchanan and Tullock extended the model of individual rational 'utility-maximising' behaviour assumed in the private sector marketplace to the public sphere. The assumption that politicians, legislators and bureaucrats behave in the public interest was replaced by that of self-interested rational behaviour. However, as Buchanan (1987) has been careful to point out in his Nobel Memorial Lecture, 'this assumption does not place economic interest in a dominating position and it surely does not imply imputing evil or malicious motives to political actors' (p. 245). While the approach does not deny that people may act to some extent in the public interest, it recognises that individuals also behave in a self-interested manner and respond to incentives. Furthermore, in Buchanan's (1987) view, 'politics is a structure of complex exchange among individuals, a structure within which persons seek to secure collectively their own privately defined objectives that cannot be efficiently secured through simple market exchanges' (p. 246).

A central contribution of *The Calculus of Consent* was the identification of, and distinction between, two levels of collective decision making: the pre-constitutional level and the post-constitutional level. The former establishes the rules or constitution ('constitutional politics') that define and set limits on what can and cannot be done via, at the post-constitutional level, 'ordinary politics'. Buchanan and Tullock recognised that in a democratic society, majority voting may be chosen by citizens as a political medium so long as the rights of minorities are protected and there is generalised consensus on the constitution. The political process is viewed as 'a means of cooperation aimed at achieving reciprocal advantages' (Nobel Foundation, 2004). Consenting individuals pay taxes in return for government goods and services and rely on the government to define the constitutional rules as to what types of goods and services, for example, are provided collectively. Given that the results of the political process depend on the so-called 'rules of the game', the importance of the choice of constitutional rules is paramount. In other words, as the outcomes of policies are largely determined by the choice of constitutional rules, emphasis is given to the importance of the design of such rules and constitutional reforms.

Buchanan has applied the analysis developed with Tullock in *The Calculus of Consent* to a wide range of issues in public economics. Among his books with important insights for this field of study are: *Public Principles of Public Debt* (1958); *Fiscal Theory and Political Economy* (1960); *Public Finance in Democratic Process* (1967); *The Demand and Supply of Public Goods* (1968); *The Limits of Liberty* (1975); *Freedom in Constitutional Contract* (1978b); *The Power to Tax* (Brennan and Buchanan, 1980); and *The Reason of Rules* (Brennan and Buchanan, 1985). The last book, co-written with Geoffrey Brennan, argues forcefully that economists should devote more attention to deriving normative procedures for establishing rules, and considers a methodological and analytical framework for their creation. A recurrent theme within Buchanan's work is an attack on many of the central premises that underlie public economics. For example, given his notion that opportunity costs are basically subjective, he departs from the traditional doctrine of marginal cost pricing of public utilities (see Buchanan, 1969).

Buchanan (Buchanan and Wagner, 1977; Buchanan et al., 1978a) has been extremely critical of traditional Keynesian economics which treats the government as an exogenous element enacting macroeconomic policies aimed at maximising social welfare. Instead the government is viewed as an endogenous element within the politico-economic system where policy makers act in a self-interested manner, rather than in the public interest, by manipulating the economy for electoral purposes. In Buchanan's view, one undesirable consequence of this is a persistent bias towards large government deficits and public debt, the burden of which is largely shouldered by future generations. As noted, given this viewpoint, attention is focused on the rules of the game and the choice of the appropriate constitution. For example, Buchanan has been a long-time supporter of a constitutional rule change for a balanced budget. His 1977 book *Democracy in Deficit*, co-authored with Richard Wagner, has acted as a catalyst for much subsequent research on political business cycles.

Buchanan is best known for his pioneering interdisciplinary work which has made him one of the leading founders of the public choice school. By applying economics to politics and studying the interaction of economic and political forces, he has changed the way economic and political decision making is analysed. One legacy of this continuing research programme is that public choice theory is now seen as an established subdiscipline within mainstream economics. In addition to his contributions to economics, Buchanan has greatly influenced the direction of contemporary political theory and is widely acknowledged as one of the great scholars of liberty of the twentieth century. *The Collected Works of James M. Buchanan* (2002) have been brought together in a 20-volume set that includes ten of his monographs (including *The Calculus of Consent* and *The Reason of Rules*) and his most important journal articles, papers and essays covering a wide range of topics (including his views on philosophical issues, especially problems of moral science and order).

Main Published Works

(1949), 'The Pure Theory of Public Finance: A Suggested Approach', *Journal of Political Economy*, **57**, December, pp. 496–505.

(1954a), 'Social Choice, Democracy, and Free Markets', *Journal of Political Economy*, **62**, April, pp. 114–23.

(1954b), 'Individual Choice in Voting and the Market', *Journal of Political Economy*, **62**, August, pp. 334–43.

(1958), *Public Principles of Public Debt: A Defence and Restatement*, Homewood, IL: Richard D. Irwin.

(1959), 'Positive Economics, Welfare Economics, and Political Economy', *Journal of Law and Economics*, **2**, October, pp. 124–38.

(1960), *Fiscal Theory and Political Economy: Selected Essays*, Chapel Hill, NC: University of North Carolina Press.

(1962), *The Calculus of Consent: Logical Foundations of Constitutional Democracy* (with G. Tullock), Ann Arbor, MI: University of Michigan Press.

(1967), *Public Finance in Democratic Process: Fiscal Institutions and Individual Choice*, Chapel Hill, NC: University of North Carolina Press.

(1968), *The Demand and Supply of Public Goods*, Chicago: Rand-McNally.

(1969), *Cost and Choice: An Inquiry in Economic Theory*, Chicago: Markham Publishing Co; reprinted by University of Chicago Press, 1979.

(1975), *The Limits of Liberty: Between Anarchy and Leviathan*, Chicago: University of Chicago Press.

(1977), *Democracy in Deficit: The Political Legacy of Lord Keynes* (with R.E. Wagner), New York: Academic Press.

(1978a), *The Consequences of Mr. Keynes* (with R.E. Wagner and J. Burton), Hobart Paper 78, London: Institute of Economic Affairs.

(1978b), *Freedom in Constitutional Contract: Perspective of a Political Economist*, Austin, TX: Texas A&M University Press.

(1980), *The Power to Tax: Analytical Foundations of a Fiscal Constitution* (with H.G. Brennan), Cambridge: Cambridge University Press.

(1985), *The Reason of Rules: Constitutional Political Economy* (with H.G. Brennan), Cambridge: Cambridge University Press.

(1987), 'The Constitution of Economic Policy', *American Economic Review*, **77**, June, pp. 243–50.

(2002), *The Collected Works of James M. Buchanan*, 20 vols, Indianapolis, IN: Liberty Fund, Inc.

Secondary Literature

Atkinson, A.B. (1987), 'James M. Buchanan's Contributions to Economics', *Scandinavian Journal of Economics*, **89** (1), pp. 5–15.

Romer, T. (1988), 'On James Buchanan's Contributions to Public Economics', *Journal of Economic Perspectives*, **2**, Fall, pp. 165–79.

See also Beaud and Dostaler (1997, pp. 199–201); Blaug (1998, pp. 29–32; 1999, pp. 168–9); Nobel Foundation (2004); Pressman (1999, pp. 170–73).

THE 1987 NOBEL MEMORIAL LAUREATE

ROBERT SOLOW

Robert M. Solow
(b. 1924)

© The Nobel Foundation

Robert Solow was born in Brooklyn, New York, USA in 1924. In receipt of a scholarship he entered Harvard College in 1940 only to interrupt his undergraduate studies in 1942 when he joined the US army during the Second World War. On his discharge from the army in 1945 Solow returned to Harvard, obtaining a BA in 1947, an MA in 1949 and a PhD in 1951. He was awarded the prestigious David A. Wells Prize for best dissertation of 1951 for his doctoral thesis on the dynamics of income distribution. The thesis was not published because Solow thought it could be improved, but he never made the revisions he deemed were necessary. Before completing his thesis he was appointed, in 1949, as Assistant Professor of Statistics at Massachusetts Institute of Technology (MIT), where he was subsequently promoted to Associate Professor of Statistics in 1954, Professor of Economics in 1958 and institute professor in 1973. Since 1995 he has been Institute Professor Emeritus at MIT.

Solow's many offices and honours include: the award of the John Bates Clark Medal of the American Economic Association in 1961 and the National Medal of Science in 1999; and election to the presidencies of the Econometric Society in 1964, the American Economic Association in 1979 and the International Economic Association from 1999 to 2002. From 1961 to 1962 he served on the US

President's Council of Economic Advisers. In 1987, Solow was awarded the Nobel Memorial Prize in Economics 'for his contributions to the theory of economic growth' (Nobel Foundation, 2004).

Solow is best known for his pioneering work on growth theory which has acted as a platform for an enormous amount of subsequent research in the field, both in terms of theorising and empirical testing. While he has written extensively on the subject over the course of his long and distinguished career, three of his early papers (Solow, 1956; 1957; 1960a), which have become classics, deserve special mention. In his *Quarterly Journal of Economics* paper entitled 'A Contribution to the Theory of Economic Growth', Solow developed a neoclassical model of growth where the aggregate production function is assumed to exhibit constant returns to scale, with substitution between two factor inputs, capital and labour, both of which experience diminishing returns. In contrast to the renowned instability property of the Harrod–Domar growth model developed in the mid-to-late 1940s, by allowing for substitutability between capital and labour, Solow was able to analyse the properties of the long-run equilibrium or steady-state growth rate where output per worker and capital input per worker are constant over time. His model predicts that: (i) an increase in the saving rate will lead to a *temporary* period of faster growth, but will not affect the steady-state growth rate; (ii) countries with higher rates of growth in their labour force will have lower steady-state levels of capital input per worker and output per worker; and (iii) in the steady state, both capital input per worker and output per worker will grow at the rate of technological progress. One of the main insights of the model is that *sustained* growth of output per worker depends on technological progress. The growth model developed by Solow has provided a framework to identify which factors determine growth in output over time and also shed light on some of the reasons why real GDP per person varies so widely between countries.

In his 1957 *Review of Economics and Statistics* paper, 'Technical Change and the Aggregate Production Function', Solow used his model to measure the contribution of capital, labour and technology to US growth experience. He estimated that over the 1909–49 period, US output per worker had doubled with about one-eighth attributable to increases in fixed capital per worker and some seven-eighths attributable to changes in technology, or what was later named the 'Solow residual'. At the time the finding that technological progress, rather than capital accumulation, is the main source of growth was a real surprise. In another very influential paper, 'Investment and Technical Progress', published in an edited volume, Solow (1960a) established a method of aggregating capital from different periods, recognising that more recent vintages incorporate more modern technology. The techniques developed in these two seminal articles spawned a vast literature on what later developed into so-called 'growth accounting'. For highly accessible discussions of Solow's growth theory, including his reflections on developments in the field since his pioneering work, the reader is referred to his Nobel Memorial Lecture (Solow, 1988), and the second edition of his intermediate textbook (Solow, 2000).

In other important work undertaken in the 1960s, Solow examined the relationship of growth theory to capital theory. For example, his 1963 book, *Capital Theory and the Rate of Return*, made an important contribution to the 'Cambridge Controversies' – between economists (such as Joan Robinson and Nicholas Kaldor) based in Cambridge, England and those (such as Paul Samuelson) in Cambridge, Massachusetts – over the nature of capital and the existence of the aggregate production function. In his book, Solow expressed the view that what is important for capital theory is how the rate of return on capital is determined rather than how capital is measured.

While Solow is best known for his seminal work on growth theory and capital theory, he has also made important contributions to macroeconomic theory and policy. In what follows we mention, in chronological order, some of his most important and influential published papers in this broad field of study. Starting in 1960 in a paper co-written with his long-time colleague at MIT, Paul Samuelson (see entry in this volume), 'Analytical Aspects of Anti-Inflation Policy' (Samuelson and Solow, 1960b), he introduced the Phillips curve to the United States by considering the relationship between the rate of wage increase and unemployment for American data. In his 1968 *Quarterly Journal of Economics* paper, co-written with Joseph Stiglitz (see entry in this volume), he presented a theory of output, employment and wages in the short run which could account for unemployment equilibrium.

Best described as an eclectic neo-Keynesian, Solow has consistently defended Keynesianism against the attacks of monetarists and new classical economists. In response to the monetarist critique that, in the long run, a bond-financed increase in government expenditure will 'crowd out' or replace private expenditure, in 1973 with Alan Blinder, he published: 'Does Fiscal Policy Matter?'. Incorporating the government budget constraint into the standard Keynesian IS–LM model of a closed economy, Blinder and Solow pointed out that a balanced budget is required for long-run equilibrium. To finance a deficit, the authorities would have to issue more bonds, which would lead to an increase in private sector wealth (owing to increased bond holdings) and an increase in private consumption expenditure and the demand for money. Solow and Blinder were able to demonstrate that if the model is stable and the wealth-induced effects on consumption outweigh those on the demand for money, then crowding out will not occur. Furthermore, if increased interest payments arising from bond finance are taken into account, the long-run multiplier for a bond-financed increase in expenditure will actually be greater than that for a money-financed increase in expenditure.

In his 1979 *Journal of Macroeconomics* paper, 'Another Possible Source of Wage Stickiness', Solow presented a model in which wage stickiness is in the employer's interest because cutting wages would lower productivity and raise costs. As such, the paper marks an important contribution to the new Keynesian literature on efficiency wage theory. In his presidential address to the American Economic Association entitled 'On Theories of Unemployment', Solow (1980) discussed why, given its characteristics, the labour market often fails to clear generating involuntary unemployment. These characteristics include: segmentation within the labour market, trade unionism, unemployment compensation and a 'code of good behaviour enforced by social pressure'. Other examples of his most widely read and cited papers in macroeconomics include his 1981 *American Economic Review* article, co-written with Ian McDonald, 'Wage Bargaining and Employment', and his 1985 *Scandinavian Journal of Economics* paper, 'Insiders and Outsiders in Wage Determination'. In other important work he has criticised the idea of a stable natural rate of unemployment; in *The Labour Market as a Social Institution* (Solow, 1990), the notion of fairness plays an important role in determining behaviour and outcomes in the labour market. As a result of this work, Solow is well known for his development and championing of neo-Keynesian economics.

In addition to his path-breaking work on growth and capital theory, and his contributions to macroeconomic theory and policy,

Solow has also made important contributions to a number of other areas including: linear programming (for example, via his classic 1958 book on the subject, co-written with Robert Dorfman and Paul Samuelson); urban economics (for example, Solow, 1972); and the economics of non-renewable or exhaustible resources (for example, Solow, 1974). A much-admired, respected and well-liked individual among fellow economists, Solow's insightful work is characterised by its readable prose, which is often laced with a keen and sharp sense of wit.

Main Published Works

(1956), 'A Contribution to the Theory of Economic Growth', *Quarterly Journal of Economics*, **70**, February, pp. 65–94.

(1957), 'Technical Change and the Aggregate Production Function', *Review of Economics and Statistics*, **39**, August, pp. 312–20.

(1958), *Linear Programming and Economic Analysis* (with R. Dorfman and P.A. Samuelson), New York: McGraw-Hill.

(1960a), 'Investment and Technical Progress', in K.J. Arrow, S. Karlin and P. Suppes (eds), *Mathematical Methods in the Social* Sciences, Stanford, CA: Stanford University Press, pp. 89–104.

(1960b), 'Analytical Aspects of Anti-Inflation Policy' (with P.A. Samuelson), *American Economic Review*, **50**, May, pp. 177–94.

(1963), *Capital Theory and the Rate of Return*, Amsterdam: North-Holland.

(1968), 'Output, Employment, and Wages in the Short Run' (with J.E. Stiglitz), *Quarterly Journal of Economics*, **82**, November, pp. 537–60.

(1972), 'Congestion, Density, and the Use of Land in Transportation', *Swedish Journal of Economics*, **74**, March, pp. 161–73.

(1973), 'Does Fiscal Policy Matter?' (with A.S. Blinder), *Journal of Public Economics*, **2**, November, pp. 319–37.

(1974), 'The Economics of Resources or the Resources of Economics', *American Economic Review*, **64**, May, pp. 1–14.

(1979), 'Another Possible Source of Wage Stickiness', *Journal of Macroeconomics*, **1**, Winter, pp. 79–82.

(1980), 'On Theories of Unemployment', *American Economic Review*, **70**, March, pp. 1–11.

(1981), 'Wage Bargaining and Employment' (with I.M. McDonald), *American Economic Review*, **71**, December, pp. 896–908.

(1985), 'Insiders and Outsiders in Wage Determination', *Scandinavian Journal of Economics*, **87** (2), pp. 411–28.

(1988), 'Growth Theory and After', *American Economic Review*, **78**, June, pp. 307–17.

(1990), *The Labour Market as a Social Institution*, Oxford: Basil Blackwell.

(2000), *Growth Theory: An Exposition*, 2nd edn, Oxford: Oxford University Press.

Secondary Literature

Blinder, A.S. (1989), 'In Honor of Robert M. Solow: Nobel Laureate in 1987', *Journal of Economic Perspectives*, **3**, Summer, pp. 99–105.

Matthews, R.C.O. (1988), 'The Work of Robert M. Solow', *Scandinavian Journal of Economics*, **90** (1), pp. 13–16.

Prescott, E.C. (1988), 'Robert M. Solow's Neoclassical Growth Model', *Scandinavian Journal of Economics*, **90** (1), pp. 7–12.

Samuelson, P.A. (1989), 'Robert Solow: An Affectionate Portrait', *Journal of Economic Perspectives*, **3**, Summer, pp. 91–7.

See also   Beaud and Dostaler (1997, pp. 410–12); Blaug (1998, pp. 268–70; 1999, p. 1050); Cate (1997, pp. 578–81); Nobel Foundation (2004); Snowdon and Vane (1999, pp. 270–91; 2002, pp. 663–8).

THE 1988 NOBEL MEMORIAL LAUREATE

MAURICE ALLAIS

Maurice F.C. Allais
(b. 1911)

Maurice Allais was born in Paris, France in 1911. He studied at the École Polytechnique in Paris, from where he graduated in 1933. After a year of military service and two years at the École Nationale Supérieure des Mines in Paris he started work in 1936 as a public service engineer. From 1937 to 1943 he served as head of the Mines and Quarries Service in Nantes and was director of the Bureau of Mines Documentation and Statistics in Paris from 1943 to 1948. In 1949 he was awarded his doctorate in engineering from the Faculty of Science at the University of Paris.

Allais's academic career began in 1944 when he was appointed Professor of Economic Analysis at the École Nationale Supérieure des Mines, a post he held until 1988. From 1946 to 1980 he was director of a research unit at the Centre National de la Recherche Scientifique (CNRS) – the National Centre for Scientific Research. He was also Professor of Theoretical Economics from 1947 to 1968 at the Institute of Statistics, University of Paris and Professor of Economics at the Graduate Institute of International Studies, Geneva from 1967 to 1970. He was a member of the editorial board of *Revue d'Économie Politique* from 1952 to 1984 and of *Econometrica* from 1959 to 1969. Among his many offices and honours are numerous prizes including, in 1978, the prestigious Gold Medal of the CNRS for his lifetime work. He was made an Officer of the French Legion of Honour in 1977. In 1988 Allais was awarded the Nobel Memorial Prize in Economics 'for his pioneering contributions to the theory of markets and efficient utilization of resources' (Nobel Foundation, 2004).

Allais was trained as an engineer and quite remarkably taught himself economics by reading the main works of Léon Walras, Vilfredo Pareto and Irving Fisher. His Nobel Memorial Prize was awarded on the basis of two major works published in French in the 1940s: *A la Recherche d'une discipline économique, première partie: L'Économie pure* (In quest of an economic discipline, Part 1: Pure economics) (Allais, 1943) and *Économie et intérêt* (Economy and interest) (Allais, 1947).

In order to place these two major works in historical context we need to first mention the work of three past eminent economists. Writing in the eighteenth century, the Scottish economist and philosopher Adam Smith (1723–90) argued that, in a market economy, the decisions of 'self-interested' agents are coordinated through the 'invisible hand' of the price system. In the nineteenth century the French economist Léon Walras (1834–1910) presented a mathematical formulation of Smith's ideas as a system of equations in which equilibrium in all markets in an economy is simultaneously determined. Walras's work was later developed by the Italian sociologist and economist Vilfredo Pareto (1848–1923). In his monumental 1943 book (which is over 900 pages in length), Allais built upon and extended the earlier work of Walras and Pareto by 'providing increasingly rigorous mathematical formulations of market equilibrium and the efficiency properties of markets' (Nobel Foundation, 2004). In doing so he presented general and rigorous proofs of two fundamental propositions of welfare theory, namely that: (i) any market equilibrium is socially efficient in the sense that no one can be made better off without someone else being made worse off; and (ii) under certain conditions, each socially efficient situation can be achieved through a market equilibrium and a redistribution of initial resources. Allais termed these two propositions the 'equivalence theorems'. In the 1970s he sought to develop ideas first put forward in his 1943 book by offering a 'general theory of surplus' (Allais, 1981). Utilising dynamic analysis, equilibrium is attained only when any surpluses have been exhausted.

Allais extended his 1943 work in his second major book *Économie et intérêt* (Allais, 1947). Interestingly the book contains a number of pioneering contributions which presage analysis subsequently developed and attributed to other leading economists. Examples include: a rigorous theoretical analysis of the transactions demand for money subsequently developed independently by William Baumol and James Tobin (see entry in this volume) in the early-to-mid-1950s; the introduction of an overlapping generations model before Paul Samuelson's work in the late 1950s; and a rigorous proof of what later came to be known as the golden rule of capital accumulation subsequently attributed to Edmund Phelps in the early 1960s.

Much of Allais's work in these two major books paralleled similar work undertaken by John Hicks (see entry in this volume) in his 1939 book *Value and Capital* and Paul Samuelson (see entry in this volume) in his 1947 book *Foundations of Economic Analysis*. However, because Allais's work was published in French it has not received the same international acclaim as that given to the work of his English-speaking fellow Nobel Memorial Laureates. In fact, outside France, Allais is best known for what has come to be popularly known as the Allais paradox. In the early 1940s, two mathematical economists John von Neumann (1903–57) and Oskar Morgenstern (1902–77), who applied game theory to economics, put forward their expected utility hypothesis, where individuals make choices under circumstances of uncertainty as though maximising their expected utility. In a series of papers published in 1952 and 1953 (see, for example, Allais, 1953), Allais presented the results of a survey he had conducted involving a hypothetical game in which the subjects routinely violated the expected utility axioms. These findings have acted as a catalyst to much subsequent research in the field of decision making under uncertainty.

For an outline of Allais's main contributions to economic science, the reader is referred to his 1988 Nobel Lecture (Allais, 1988). Finally, in addition to his contributions to economics, mention should also be made of his work undertaken on the history of civilisations, and in theoretical and applied physics.

Main Published Works

(1943), *A la Recherche d'une discipline économique, première partie: l'Économie pure*, Paris: Ateliers Industria; 2nd edn published as *Traité d'économie pure*, Paris: Imprimerie Nationale, 1952.

(1947), *Économie et intérêt*, 2 vols, Paris: Imprimerie Nationale.

(1953), 'Le Comportement de l'homme rationnel devant le risque: critique des postulats et axioms de l'école américaine', *Econometrica*, **21**, October, pp. 503–46.

(1981), *The General Thory of Surpluses*, 2 vols, Paris: Institut de Sciences Mathématiques et Économiques.

(1988), 'An Outline of My Main Contributions to Economic Science', in K.-G. Maler (ed.), *Nobel Lectures, Economics 1981–1990*, Singapore: World Scientific Publishing Co., 1992.

Secondary Literature

Drèze, J.H. (1989), 'Maurice Allais and the French Marginalist School', *Scandinavian Journal of Economics*, **91** (1), pp. 5–16.

Grandmont, J.-M. (1989), 'Report on Maurice Allais' Scientific Work', *Scandinavian Journal of Economics*, **91** (1), pp. 17–28.

Munier, B.R. (1991), 'The Many Other Allais Paradoxes', *Journal of Economic Perspectives*, **5**, Spring, pp. 179–99.

See also   Beaud and Dostaler (1997, pp. 165–7); Blaug (1999, pp. 20–22); Nobel Foundation (2004).

THE 1989 NOBEL MEMORIAL LAUREATE
TRYGVE HAAVELMO

Trygve Haavelmo
(1911–99)

© The Nobel Foundation

Trygve Haavelmo was born in Skedsmo, near Oslo in Norway in 1911. He studied economics at the University of Oslo and was awarded his degree in 1933. The 1969 Nobel Laureate Ragnar Frisch (see entry in the present volume) was Professor of Economics at Oslo at this time, and Haavelmo started working for Frisch after his graduation at the newly established Institute of Economics. In 1938 Haavelmo moved to Denmark, taking up an appointment as Lecturer in Statistics at the University of Århus. The following year he left for the United States on a Fulbright scholarship and stayed there for the duration of the Second World War, both as a student (supported by the Rockefeller Foundation in 1940–41), and as a civil servant employed by the Norwegian government. Haavelmo completed his doctoral thesis at Harvard University in 1941 and submitted it to the University of Oslo after the war (he was awarded a PhD in 1946); in the interim the thesis was published in *Econometrica* as 'The Probability Approach in Economics'. This work (Haavelmo, 1944) was instrumental in the Royal Swedish Academy's decision to award the Nobel Prize to Haavelmo (Nobel Foundation, 2004). In 1946, Haavelmo joined the Cowles Commission – then in Chicago – before returning to Oslo in 1947 to work on plans for the reconstruction of the Norwegian economy. In 1948 he was appointed Professor of Economics and Statistics at the University of Oslo; he retired from this post in 1979.

Haavelmo is remembered by those who knew him as a modest, even shy man who refused many of the honours that were offered to him, although he was president of the Econometric Society in 1957 and he accepted membership of the Danish Academy of Sciences in 1975. His gracious Nobel banquet speech suggests that it is economists in general that are being honoured by his award, rather than him in particular. Haavelmo was awarded the Nobel Memorial Prize in Economics in 1989 'for his clarification of the probability theory foundations of econometrics and his analyses of simultaneous economic structures' (Nobel Foundation, 2004).

Haavelmo's doctoral thesis provided 'the foundation of modern econometric methods' (Nobel Foundation, 2004). This work proposed a new 'probability approach' in attempting to resolve some of the key problems in econometrics that had been previously explored by Ragnar Frisch. The most fundamental of these is the identification problem: that is, isolating causal parameters in economic data. A major challenge here is that a range of different economic models may be consistent with the same data (Heckman, 2000). How are appropriate choices to be made across this range? In the 1930s, Frisch had attempted to uncover causal economic relationships by means of 'confluence analysis'. This involved running regressions on all possible relationships on a set of variables in order to work towards the true causations lurking in the data (Moene and Rodseth, 1991). Haavelmo, while generously attributing many of his ideas to Frisch, proposed an alternative method: the prior specification of an economic model – formulated in probabilistic terms – that could be used to guide the statistical measurement, collection and interpretation of data (ibid.; Nobel Foundation, 2004). Haavelmo was also the first to clearly distinguish the identification and estimation problems in econometrics (Heckman, 1992; see also Morgan, 1990).

Again following Frisch, Haavelmo stressed the importance for policy analysis of delineating highly 'autonomous' structural relationships in economic models (Nerlove, 1990). More autonomous relationships hold under a wider variety of circumstances and are therefore particularly useful for the evaluation of alternative economic policies and institutional arrangements (Christiansen and Rodseth, 2000). It has also been suggested that Haavelmo's emphasis on the significance of autonomy in economic modelling might have obviated the need for the Lucas critique:[5] there would have been no temptation to predict the consequences of alternative policy changes within a macroeconomic model as the behaviour of economic agents cannot be modelled at the necessary level of autonomy (Moene and Rodseth, 1991). Although Haavelmo's Nobel citation focuses on his doctoral thesis, two other papers in which he extended and applied his insights are also highlighted: Haavelmo (1943) and, with M.A. Girshick, Haavelmo (1947).

According to the Nobel Foundation (2004), 'Haavelmo's doctoral thesis had a swift and path-breaking influence on the development of econometrics'. In particular it was adopted by the Cowles Commission as its econometric *modus operandi*, and directly influenced the work of other Nobel Laureates such as Koopmans and Klein (Haavelmo, 1997; Heckman, 1992).[6]

In the 1950s, Haavelmo turned his attentions away from econometrics narrowly defined and concentrated instead on economic theory. His reasons for this switch – mostly to do with the need to improve theory – were outlined in his 1957 presidential address to the Econometric Society and reprised in his Nobel lecture (Haavelmo, 1958; 1997). The practical outcome included six books, two of which have been published in English: *A Study in the Theory of Economic Evolution* (1954) and *A Study in the Theory of Investment* (1960). Haavelmo's name is also commonly associated with the theorem discussed in 'Multiplier Effects of a Balanced Budget', published in *Econometrica* in 1945. Although he was not the first to highlight the non-neutrality of increases in government expenditure balanced by higher taxes, his proof of the phenomenon was sufficient for it to become known as 'Haavelmo's theorem' (Nerlove, 1990).

Main Published Works

(1943), 'The Statistical Implications of a System of Simultaneous Equations', *Econometrica*, **11**, January, pp. 1–12.
(1944), 'The Probability Approach in Economics', *Econometrica*, Supplement, **12**, July, pp. 1–118.
(1945), 'Multiplier Effects of a Balanced Budget', *Econometrica*, **13**, October, pp. 311–18.

[5] Named after Robert Lucas Jr, the 1995 Nobel Laureate – see entry in this volume.
[6] For discussions of the limits to the work of the Cowles Commission, see Heckman (1992; 2000).

(1947), 'Statistical Analysis of the Demand for Food: Examples of Simultaneous Estimation of Structural Equations' (with M.A. Girshick), *Econometrica*, **15**, April, pp. 79–110.
(1954), *A Study in the Theory of Economic Evolution*, Amsterdam: North-Holland.
(1958), 'The Role of the Econometrician in the Advancement of Economic Theory', *Econometrica*, **26**, July, pp. 351–7.
(1960), *A Study in the Theory of Investment*, Chicago: University of Chicago Press.
(1997), 'Econometrics and the Welfare State', *American Economic Review*, **87**, December, pp. 13–15.

Secondary Literature

Christiansen, V. and A. Rodseth (2000), 'In Memoriam: Trygve Haavelmo, 1911–1999', *Scandinavian Journal of Economics*, **102** (2), pp. 181–91.
Heckman, J.J. (1992), 'Haavelmo and the Birth of Modern Econometrics: A Review of *The History of Economic Ideas* by Mary Morgan', *Journal of Economic Literature*, **30**, June, pp. 876–86.
Heckman, J.J. (2000), 'Causal Parameters and Policy Analysis in Economics: A Twentieth Century Retrospective', *Quarterly Journal of Economics*, **115**, February, pp. 45–97.
Moene, K.O. and A. Rodseth (1991), 'Nobel Laureate Trygve Haavelmo', *Journal of Economic Perspectives*, **5**, Summer, pp. 175–92.
Morgan, M. (1990), *The History of Econometric Ideas*, Cambridge: Cambridge University Press.
Nerlove, M. (1990), 'Trygve Haavelmo: A Critical Appreciation', *Scandinavian Journal of Economics*, **92** (1), pp. 17–24.

See also Beaud and Dostaler (1997, pp. 253–5); Cate (1997, pp. 218–20); Nobel Foundation (2004).

THE 1990 NOBEL MEMORIAL LAUREATES

HARRY MARKOWITZ, MERTON MILLER AND WILLIAM SHARPE

© The Nobel Foundation

Harry M.
Markowitz
(b. 1927)

Harry Max Markowitz was born in Chicago, Illinois, USA in 1927. He remembers reading David Hume and Charles Darwin while still in high school and being especially taken with the problem of induction and by Darwin's carefully drawn arguments. Markowitz studied at the University of Chicago on a bachelor's programme for two years before electing to specialise in economics. His choice turned particularly on his interest in the economics of uncertainty; he was awarded a BPh in 1947, followed by an MA in 1950. Markowitz's teachers at Chicago included subsequent Nobel Laureates Milton Friedman and Tjalling Koopmans. Markowitz clearly impressed as a student as he was invited to take up a junior research position at the Cowles Commission at Chicago, then directed by Koopmans (Nobel Foundation, 2004). He was awarded a PhD by the University of Chicago in 1954.

In 1952 Markowitz took a job as a research associate with the RAND Corporation. Following an invitation from James Tobin (see entry in this volume) he spent the academic year 1955–56 at the Cowles Foundation at Yale University writing a book *Portfolio Selection: Efficient Diversification of Investment*, published in 1959. He briefly left the RAND Corporation for a consultant's position with General Electric in 1960 before returning in 1961. After further work in the business sector, Markowitz began to combine business and academic life. He has held professorial posts at the University of California, Los Angeles (1968–69), the Wharton School, University of Pennsylvania (1972–74), and Rutgers University (1980–82), and worked for IBM and Daiwa Securities Trust Company, before becoming president of his own firm. He has also been visiting professor at Hebrew University in Israel, the University of Tokyo and the London Business School. From 1982 to 1993, Markowitz was the Marvin Speiser Distinguished Professor of Finance and Economics at Baruch College, City University of New York; his institutional affiliation at the time of his Nobel Award. He is presently research professor at the University of California, San Diego.

Markowitz's offices and honours include presidency of the American Finance Association in 1982, election to membership of the American Academy of Arts and Sciences in 1987, and the award of the John von Neumann Theory Prize in 1989 by the Operations Research Society of America and the Institute of Management Sciences. He is also a fellow of the Econometric Society. In 1990 he was awarded the Nobel Memorial Prize in Economics, together with Merton Miller and William Sharpe, 'for their pioneering work in the theory of financial economics', and more specifically in Markowitz's case 'for having developed the theory of portfolio choice' (Nobel Foundation, 2004).

In his Nobel lecture, Markowitz (1991, p. 476) recalls a slightly ticklish episode during the defence of his PhD at Chicago: 'Milton Friedman argued that portfolio theory [the subject of Markowitz's dissertation] was not Economics, and that they could not award me a PhD degree in Economics for a dissertation which was not in Economics'. We shall come to the result of this apparent impasse later, but the debate itself is instructive – and this is Markowitz's point in relating it – because it illustrates the novelty of his work on portfolio theory in the early 1950s. As Professor Assar Lindbeck noted in his Nobel Presentation Speech on behalf of the Royal Swedish Academy, before Markowitz's pioneering contribution 'there was hardly any theory whatsoever in financial markets'.

Markowitz's initial paper on portfolio theory – 'Portfolio Selection' – was published in 1952 in the *Journal of Finance*. The paper began by rejecting the hypothesis that investment behaviour should seek to maximise discounted anticipated returns on a portfolio. Markowitz pointed out that such a strategy might easily underplay the role of diversification in portfolio choice when, in truth, 'diversification is both observed and sensible' (Markowitz, 1952, p. 77). The point of diversification, of course, is that it reduces uncertainty. An investment decision that turned solely on expected return could lead to either a portfolio composed of just one security, or one of several where securities have equal expected returns. The problem here is that investor-return myopia abstracts from any considerations about portfolio risk. Following this line of argument, for Markowitz (1991, p. 470), 'It seemed obvious that investors are concerned with risk and return and that these should be measured for the portfolio as a whole'. However, he also pointed out that diversification *per se* might not be enough to reduce the risk associated with a portfolio. Previously, it had been 'hinted' by, for example, John Hicks, that the law of large numbers meant that risk could be eliminated by sufficient diversification (Brealey, 1991). Markowitz argued that because the returns from securities are too intercorrelated, the law of large numbers was not applicable. This meant that diversification had to be of an appropriate form – in other words it had to take account of the variance of portfolio return. Here then was Markowitz's approach to portfolio choice: it had to balance 'two dimensions ... the expected return on the portfolio and its variance' (Royal Swedish Academy of Sciences, 1991, p. 2). This gave rise to his 'expected returns–variance of returns' or E–V rule which states that investors should choose from a set of efficient portfolios that have a 'minimum variance for a given expected return or more and maximum expected return for a given variance or less' (Markowitz, 1952, p. 82). The paper identified the efficient portfolio set using graphical analysis. A central characteristic of the E–V rule is that it requires fruitful diversification. Markowitz highlights the futility of assembling a portfolio of securities based on firms from the same industry: their performances are likely to be highly correlated, and no matter how many securities are held, the problem will persist unless covariances are recognised as a critical issue in portfolio choice. For Brealey (1991, p. 15) this highlights Markowitz's most important contribution to financial economics – his demonstration 'that there is a role for a portfolio manager that is distinct from that of the security analyst and that this role has a formal economic logic'. In Markowitz's (1952, p. 87) own words 'The rule serves better...as an explanation of, and guide to, "investment" as distinguished from "speculative" behaviour'. In subsequent work (Markowitz, 1956; 1959; 1987; Markowitz et al., 1999) he provided an algorithm for tracing the efficient frontier of portfolio choice and offered elaborations on his earlier analyses.

In addition to his Nobel Prize-winning work on portfolio theory, Markowitz has also made important contributions to mathematical programming and the development of a computer programming language SIMSCRIPT, both of which were recognised in the award of the von Neumann Theory Prize.

Finally, we return to the debate initiated by Milton Friedman over the economic credentials of Markowitz's PhD. Markowitz supposes Friedman to have been only 'half serious' as his degree was awarded with no undue delay. However, at a distance of almost 40 years, Markowitz is content to acknowledge that, *then*, Friedman may well have been right, yet he adds a twist: 'at the time I defended my dissertation, portfolio theory was not part of economics. But now it is' (Markowitz, 1991, p. 476). He might well have continued that the difference was initiated by his own pioneering work (Brealey, 1991; Royal Swedish Academy of Sciences, 1991; Varian, 1993).

Main Published Works

(1952), 'Portfolio Selection', *Journal of Finance*, **7**, March, pp. 77–91.
(1956), 'The Optimization of a Quadratic Function Subject to Linear Constraints', *Naval Research Logistics Quarterly*, **3**, March–June, pp. 111–33.
(1959), *Portfolio Selection: Efficient Diversification of Investment*, New York: Wiley & Sons.
(1987), *Mean-Variance Analysis in Portfolio Choice and Capital Markets*, New York: Basil Blackwell.
(1991), 'Foundations of Portfolio Theory', *Journal of Finance*, **46**, June, pp. 469–77.
(1999), 'A More Efficient Frontier' (with F. Schirripa and N.D. Tecotzky), *Journal of Portfolio Management*, **25**, May, pp. 99–108.

Secondary Literature

Brealey, R.A. (1991) 'Harry M. Markowitz's Contributions to Financial Economics', *Scandinavian Journal of Economics*, **93** (1), pp. 7–17.
Royal Swedish Academy of Sciences (1991), 'The Nobel Memorial Prize in Economics 1990', *Scandinavian Journal of Economics*, **93** (1), pp. 1–6.
Varian, H. (1993), 'A Portfolio of Nobel Laureates: Markowitz, Miller and Sharpe', *Journal of Economic Perspectives*, **7**, Winter, pp. 159–69.

See also Blaug (1999, pp. 737–8); Cate (1997, pp. 395–8); Nobel Foundation (2004).

© The Nobel Foundation

Merton H. Miller
(1923–2000)

Merton Miller was born in Boston, Massachusetts, USA in 1923. He studied economics as an undergraduate at Harvard University, where one of his contemporaries was fellow Nobel Laureate Robert Solow. Miller was awarded a BA in 1944. After graduation he worked as an economist, first in the US Treasury's Division of Tax Research from 1943 to 1947, and subsequently in the Research and Statistics Division of the Board of Governors of the Federal Reserve. In 1949, Miller left government service for postgraduate research at Johns Hopkins University. He was awarded a PhD by Johns Hopkins in 1952.

Miller's academic life began in the UK, where he was assistant lecturer at the London School of Economics in 1952–53. He returned to the United States in 1953 as Assistant Professor of Economics and Industrial Administration at Carnegie Institute of Technology (now Carnegie-Mellon University); he was promoted to associate professor in 1958. In 1961 Miller moved to the University of Chicago as Professor of Finance and Economics, before becoming Edward Eagle Brown Professor of Banking and Finance in 1966. Apart from two visiting professorial appointments at the University of Louvain and the University Faculty of Mons, both in Belgium, in 1966 and 1973, respectively, Miller remained at Chicago for the rest of his career where he was subsequently Leon Carroll Marshall Distinguished Service Professor (1981–87), Robert R. McCormick Distinguished Service Professor (1987–93) and, from 1993, Robert R. McCormick Distinguished Service Professor Emeritus. Miller died on 3 June 2000.

Miller's professional activities were wide ranging. He was public director of the Chicago Board of Trade from 1983 to 1985 and public director of the Chicago Mercantile Exchange from 1990. Also in 1990, Miller was a member of the New York Stock Exchange Advisory Panel on Market Volatility and Investor Confidence.

Miller was a fellow both of the Econometric Society and the American Academy of Arts and Sciences, and a distinguished fellow of the American Economic Association. He was also a senior fellow of the American Association of Financial Engineers. In 1975 he served as vice-president of the American Finance Association and in 1976 he was the association's president. In 1990 Miller was awarded the Nobel Memorial Prize in Economics, together with Harry Markowitz and William Sharpe, 'for their pioneering work in the theory of financial economics', and more specifically in Miller's case 'for his fundamental contributions to the theory of corporate finance' (Nobel Foundation, 2004).

Miller, together with the 1985 Nobel Laureate Franco Modigliani, his co-author in papers specifically acknowledged by the Royal Swedish Academy, is a founder of the modern theory of corporate finance (Myers, 1991). In a path-breaking article in the *American Economic Review*, 'The Cost of Capital, Corporation Finance and the Theory of Investment', Modigliani and Miller (1958) argued that discussions of rational investment and financial policy had up until then lacked theoretical foundation (see also Modigliani and Miller, 1959). The purpose of their paper was to construct an appropriate theory based on the relationship between corporate financial structure and market valuation. In doing so, they reached what was at the time a startlingly novel conclusion: that the value of a firm was independent of its capital structure. So long as capital markets functioned perfectly, an implication of equilibrium was that the issuing of new debt or equity did not appear to carry any particular valuation consequences for the firm. This has since become known as the first Modigliani and Miller value-invariance proposition. Modigliani and Miller developed their initial 1958 contribution in two further papers that are also acknowledged in Miller's Nobel citation: Modigliani and Miller (1963; 1966).

Modigliani and Miller's analysis can be understood by reference to the absence of opportunities for arbitrage by both firms and investors in debt and equity transactions. If a firm could alter its market value by modifying its debt–equity structure, it would be possible for individual bond and shareholders to undertake parallel transactions that would guarantee them arbitrage profits. An investor could modify his or her portfolio of bonds and shares and realise the resulting increase in portfolio value as profit. That investors *cannot* act in this way implies that the value of a firm must indeed be independent of its capital structure in the context of equilibrium in perfect capital markets.

Following Varian (1987; 1993), note that this argument does not contradict the fundamental insight due to Markowitz (see entry in this volume) that asset diversification is an essential element in investor portfolio choice. As Markowitz argued, diversification among assets is sensible because it reduces uncertainty for investors. Given the value additivity principle – which states that the value of a portfolio simply reflects the combined prices of the assets of which it is composed – it is apparent that equilibrium asset prices already incorporate any value that could be achieved by portfolio restructuring. Moreover, because investors have the same free access to capital markets as firms, it follows that diversification for risk-management purposes can be done by investors themselves through the medium of portfolio choice; all investors require of firms is that they maximise value (Myers, 1991). The simple message of Modigliani and Miller's first value-invariance proposition is that this cannot be achieved by changes in capital structure.

Modigliani and Miller's second value-invariance proposition states that, given a firm's investment decision, its dividend policy has no influence on the value of its shares and, therefore, its market value (Miller, 1988; Royal Swedish Academy of Sciences, 1991). Miller (1988) offers a simple explanation of this second proposition. To finance, for example, a higher dividend, as investment is held given, part of the firm must be sold off. In this way, dividend policy becomes 'just a wash – a swap of equal values not much different in principle from withdrawing money from a passbook savings account' (ibid., p. 104). It has, in other words, no impact on the share price or the market value of the firm.

In a retrospective on the Modigliani–Miller propositions, Miller (1988) considered that the first invariance proposition – that a firm's capital structure does not influence its market value – had been fully incorporated into economic theory. He noted, however, that doubts about the *practical* application of the proposition persisted on the back of many instances of real-world association between changes in the capital structures of firms and their values. Similar concerns regarding the second invariance proposition had also surfaced as numerous announced dividend changes appeared to prompt share price reactions. In fact, as Myers (1991) notes, Modigliani and Miller in their 1958 paper had anticipated that market frictions attributable to, for example, taxes might result in empirical challenges to their analysis. In the context of the first proposition, Miller (1977; 1988) disputed the argument that the tax advantages of debt financing gave rise to some optimal tax structure for the firm (the Modigliani and Miller contention, of course, was that there was none). Similarly, Modigliani and Miller (1961) suggested that share price reactions to dividend announcements were not an empirical refutation of the second proposition but reflected informational asymmetries between a firm's executives and other agents in the market: in other words, dividends could carry some 'informational content' about a firm's future earnings prospects (see also Miller, 1988; Myers, 1991).

Miller (1988, p. 118) acknowledges that 'the open questions about [the invariance] propositions have long been empirical ones' (see also Miller, 1991). Implicit in this statement is the justified claim that Modigliani and Miller's work has provided the foundation upon which the development of research in corporate finance has subsequently been based (Royal Swedish Academy of Sciences, 1991; see also Miller's 1972 book, with Eugene Fama, *The Theory of Finance*). A selection of Miller's contributions to finance and economics has been published in two volumes edited by Bruce Gundy (Miller, 2002).

Main Published Works

(1958), 'The Cost of Capital, Corporation Finance and the Theory of Investment', (with F. Modigliani), *American Economic Review*, **48**, June, pp. 261–97.

(1959), 'The Cost of Capital, Corporation Finance and the Theory of Investment. Reply' (with F. Modigliani), *American Economic Review*, **49**, September, pp. 655–69.

(1961), 'Dividend Policy, Growth and the Valuation of Shares' (with F. Modigliani), *Journal of Business*, **34**, October, pp. 411–33.

(1963), 'Corporate Income Taxes and the Cost of Capital: A Correction' (with F. Modigliani), *American Economic Review*, **53**, June, pp. 433–43.

(1966), 'Some Estimates of the Cost of Capital in the Electric Utility Industry, 1954–57' (with F. Modigliani), *American Economic Review*, **56**, June, pp. 333–91.

(1972), *The Theory of Finance* (with E.F. Fama), New York: Holt, Reinhart & Winston.

(1977), 'Debt and Taxes', *Journal of Finance*, **32**, May, pp. 261–75.

(1988), 'The Modigliani–Miller Propositions After Thirty Years', *Journal of Economic Perspectives*, **2**, Fall, pp. 99–120.

(1991), 'Leverage', *Journal of Finance*, **46**, June, pp. 479–88.

(2002), *Selected Works of Merton H. Miller: A Celebration of Markets* (ed. B.D. Gundy), 2 vols, Chicago: University of Chicago Press.

Secondary Literature

Myers, S.C. (1991), 'Merton H. Miller's Contributions to Financial Economics', *Scandinavian Journal of Economics*, **93** (1), pp. 23–32.

Royal Swedish Academy of Sciences (1991), 'The Nobel Memorial Prize in Economics 1990', *Scandinavian Journal of Economics*, **93** (1), pp. 1–6.

Varian, H.R. (1987), 'The Arbitrage Principle in Financial Economics', *Journal of Economic Perspectives*, **1**, Fall, pp. 55–72.

Varian, H.R. (1993), 'A Portfolio of Nobel Laureates: Markowitz, Miller and Sharpe', *Journal of Economic Perspectives*, **7**, Winter, pp. 159–69.

See also   Blaug (1999, pp. 778–9); Nobel Foundation (2004).

William F. Sharpe
(b. 1934)

© The Nobel Foundation

William Sharpe was born in Boston, Massachusetts, USA, in 1934. In the 1940s his family moved to California and Sharpe enrolled at the University of California at Berkeley intending to study medicine. However, the preparatory courses were not to his taste and after a year he switched to a business administration degree at the University of California at Los Angeles (UCLA). He graduated from UCLA in 1955 with a BA and was awarded an MA, also by UCLA, in 1956.

After a short period of service in the US Army, Sharpe started work as an economist for the RAND Corporation in 1956. At the same time he registered for a PhD at UCLA. Sharpe's PhD research benefited from advice given by his fellow Laureate, Harry Markowitz, then also at RAND. After completing his PhD in 1961, Sharpe was appointed assistant professor at the University of Washington in Seattle; he was promoted to associate professor in 1963 and professor in 1967. In 1968, Sharpe took up a professorial post at the University of California at Irvine, attracted by the prospect of interdisciplinary quantitative work in the social sciences (Nobel Foundation, 2004). However, the venture was not a success and in 1970 Sharpe moved as professor to Stanford University, where he stayed for the remainder of his academic career. In 1973 he became the Timken Professor of Finance at Stanford and then, from 1989 to 1992, the Timken Professor Emeritus of Finance, as he simultaneously branched out into private practice. He had also been senior research associate at the National Bureau of Economic Research in 1976–77. From 1992 to 1995, Sharpe was Professor of Finance at Stanford and from 1995 to 1999 STANCO 25 Professor of Finance. Since 1999 he has been STANCO 25 Professor Emeritus of Finance. Sharpe has extensive experience in the corporate sector. He has been consultant to more than 20 firms and has been chairman or president of several others.

Sharpe was director of the American Finance Association in 1977–78, the association's vice-president in 1979 and its president in 1980. He was director of the Western Finance Association from 1978 to 1980. He is also a recipient of the UCLA Medal, UCLA's highest honour. In 1990, Sharpe was awarded the Nobel Memorial Prize in Economics, together with Harry Markowitz and Merton Miller, 'for their pioneering work in the theory of financial economics', and more specifically in Sharpe's case 'for his contribution to the theory of price formation for financial assets' (Nobel Foundation, 2004).

Sharpe's Nobel citation highlights his work on the capital asset pricing model (CAPM), which the Royal Swedish Academy of Sciences (1991, p. 4) calls 'the backbone of modern price theory for financial markets'. His research interest in financial economics was confirmed by his choice of PhD topic. Under the aforementioned unofficial supervision of his RAND colleague Markowitz, Sharpe tried to produce a model that would simplify Markowitz's prescription for portfolio choice.[7] Sharpe's PhD was entitled 'Portfolio Analysis Based on a Simplified Model of the Relationship Among Securities'. His approach involved fastening co-variances between asset returns to the aggregate movement of returns for the market as a whole. Sharpe was adroitly using the observation that assets tend to move together broadly with the market. This allowed him to express asset co-variances with a common feature – the market – instead of pair-wise with each other as Markowitz had done, thus making for a much leaner calculation to arrive at an efficient portfolio. Sharpe (1963) called his finding the 'single index model', though it is now more generally known as the 'market model' (see Varian, 1993).

[7] For which Markowitz himself was awarded the Nobel Prize – see entry for Markowitz in this volume.

Although the market model was the first published outcome of Sharpe's dissertation, its final chapter also contained the seeds of his work on the CAPM (Nobel Foundation, 2004). The paper that proposed the CAPM – 'Capital Asset Prices: A Theory of Market Equilibrium Under Conditions of Risk' – was published in the *Journal of Finance* in 1964.[8] At about the same time, the late John Lintner independently derived the CAPM (see Lintner, 1965). The CAPM is a positive or descriptive theory of the relationship between a security's expected rate of return and its risk. Although Sharpe's research built primarily on Markowitz's theory of portfolio choice, Markowitz's approach had been to consider choice only among the family of risk-bearing assets, such as stocks, and not risk-free assets such as government securities. James Tobin[9] extended Markowitz's analysis by including the risk-free asset in the spectrum of portfolio choice. This produced the important result that the trade-off between risk and return for investors becomes linear. Its implication in the CAPM is that an *identical* portfolio of risky assets is appropriate for all investors. The only decision individuals have to make is how they should apportion investment between the risk-free asset and the risky asset portfolio. The outcome turns on their risk preferences. Sharpe's insight was to recognise that the risky portfolio would, in equilibrium, precisely mirror that held by the market as a whole (Varian, 1993). The market portfolio is simply the aggregation of identical portfolios of the individuals who make up the market.

Sharpe employed the 'beta' of a risky asset to indicate the contribution of its specific risk to that of the market-wide portfolio of risky assets. The return on an asset with a beta of 1 will tend to move in tandem with the market. However, a risky asset with a beta of more than 1 will tend to be more volatile than the market as a whole with higher expected returns. A beta of less than 1 indicates an asset that carries less risk than the market with a lower expected return.

Adding an asset to a portfolio presents an investor with the opportunity to adopt an aggressive or defensive posture; for example, an asset with a beta greater than 1 is considered an aggressive asset. Note, however, that the CAPM demonstrates that, in all cases, in-

[8] Publication was not a smooth process – Sharpe recollects that the paper was initially greeted by a negative referee's report (Nobel Foundation, 2004).
[9] Tobin was the 1981 Nobel Laureate – see entry in this volume.

vestors are rewarded according to the co-variance of a risky asset with the market portfolio and not according to the volatility of the asset itself. This is because any specific risk associated with an asset can be easily eliminated by appropriate diversification. In other words, the CAPM shows that expected returns are related to market risk rather than to total risk. Prior to Sharpe's contributions it was understood that the risk associated with an asset simply reflected the dispersion of its returns.

In addition to his work on the CAPM and the market model (see also Sharpe, 1991), Sharpe is also known for his contributions to the analysis of mutual fund performance (Sharpe, 1966), the pricing of American options (Sharpe, 1978a), and for his analytical concerns regarding the distortions associated with deposit insurance in the banking sector (Sharpe, 1978b; and see Litzenberger, 1991). Finally, his books on finance include Sharpe (1970; 1985).

Main Published Works

(1963), 'A Simplified Model for Portfolio Analysis', *Management Science*, **9**, January, pp. 277–93.

(1964), 'Capital Asset Prices: A Theory of Market Equilibrium Under Conditions of Risk', *Journal of Finance*, **19**, September, pp. 425–42.

(1966), 'Mutual Fund Performance', *Journal of Business*, **39**, January, pp. 119–38.

(1970), *Portfolio Theory and Capital Markets*, New York: McGraw-Hill; 2nd edn 2000.

(1978a), *Investments*, Englewood Cliffs, NJ: Prentice Hall; 2nd edn 1981; 3rd edn 1985; 4th edn (with G.J. Alexander), 1990; 5th edn (with G.J. Alexander and J.V. Bailey), 1995; 6th edn (with G.J. Alexander and J.V. Bailey), 1999.

(1978b), 'Bank Capital Adequacy, Deposit Insurance, and Security Values', *Journal of Financial and Quantitative Analysis*, **13**, November, pp. 701–18.

(1985), *Asset Allocation Tools*, The Scientific Press; 2nd edn 1987.

(1991), 'Capital Asset Prices With and Without Negative Holdings', *Journal of Finance*, **46**, June, pp. 489–509.

Secondary Literature

Lintner, J. (1965), 'The Valuation of Risk Assets and the Selection of Risky Investments in Stock Portfolios and Capital Budgets', *Review of Economics and Statistics*, **47**, February, pp. 13–37.

Litzenberger, R.H. (1991), 'William F. Sharpe's Contributions to Financial Economics', *Scandinavian Journal of Economics*, **93** (1), pp. 37–46.

Royal Swedish Academy of Sciences (1991), 'The Nobel Memorial Prize in Economics 1990', *Scandinavian Journal of Economics*, **93** (1), pp. 1–6.

Varian, H. (1993), 'A Portfolio of Nobel Laureates: Markowitz, Miller and Sharpe', *Journal of Economic Perspectives*, **7**, Winter, pp. 159–69.

See also Blaug (1999, pp. 1018–19); Cate (1997, pp. 576–8); Nobel Foundation (2004).

THE 1991 NOBEL MEMORIAL LAUREATE

RONALD COASE

Ronald H. Coase
(b. 1910)

© The Nobel Foundation

Ronald Coase was born in Willesden, London, UK in 1910. He went to school in London and won a place at a high (secondary) school which, at that time, allowed pupils after they had completed their secondary education to study as external students of the University of London for a year. Coase reports that this prompted the first of a number of fortunate incidents that shaped his career as an economist (Nobel Foundation, 2004). His initial intention was to take a degree in history but a late start at high school meant that he had not taken the required prior course in Latin. As an alternative Coase chose chemistry – a subject in which he had demonstrated some earlier promise – but he found the associated mathematics 'not to my taste'. This left him with only one option: commerce. He passed his first year's work and enrolled at the London School of Economics (LSE) (part of the University of London) to continue as an undergraduate on a bachelor of commerce degree. He was awarded a BCom by the University of London in 1932. In 1951 he was awarded a PhD in economics by the same institution.

Coase's first academic appointment was as an assistant lecturer at the Dundee School of Economics and Commerce in 1932. In 1934 he was appointed as assistant lecturer at the University of Liverpool and in 1935 he returned to the London School of Economics, initially as an assistant lecturer, then lecturer (1938) and finally reader (1947). During the Second World War he did statistical work at the Forestry Commission and in the Offices of the War Cabinet. His war service lasted from 1940 to 1946. In 1951, Coase left the UK for the United States where he was appointed Professor of Economics at Buffalo University, New York. In 1958 he moved to the University of Virginia as professor, and in 1964 he joined the University of Chicago, first as professor and from 1971 as the Clifton R. Musser Professor of Economics. Coase spent 1991 as Distinguished Professor (visiting) of Law and Economics at the University of Kansas. Since 1982 he has been Clifton R. Musser Professor Emeritus of Economics and Senior Fellow in Law and Economics at Chicago.

Among Coase's offices and honours are honorary degrees from a number of universities around the world. He is a distinguished fellow of the American Economic Association and a fellow of the American Academy of Arts and Sciences. Coase is also an honorary fellow of the LSE, a corresponding fellow of the British Academy and a Membre Titulaire of the European Academy. In 1980 he won the Law and Economics Center Prize from the University of Miami and in 1988 he received the D. Francis Bustin Prize from the University of Chicago. In 1991 Coase was awarded the Nobel Memorial Prize in Economics 'for his discovery and clarification of the significance of transaction costs and property rights for the institutional structure and functioning of the economy' (Nobel Foundation, 2004).

As noted, Coase spent the first year of his undergraduate career as an external student of the University of London. He then took the usual two further years to complete his degree. However, university regulations required him to be 'resident' at the LSE for three years before he could graduate. This presented Coase with the problem of finding something to do to fulfil his final year of residency. Again, Coase records an incident of serendipity that would decisively influence his life and career. He confesses that even as late as five months before his final examinations his 'notions on how the economy worked were extremely woolly' (Coase, 1992, p. 715). However, attending the seminars of a newly appointed professor – Arnold Plant – proved to be a turning point. Plant introduced Coase to Adam Smith's 'invisible hand' and gave him a revelatory and 'coherent view of the economic system'. It seems that Coase also impressed Plant, as under his influence the University of London awarded Coase a Sir Ernest Cassel Travelling Scholarship. Coase used this to spend a year in the United States doing the research that would many years later form a major part of his Nobel citation. Prior to learning of his award, Coase had planned to spend his last year as an undergraduate studying industrial law and he observes that 'had I done so I would undoubtedly have gone on to become a lawyer' (Nobel Foundation, 2004).

Coase travelled to the United States intent on 'studying the structure of American industries, with the aim of discovering why industries were organized in different ways' (Nobel Foundation, 2004). He was also exercised by a puzzle posed for him by the teachings of Smith (and Plant). The metaphorical invisible hand demonstrated the power that the competitive process had to organise and coordinate production. But in his visits to American firms and factories, Coase was meeting a tier of management whose very function was also to coordinate and organise: 'Why was it needed if the pricing system provided all the coordination necessary?' (Coase, 1992, p. 715). The answer to this question, Coase realised, was that 'there were costs of using the price mechanism. What the prices are have to be discovered. There are negotiations to be undertaken, contracts have to be drawn up, inspections have to be made … and so on. These costs have come to be known as transaction costs' (Coase, 1992, p. 715). In his 1937 paper in *Economica*, 'The Nature of the Firm', cited by the Royal Swedish Academy of Sciences as part of the reason for his Nobel award, Coase argues that it is the presence of transaction costs that explains the very existence of firms: the contractual and other tasks and processes that give rise to such costs are simply more efficiently managed by the institution of the firm. Markets and the individuals within them could do the job but less efficiently. Coase (ibid., p. 716) characterises the firm as a 'little planned society'; he argues that the boundary between what is done through the market and what is done by the firm is decided by the competitive process.

Coase's Nobel citation makes reference to one other paper: 'The Problem of Social Cost', published in the *Journal of Law and Economics* (which Coase was later to edit) in 1960. This work gave rise to the famous Coase theorem, which Coase himself credits to fellow Nobel Laureate, George Stigler (see entry for Stigler in the present volume and Stigler, 1989). Coase's purpose in the 'Problem of Social Cost' paper was to offer a critique of the convention established by A.C. Pigou that, in the presence of negative externalities, some form of corrective government action – such as the imposition of a tax – could 'internalise' and therefore limit damage to third parties. Coase showed that, where transaction costs are zero, negotiations freely entered into by the offending and offended parties will both eliminate negative externalities and provide for an efficient allocation of resources. Moreover, Coase was able to demonstrate that this outcome will occur however property rights are defined between the parties. For example, a firm at risk of polluting a river would be willing to compensate the riparian owner were a pollution event to arise. On the other hand, if the firm were the riparian owner, then a third-party river user would be willing to pay it to take steps not to pollute. Payments in either direction would vary according to the value each side placed on its output (the firm), or amenity (the river user): the most valued option prevails regardless of who has rights over the river. Of course, where transaction costs *are* present, affected parties may find it too costly or difficult to undertake the necessary negotiations. In such circumstances, Coase recognised that the assignment of property rights can affect resource allocation and, as Brunner (1992, p. 10) notes, 'The social problem then is the optimal assignment of rights'. For Coase (1992, p. 718), and those his work has encouraged, this raises the significance of the links between economics and the institutional arena where rights are decided: that of the law. In a wonderful passage from his Nobel lecture he emphasises the importance of the institutional context for economic analysis:

> It makes little sense for economists to discuss the process of exchange without specifying the institutional setting within which the trading takes place, since this affects the incentives to produce and the costs of transacting. I think this is now beginning to be recognized and made crystal-clear by what is going on in Eastern Europe today. The time has surely gone in which economists could analyze in great detail two individuals exchanging nuts for berries on the edge of the forest and then feel that their analysis of the process of exchange was complete, illuminating though this analysis may be in certain respects.

Brunner (1992, p. 10) has called 'The Problem of Social Cost', one of the outstanding papers published in the postwar period. Blaug (1998, p. 41) is perhaps even more fulsome:

> It is rare for a single article to generate an entire branch of economics, much less two branches of economics, but the Economics of Property Rights ... and the Economics of Law ... two rapidly growing sub-disciplines within econom-

ics in the last decade or so, can be traced directly to Coase's article on social cost ...

Posner (1993, p. 195) claims that it 'is widely believed to be the most frequently cited article in all of economics'.

Coase's other notable work includes a study of the allocation of the radio frequency spectrum in the United States published as 'The Federal Communications Commission' in the *Journal of Law and Economics* in 1959. Against the grain of popular wisdom at the time in the industry and in government circles, Coase argued in the paper 'that it would be better if use of the spectrum was determined by the pricing system and was awarded to the highest bidder' (Nobel Foundation, 2004). He relates an interesting story of an invitation from a number of Chicago economists (Coase was then at the University of Virginia) to discuss what they thought was an error in this work. At the meeting, Coase persuaded his critics that he was in the right and he was asked to write up his argument for a second paper in the *Journal of Law and Economics*. This subsequently appeared in 1960 as 'The Problem of Social Cost'. Coase supposes that without the prompt from Chicago his most famous paper would never have been written (Nobel Foundation, 2004). The central argument in 'The Federal Communications Commission' is itself of some contemporary relevance. The economist consultants to the British government on its auction of the '3rd generation' mobile phone licences – which raised some £22.5 billion ($34bn) or 2.5 per cent of UK GDP – cite Coase as the original advocate of the kind of work on which they were engaged (see Binmore and Klemperer, 2002).

Coase's lifetime work has been drawn together in two volumes: Coase (1988; 1994). The former includes his two classic articles from 1937 and 1960. The latter consists of 15 essays in which Coase evaluates the contributions of outstanding economists, including Adam Smith, Alfred Marshall and George Stigler. The legacy of Coase in economic analysis is explored in a collection of 40 articles edited by Steven Medema (1995).

Main Published Works

(1937), 'The Nature of the Firm', *Economica*, **4**, November, pp. 386–405.
(1959), 'The Federal Communications Commission', *Journal of Law and Economics*, **2**, October, pp. 1–40.
(1960), 'The Problem of Social Cost', *Journal of Law and Economics*, **3**, October, pp. 1–44.

(1988), *The Firm, the Market and the Law*, Chicago: University of Chicago Press.

(1992), 'The Institutional Structure of Production', *American Economic Review*, **82**, September, pp. 713–19.

(1994), *Essays on Economics and Economists*, Chicago: University of Chicago Press.

Secondary Literature

Barzel, Y. and L.A. Kochin (1992), 'Ronald Coase on the Nature of Social Cost as a Key to the Problem of the Firm', *Scandinavian Journal of Economics*, **94** (1), pp. 19–31.

Binmore, K. and P. Klemperer (2002), 'The Biggest Auction Ever: The Sale of the British 3G Telecom Licences', *Economic Journal*, **112**, March, C74–C96.

Brunner, K. (1992), 'Ronald Coase: Old Fashioned Scholar', *Scandinavian Journal of Economics*, **94** (1), pp. 7–17.

Medema, S.G. (ed.) (1995), *The Legacy of Ronald Coase in Economic Analysis*, Cheltenham, UK and Northampton, MA, USA: Edward Elgar.

Posner, R.A. (1993), 'Ronald Coase and Methodology', *Journal of Economic Perspectives*, **7**, Fall, pp. 195–210.

Stigler, G.J. (1989), 'Two Notes on the Coase Theorem', *Yale Law Journal*, **99**, December, pp. 631–3.

See also   Beaud and Dostaler (1997, pp. 208–11); Blaug (1998, pp. 40–42; 1999, p. 236); Nobel Foundation (2004).

THE 1992 NOBEL MEMORIAL LAUREATE

LAUREATE

GARY BECKER

Gary S. Becker
(b. 1930)

© The Nobel Foundation

Gary Becker was born in Pottsville, Pennsylvania, USA, in 1930. When he was still a young child his family moved to Brooklyn, New York where he went to school (interestingly, Becker and the 1987 Nobel Laureate Robert Solow both graduated from the same high school: James Madison; Fuchs, 1994). Becker was a good student with a particular interest in mathematics. His family life was stimulating and he recalls 'many lively discussions in the house about politics and justice', to which he credits a growing desire he felt 'to do something useful for society' (Nobel Foundation, 2004).

Becker's first encounter with economics happened 'accidentally' at Princeton University – where he was taking mostly mathematical courses. However, the subject seemed to blend social concerns with mathematical rigour and this made it attractive to him. In his final year at Princeton, some of this allure had worn off and Becker says he contemplated switching to sociology but he 'found that subject too difficult' (Nobel Foundation, 2004). He graduated with a BA from Princeton in 1951. Becker's graduate study was in economics at the University of Chicago, where he excelled. Jacob Viner, a faculty member at Chicago during the time when Milton Friedman and George Stigler studied there, credits Becker with being 'the best student I ever had' (quoted in Fuchs, 1994, p. 183). The university awarded Becker an MA in 1953 and a PhD in 1955. By the time Becker arrived at Chicago, Friedman was himself on the faculty and Friedman's teaching and wider academic influence both revived Becker's excitement about economics and 'had a profound effect on the direction taken by my research' (Nobel Foundation, 2004). Becker also mentions, among others, the 1979 Nobel Laureate Theodore Schultz – with his pioneering work on human capital – as an important influence at Chicago.

In 1954 Becker was appointed to his first academic post as assistant professor at Chicago. In 1957 he moved to Columbia University, New York – again as assistant professor but combined this with an appointment at the National Bureau of Economic Research, also in New York. Becker had been offered a lot more money to stay at Chicago but,

> I felt I would become intellectually more independent if I left the nest and had to make it on my own ... I have always believed this was the correct decision, for I developed greater independence and self-confidence than seems likely if I remained at Chicago. (Nobel Foundation, 2004)

At Columbia, Becker became associate professor, professor and then Arthur Lehman Professor of Economics. After 12 years in New York and beginning to feel 'intellectually stale' he decided to return to Chicago where he was Ford Foundation Visiting Professor of Economics from 1969 to 1970 and Professor of Economics from 1970 to 1983. In 1983 Becker was offered a joint appointment by the Sociology Department at Chicago, a post he still holds alongside that in economics. Since 1990 he has also been a senior fellow at the Hoover Institution at Stanford University, California.

Becker's offices and honours include the W.S. Woytinsky Award from the University of Michigan (1964) and – in 1967 – the receipt of the American Economic Association's John Bates Clark Medal. He is a fellow of the American Statistical Society, the Econometric Society and the American Academy of Arts and Sciences. In 1974 Becker served as vice-president and in 1987 as president of the American Economic Association. He is a member of the National Academy of Sciences and from 1990 to 1992 served as president of the Mont Pelerin Society. He also received the National Medal of Science Award in 2000. In 1992 Becker was awarded the Nobel Memorial Prize in Economics 'for having extended the domain of microeconomic analysis to a wide range of human behaviour and interaction, including nonmarket behaviour' (Nobel Foundation, 2004).

As we have seen, in Becker's upbringing and in his student life he developed a concern about social issues and what might be done about them. A reasonable characterisation of his work would be that it has sought to apply a basic economic approach to a diffuse range of social problems and institutions, many of which – such as discrimination, crime and punishment, and considerations of the family – were previously thought to be beyond the remit of economic analysis. Moreover, Becker has accomplished this feat often in the face of doubt and hostility from others in his own profession, as well as practitioners in other disciplines affronted by what they perceive as an interloper in their intellectual domain.

Becker's method is to apply an *enriched* model of rational choice to try to understand the behaviour of individual agents in particular contexts. It is his contention that this approach is a powerful and general means of producing explanations and predictions that are open to empirical resolution.[10] Becker's working assumption is *not* that individuals 'are motivated solely by selfishness or gain' but that they try, consistently, to 'maximize welfare *as they conceive it*, whether they be selfish, altruistic, loyal, spiteful or masochistic' (Becker, 1993, p. 38, emphasis in original). Their choices in turn are constrained by a variety of factors such as income, opportunity and, importantly for Becker, time.

Becker's first significant publication was a book, *The Economics of Discrimination*, based on his Chicago PhD thesis (Becker, 1957a).[11] Becker thought that discrimination against minorities was an important social concern but he was aware that, hitherto, economists had displayed no great interest in the matter.[12] Although the book was favourably reviewed in some journals, Becker was aware of the hostility and doubt that it also generated. Perhaps this was to be expected. As Rosen (1993, p. 33) notes,

[10] Although Becker does not specifically acknowledge it in his Nobel lecture, Friedman's methodological influence might be inferred here – see entry on Friedman in this volume.
[11] This was not his first publication. Becker had already produced two papers arising from his time at Princeton and co-authored an article with Friedman (Becker, 1952a; Becker and Baumol, 1952b; Friedman and Becker, 1957b).
[12] Gunnar Myrdal was an exception. His book *American Dilemma* (1944) is specifically acknowledged as such by Becker. See entry on Myrdal in this volume.

It is hard to describe what a daring work this was back then, given the general tenor of the times in the United States, and the general scepticism of economists and other social scientists for work that strayed too far from familiar turf.

Becker's simple but effective approach was to explore the economic implications of discrimination using a model analogous to that employed in the study of international trade. This allows the incidence of discrimination to be interpreted as a tariff: in the case of a discriminating employer the tariff is a tax the employer is willing to pay (a rational choice in spiteful subjective terms) to hire a less-productive white person instead of a more productive black person (see Sandmo, 1993). Such a reading allowed Becker to demonstrate that discrimination harms both its victims and its perpetrators (Nobel Foundation, 2004). Just as trade protection reduces social welfare in international goods markets, so does discrimination-based protection in the job market. However, Becker also showed that where the discriminating majority is large, such as in the United States, 'discrimination by the majority hardly lowers their incomes, but may greatly reduce the incomes of the minority' (Becker, 1993, p. 40).

Becker's Nobel citation suggests that his work on human capital may be his most notable contribution to the canon of economics. It is generally recognised that while he was not the first modern economist to offer new insights into this subject – Becker himself credits *inter alia* Theodore Schultz with that distinction (see entry on Schultz in this volume) – he has certainly done most to underpin its microeconomic foundations and to explore its empirical applications. The key references here are Becker's 1962 article in the *Journal of Political Economy* and his 1964 book, *Human Capital: A Theoretical and Empirical Analysis with Special Reference to Education*. The choice of book title is interesting. Becker expected the phrase 'human capital' to generate a hostile reaction given its (at that time) demeaning human-as-machine connotations and because it would be read as devaluing the cultural enrichment associated with education. He recollects: 'As a result, I hesitated a long time before deciding to call my book *Human Capital*, and hedged the risk by using a long subtitle' (Becker, 1993, p. 43).

Although he was in uncertain territory in the early 1960s, the rational choice approach to human capital Becker pioneered has bequeathed what is today 'a uniform and generally applicable analytical framework' (Nobel Foundation, 2004). Becker's starting point is to interpret the decisions by individuals to invest in their own capabilities through education, training, medical care and so on as turning on the balance of benefits and costs of such investments. This is not simply a narrow appeal to self-interest as individuals maximise welfare subjectively and they may be as much motivated by altruism as greed. (Recall that Becker's own interest in economics originated partly because of its relevance to social improvement; if he had just wanted to make money he might have chosen to augment his human capital in another way.) The benefits of investing certainly include higher earnings and better jobs but they also encompass, for example, cultural enrichment where individuals think this is important. The costs centre on the value of the time surrendered in making investments.

This approach has wide application. To give just one example used by Becker in his Nobel lecture, human capital theory can be used to understand recent changes in the 'gender gap' in earnings (see Becker, 1993). He argues that the traditional obligations of childcare gave women fewer incentives to invest in education and training – hence their lower earnings. But in most advanced societies, labour markets have changed substantially in recent decades. Smaller families, more single-parent families, the growth in service sector employment and changes in the legislative framework have all encouraged more women to enter the labour market, and this has provided an incentive for them to invest in their own skills. The consequence has been a narrowing of the gender gap in earnings.

After Becker returned to Chicago at the beginning of the 1970s, his work found a new focus. He began to try to use his economic approach to explore a 'whole range of family issues: marriage, divorce, altruism toward other members, investments by parents in children, and long-term changes in what families do' (Nobel Foundation, 2004). The results were brought together in 1981 in his book, *A Treatise on the Family*.[13] This was not entirely new territory to Becker. He had, for example, previously considered questions about fertility (Becker, 1960) and the way that households allocate time (Becker, 1965). Building upon the foundations laid in the latter pa-

---

[13] An interesting and revealing admission in Becker's Nobel lecture: the six years he devoted to the *Treatise* left him 'intellectually and emotionally exhausted' and it took him about two years to recover. Academic success, even for the most able, demands major sacrifice.

per, Becker has arrived at a general theory of family behaviour in which, for example, increases in real wages and greater opportunities for substituting capital for labour in household tasks have created new incentives and opportunities for families to function in different ways, with more time allocated to paid work and less to unpaid household labour (Sandmo, 1993). With Nigel Tomes, he has argued that these trends account for both increases in the participation of married women in the labour market and the rising tendency towards divorce, particularly for poorer couples (Becker and Tomes, 1986; and see Becker, 1993).

A final dimension to Becker's work acknowledged in his Nobel citation is his application of the rational model to considerations of crime and punishment. A personal anecdote reveals how he got started. Late for an appointment he weighed the cost of parking his car legally in a car park against the probability of a fine for parking illegally and took the size of the fine into account. He risked parking illegally and was not caught. Becker thought that this kind of experience could be used to analyse criminal behaviour: 'I was not persuaded that criminals had radically different motivations from everyone else' (Becker, 1993, p. 41). Criminality, in other words, could be considered rational: 'some individuals become criminals because of the financial rewards from crime compared to legal work, taking account of the likelihood of apprehension and conviction and the severity of punishment' (ibid., p. 42). The key references here are Becker (1968) and Becker and Landes (1974).

Main Published Works

(1952a), 'A Note on Multi-Country Trade', *American Economic Review*, **42**, September, pp. 558–68.

(1952b), 'The Classical Monetary Theory: The Outcome of the Discussion' (with W.J. Baumol), *Economica*, **19**, November, pp. 355–76.

(1957a), *The Economics of Discrimination*, Chicago: University of Chicago Press.

(1957b), 'A Statistical Illusion in Judging Keynesian Models' (with M. Friedman), *Journal of Political Economy*, **65**, February, pp. 64–75.

(1960), 'An Economic Analysis of Fertility', in *Demographic and Economic Change in Developed Countries*, Conference of the Universities – National Bureau Committee for Economic Research, A Report of the National Bureau of Economic Research, Princeton, NJ: Princeton University Press, pp. 209–40.

(1962), 'Investment in Human Capital: A Theoretical Analysis', *Journal of Political Economy*, **70**, October, pp. 9–49.

(1964), *Human Capital: A Theoretical and Empirical Analysis with Special Reference to Education*, New York: Columbia University Press; expanded edn 1993, Chicago: University of Chicago Press.

(1965), 'A Theory of the Allocation of Time', *Economic Journal*, **75**, September, pp. 493–508.

(1968), 'Crime and Punishment: An Economic Approach', *Journal of Political Economy*, **76**, March/April, pp. 169–217.

(1974), *Essays in the Economics of Crime and Punishment* (ed. with W.M. Landes), New York: Columbia University Press.

(1981), *A Treatise on the Family*, Cambridge, MA: Harvard University Press.

(1986), 'Human Capital and the Rise and Fall of Families' (with N. Tomes), *Journal of Labour Economics*, **4**, July, S1–S39.

(1993), 'The Economic Way of Looking at Life', *Journal of Political Economy*, **101**, June, pp. 38–58.

Secondary Literature

Fuchs, V.R. (1994), 'Gary S. Becker: Ideas About Facts', *Journal of Economic Perspectives*, **8**, Spring, pp. 183–92.

Rosen, S. (1993), 'Risks and Rewards: Gary Becker's Contributions to Economics', *Scandinavian Journal of Economics*, **95** (1), pp. 25–36.

Sandmo, A. (1993), 'Gary Becker's Contributions to Economics', *Scandinavian Journal of Economics*, **95** (1), pp. 7–23.

See also   Beaud and Dostaler (1997, pp. 182–4); Blaug (1998, pp. 16–18); Blaug and Vane (2003, pp. 65–6); Nobel Foundation (2004); Pressman (1999, pp. 185–8).

THE 1993 NOBEL MEMORIAL LAUREATES

ROBERT FOGEL
AND
DOUGLASS NORTH

Robert W. Fogel
(b. 1926)

© The Nobel Foundation

Robert Fogel was born in New York City, USA, in 1926. His parents and elder brother had arrived in America four years earlier from Odessa, on the Black Sea coast of Russia. Fogel remembers that his mother and father had a 'reverence for learning [that] encouraged both my brother and me toward academic pursuits' (Nobel Foundation, 2004). Although the Great Depression made times generally hard during his childhood, Fogel suggests that one of its effects was to 'attract a remarkably talented and dedicated collection of teachers' into the New York public school system. This stimulating environment prompted him to aspire initially to a career in science.

Fogel attended Cornell University where he was awarded a BA in 1948. Although he began studying physics and chemistry at Cornell, he later switched to economics and history. The change was prompted by the spectre of a return to depression after the end of the Second World War. Fogel wanted to 'find solutions to the current problems of instability and equity' (Nobel Foundation, 2004). He later enrolled at Columbia University, where he was taught microeconomics by George Stigler (see entry in this volume) and American economic history by Carter Goodrich. Goodrich was undertaking research into government support for the development of transport and on his advice Fogel wrote his master's thesis on the

Union Pacific Railroad. This work was published in 1960 as Fogel's first book and he obtained his MA from Columbia in 1960. Fogel completed his training at Johns Hopkins University with the award of a PhD in 1963. At Johns Hopkins his teachers included Abba Lerner, Fritz Machlup and Evsey Domar. Fogel's dissertation, from which he derived one of his most important books – *Railroads and American Economic Growth: Essays in Econometric History* (1964) – was supervised by Simon Kuznets (Goldin, 1995, and see entry in this volume). This book was included in Fogel's Nobel citation.

Fogel's academic career began in 1958 when he obtained an instructor post at Johns Hopkins. In 1960 he became an assistant professor at the University of Rochester, with promotion to associate professor in 1964. In 1965, Fogel was appointed professor at the University of Chicago, a post he held until 1975; although between 1968 and 1975 he was also visiting professor at Rochester. In 1975 he moved to Harvard University as professor until 1981, although he spent 1975–76 as Pitt Professor of American History and Institutions at Cambridge University. In 1981 he returned to Chicago as George Stigler's successor as the Charles R. Walgreen Professor of American Institutions and director of the Walgreen Foundation and the Center for Population Economics.

Turning to his offices and honours, Fogel has been an associate of the Columbia University Seminar in Economic History since 1969. He has also been a member of the Board of Trustees of the Economic History Association since 1972 and he served as its president in 1977–78. Since 1978 he has been research associate and programme director at the National Bureau of Economic Research. In 1980–81, Fogel was president of the Social Science History Association and in 1998 president of the American Economic Association. In 1993 he was awarded the Nobel Memorial Prize in Economics jointly with Douglass North 'for having renewed research in economic history by applying economic theory and quantitative methods in order to explain economic and institutional change' (Nobel Foundation, 2004).

Fogel and his fellow Laureate, Douglass North, are generally acknowledged as the founders and major protagonists in the field of *cliometrics*. This involves the application to economic history of 'economic theory, quantification and formal hypothesis tests' (Eichengreen, 1994, p. 167). Cliometrics is credited with adding a degree of robustness to what had previously been a narrative emphasis on events in economic history; it has also engendered a new understanding of the importance of history to economic analysis (Eichengreen, 1994; McCloskey, 1994; Goldin, 1995; Nobel Foundation, 2004). Fogel's tentative thinking in this area began when he was a graduate student at Columbia. He supposed that a blend of history and economics could uncover the grand forces behind technological and institutional change and yield answers to contemporary social and economic problems. Naïve? Fogel now thinks so but he had started down what might be best termed a promising *funnel* of exploration. Realising that there was a general ignorance about the 'large processes' of social innovation and change, Fogel 'began to focus on more discrete issues', for example: 'What was the nature and the magnitude of the contribution of particular new technologies, such as railroads or steel mills to economic growth?' (Nobel Foundation, 2004). It was possible to be more certain about these narrower concerns because they lent themselves to more precise theorisation and quantification: in other words, they could be directly approached using what would become known as cliometrics.

McCloskey (1994, p. 164) describes Fogel's work as exercises in comparative statics – 'snapshots of the rationale for institutions at a single time'. Goldin (1995, p. 195) labels him 'the premier empiricist, who establishes a fact and then establishes it over and over again until he is confident he can persuade the most determined sceptic'. Fogel's Nobel citation concurs: 'Fogel's painstaking criticism of his sources, along with applications of innumerable and highly varied economic data, make it difficult for his critics to argue against him on purely empirical grounds' (Nobel Foundation, 2004). Herein lies Fogel's distinct and highly influential methodology: his concern is to produce analyses of institutions in economic history that employ precise forms of theoretisation and which are open to empirical validation or refutation.

This is not, however, Fogel's only methodological breakthrough. His 1964 book on the role of railroads in the development of the American economy employed *'counterfactual historiography'* to empirically test the validity of the widely held contention that rail had been integral to American growth. This position had been advanced, for example, by Rostow (1960), who argued that the 'take-off' of an economy into a stage of steady growth was predicated on the development of certain key sectors. Fogel's approach was to compare the actual growth of the American economy in 1890 with the hypothesised alternative of development in the absence of a rail network.

Measuring the difference would provide an estimate of the 'social savings' derived from railroads, together with the reciprocal cost in growth lost from the reliance on inferior modes of transport. Fogel found that the reduction in GDP growth was unexpectedly small: railroads could hardly be considered an indispensable element in American economic history. The book stimulated a substantial literature, indeed 'few books in economic history have made such an impression as Fogel's' (Nobel Foundation, 2004).

One exception may well be *Time on the Cross: The Economics of American Negro Slavery*, a book Fogel wrote with Stanley Engerman. When this book was published in 1974 there was still a presumption that slavery was an inefficient and unprofitable form of activity and that the Southern states where it had been practised did not gain economically from it (Eichengreen, 1994). Using a considerable volume of evidence to show that bigger plantations that used slaves in large numbers were able to reap economies of scale, Fogel (and Engerman) demonstrated that the institution of slavery gave the South 'a strong comparative advantage in the production of cotton' and, instead of leaving it 'backward', this alternative 'specialism' simply militated against Southern industrialisation (Goldin, 1995, p. 200). One implication is that the ending of slavery in the United States arose from political rather than economic imperatives: it did not wither, it was crushed (Nobel Foundation, 2004). *Time on the Cross* was a highly controversial work. Blaug (1998, p. 66) calls it 'perhaps the most controversial book that has ever been published in American history, on a subject known for its controversies'. Fogel's more recent work on slavery, *Without Consent or Contract: The Rise and Fall of American Slavery* (1989), is based on more qualitative evidence and is supplemented by three additional technical volumes: (Fogel et al., 1992a; 1992b; 1992c).

Fogel's present project is an enormous multi-disciplinary study of the links between long-term improvements in human health and economic growth. The work also considers the implications of patterns in health and economic performance for such issues as the demand for leisure, pensions and health care. A summary can be found in Fogel (1994). This research involves 'scholars from economics, history, medicine, physiology, demography, and statistics, and a data collection that is the largest ever in the field of economic history and one of the largest that has been privately amassed in economics' (Goldin, 1995, p. 203). Fogel's Nobel citation highlights findings on nineteenth-century mortality from this wide-ranging and continuing project: Fogel (1992d) is the relevant reference.

Main Published Works

(1960), *The Union Pacific Railroad: A Case in Premature Enterprise*, Baltimore, MD: Johns Hopkins University Press.

(1964), *Railroads and American Economic Growth: Essays in Econometric History*, Baltimore, MD: Johns Hopkins University Press.

(1974), *Time on the Cross: The Economics of American Negro Slavery* (with S.L. Engerman), vols 1 and 2, New York: Little, Brown & Co.

(1989), *Without Consent or Contract: The Rise and Fall of American Slavery*, New York: W.W. Norton.

(1992a), *Without Consent or Contract: The Rise and Fall of American Slavery: Evidence and Methods* (with others), New York: W.W. Norton.

(1992b), *Without Consent or Contract: The Rise and Fall of American Slavery: Markets and Production: Technical Papers, Volume I* (with S.L. Engerman and others), New York: W.W. Norton.

(1992c), *Without Consent or Contract: The Rise and Fall of American Slavery: Conditions of Slave Life and the Transition to Freedom: Technical Papers, Volume II* (with S.L. Engerman and others), New York: W.W. Norton.

(1992d), 'Second Thoughts on the European Escape from Hunger: Famines, Chronic Malnutrition and Mortality', in S.R. Osmani (ed.), *Nutrition and Poverty*, Oxford: Clarendon Press, pp. 243–86.

(1994), 'Economic Growth, Population Theory, and Physiology: The Bearing of Long-Term Processes on the Making of Economic Policy', *American Economic Review*, **84**, June, pp. 369–95.

Secondary Literature

Eichengreen, B. (1994), 'The Contributions of Robert W. Fogel to Economics and Economic History', *Scandinavian Journal of Economics*, **96** (2), pp. 167–79.

Goldin, C. (1995), 'Cliometrics and the Nobel', *Journal of Economic Perspectives*, **9**, Spring, pp. 191–208.

McCloskey, D.N. (1994), 'Fogel and North: Statics and Dynamics in Historical Economics', *Scandinavian Journal of Economics*, **96** (2), pp. 161–6.

Rostow, W.W. (1960), *The Stages of Economic Growth*, Cambridge: Cambridge University Press.

See also   Beaud and Dostaler (1997, pp. 232–3); Blaug (1998, pp. 66–7); Blaug and Vane (2003, pp. 255–6); Nobel Foundation (2004).

Douglass C. North
(b. 1920)

© The Nobel Foundation

Douglass North was born in Cambridge, Massachusetts, USA in 1920. His early education was peripatetic, primarily because his father's job as an insurance company manager necessitated a number of family relocations – including a spell in Ottawa, Canada. As North's mother 'believed in education broadly construed', the family also lived for a time in Europe and North went to school in Switzerland in 1929–30 (Nobel Foundation, 2004). Returning to America, North completed his high-school education in Wallingford, Connecticut, where he became an accomplished amateur photographer, something he was to later consider taking up as a profession.

Although accepted by Harvard University, North elected to attend the University of California at Berkeley following another family move, on this occasion to San Francisco. He judges himself to have been at best a 'mediocre' undergraduate; possibly he spent a little too much time engaged in student politics – North says he became a 'convinced Marxist' at Berkeley. He was awarded a BA in political science, philosophy and economics in 1942. Plans he had to enrol in law school after graduation were abandoned after the American entry into the Second World War (following the Japanese attack on Pearl Harbour in December 1941), and on leaving university North joined the Merchant Marine 'because of the strong feeling that I did not want to kill anybody' (Nobel Foundation, 2004). He became a navigator and made repeated trips to Australia and into the Pacific war zone.

North recollects that his time at sea, and a period towards the end of the war as a navigation instructor back in California, gave him an opportunity for three years of continuous reading; this reading convinced him that he should become an economist (Nobel Foundation, 2004). It was, however, a close-run thing. As an undergraduate North had worked a summer as a photographer and had encouragement to return to that profession, but he was persuaded to stick with economics and so went back to Berkeley to enrol as a graduate student. This decision was informed by a conviction 'that what I wanted to do with my life was to improve societies, and the way to do that was to find out what made economies work the way they did or fail to work' (Nobel Foundation, 2004). While the formal economics he learned at Berkeley did not inspire him – and he claims not to have learned much – it was during his postgraduate studies that he began to embrace economic history under his thesis adviser M.M. Knight. North was awarded his PhD in 1952.

After the war, Berkeley also provided North with his first academic appointment as graduate teaching fellow, a post he held from 1946 to 1949. In 1950 he began a 33-year association with the University of Washington in Seattle where he was first assistant, then associate professor, becoming Professor of Economics in 1960. North also served as director of the university's Institute for Economic Research between 1961 and 1966 and then chairman of the same body from 1967 to 1969. He has also held posts at Rice University, Houston, Texas, where he was Peterkin Professor of Political Economy in 1979, and the University of Cambridge, where he was Pitt Professor from 1981 to 1982. Since 1983, North has been Professor of Economics at Washington University in St Louis.

North's offices and honours include membership of the Board of Directors of the National Bureau of Economic Research (NBER) from 1967 to 1987; in 1972–73 he was president of the American Economic History Association. North was visiting associate director of the Centre de Recherche Historique at the École Pratique des Hautes Études in Paris in 1973 and in 1975–76 he was president of the American Western Economic Association. In 1993 North was awarded the Nobel Memorial Prize in Economics jointly with Robert Fogel 'for having renewed research in economic history by applying economic theory and quantitative methods in order to explain economic and institutional change' (Nobel Foundation, 2004).

North's involvement with what has become known as the 'new economic history' or 'cliometrics'[14] – he and Fogel are generally acknowledged as its founders – began at a joint conference of the NBER and the Economic History Association on the growth of the American economy. He credits this meeting – which had a *quantitative* focus – with actually launching cliometrics; which is the use, *inter alia*, of quantitative techniques, hypothesis testing, economic theory and counterfactual analysis to explain economic growth and decline (Nobel Foundation, 2004). North joined the NBER as a research associate in 1956 and, working alongside Simon Kuznets (see entry in this volume), began the empirical analysis that would lead to his important quantitative study of the US balance of payments 1790–1860 (Nobel Foundation, 2004 and see North, 1960). North reflects that this 'was an enormously important year of my life'; in effect it both prompted and nurtured his ground-floor work in cliometrics (Nobel Foundation, 2004).

North's Nobel citation credits him specifically with pioneering studies of long-term development in Europe and the United States and with penetrating analyses of the role of institutions in fostering economic growth. North characterises his own approach to economic history as concerning 'the performance of economies through time' (North, 1994, p. 359). McCloskey (1994, p. 165) provides perhaps the most illuminating representation of North's work in describing it as 'narrative', and more compellingly, 'moving pictures'. North's dynamic methodology evolved out of the shortcomings he perceived in standard neoclassical theory as applied to such basic questions as why some economies grow and others stagnate. The neoclassical model might be precise and elegant but, for North, it is also 'frictionless and static': it can, for example, say much about the operation of markets but little about how they arise and how they develop over time (North, 1994, p. 359). North argues that the neoclassical approach neglects two crucial factors that profoundly influence economic performance: the *institutional framework* that structures human relations, and the *dimension of time* through which, and here North borrows a phrase from Friedrich von Hayek, a

---

[14] The name is derived from Clio, the muse of history, so its literal interpretation might be taken as 'history measuring'.

society's 'accumulated stock of knowledge' is transmitted (and via which institutions evolve). Institutions are the formal constraints that govern a society – rules, laws, constitutions – together with the informal constraints that also condition the behaviour of its members: codes of conduct and conventions, for example (North, 1994). An analytical framework based on an appreciation of the dynamic significance of institutions has enabled North to offer some convincing explanations of economic performance in a variety of historical and contemporary contexts (Myhrman and Weingast, 1994).

North traces the development of his work through a series of books, most of which are referenced in his Nobel citation. The first of these – *The Economic Growth of the United States, 1790–1860* – published in 1961, he describes as a 'straightforward analysis of how markets work in the context of an export staple model of growth' (Nobel Foundation, 2004). Others are more effusive. Myhrman and Weingast (1994, p. 186) consider it to be 'one of the founding contributions to cliometrics and the new economic history', while the Nobel Committee credits it with influencing the research agenda in the United States and elsewhere (see also McCloskey, 1994). Its major (cliometric) innovation was to incorporate significant amounts of quantitative data into the analysis of historical economic performance (see Pressman, 1999; Myhrman and Weingast, 1994).

In the mid-1960s, North switched the focus of his research from the United States to Europe. In doing so he came up against a problem: in his own words he 'quickly became convinced that the tools of neo-classical economic theory were not up to the task of explaining the kind of fundamental societal change that had characterized European economies from medieval times onward' (Nobel Foundation, 2004). In North's view, adequate explanations of the markedly different trajectories of European economies could not be produced from 'frictionless and static' methods. The neoclassical approach had, for example, little to say about why some countries in Western Europe flourished economically – England and the Netherlands were the beacon cases – and others, such as Spain and Portugal, failed. North's 'new institutional economics' was the means by which he began to address such questions.

This new emphasis on the role of institutions in conditioning economic growth resulted in two further books: with Lance Davis, North produced a reinterpretation of growth in the United States,

Institutional Change and American Economic Growth (1971a); and with Robert Thomas he wrote *The Rise of the Western World: A New Economic History* (1973). Both books demonstrated the importance of the institutional context of growth promotion, as opposed to the traditional neoclassical concern with factor accumulation (North, 1994). For example, in the early United States, canal building played a central role in growth because it both provided for unprecedented savings in transport costs and extended the physical and functional range of markets. What Davis and North (1971a) showed was that this new transport technology did not emerge spontaneously or naturally out of the ether, rather it was predicated on historically contingent institutional change. Similarly, North and Thomas (1973) demonstrated that the economic growth in England that propelled it from a second-class economy in 1600 to the world's greatest power by 1700 (Hill, 1980) largely rested on a new institutional framework: property rights and the fillip to individualism underwritten by the nascent parliamentary system. Spain, on the other hand, got 'stuck' with the wrong institutions and floundered economically (see also North, 1994; Goldin, 1995). Although both books explicitly understood the significance of institutional forms in the growth process, North later acknowledged that they also had shortcomings: for example, they could not explain 'why institutions produced results that in the long run did not manage to produce economic growth' (Nobel Foundation, 2004). Why, in other words, *pace* the neoclassical rationality assumption, would societies, apparently actively and consistently, choose poor institutional arrangements?

North approached an answer to this question in two further books: *Structure and Change in Economic History* (1981) and *Institutions, Institutional Change and Economic Performance* (1990). In the first of these he modelled the state in history – the arbiter of institutional rules – as a maximising agency that provides state services, such as security and justice, in exchange for revenue, and which also operates under the risk of replacement by rivals (Myhrman and Weingast, 1994). This approach enabled North to demonstrate that, in his phrase, 'inefficient' rules – in the sense that they were preferred by the state but were not greatly conducive to the promotion of economic growth – could emerge and persist (Nobel Foundation, 2004). However, this reading still left him with a rather unsatisfactory understanding of the political process and it is politics, in the final analysis, which decisively conditions the rules by which societies operate.

The second book moves on to consider the relationship between the political process, institutional forms and the economic performance of nations. North argues here that what he calls 'political markets' tend to be inefficient because of the difficulty in measuring and enforcing agreements between participants (the electors and electoral candidates in democracies). Given that electors tend to be generally underinformed and the issues complex, 'ideological stereotyping takes over and [in many cases adversely] shapes the consequent performance of economies' (North, 1994, p. 361). However, North also stresses that economic progress is not just a matter of selecting 'appropriate' institutions: this can be done relatively quickly but the 'informal norms' that condition people to behave in particular ways (customs, beliefs, dogmas, prejudices and so on), and which also shape economic performance, change much more slowly. North's Nobel citation recognises that his work in this area has important implications for policy making in developed and transition economies.

In addition to his books (see also North, 1966; North and Miller 1971b), North has written some highly influential journal articles. For example, his 1968 *Journal of Political Economy* paper on productivity in ocean shipping is 'one of the most quoted studies in economic history' (Nobel Foundation, 2004).

Main Published Works

(1961), *The Economic Growth of the United States, 1790–1860*, Englewood Cliffs, NJ: Prentice-Hall.

(1960), 'The United States Balance of Payments 1790–1860', *Trends in the American Economy in the Nineteenth Century*, 24th Conference on Income and Wealth, National Bureau of Economic Research, Princeton, NJ: Princeton University Press.

(1966), *Growth and Welfare in the American Past: A New Economic History*, Englewood Cliffs, NJ: Prentice-Hall.

(1968), 'Sources of Productivity Change in Ocean Shipping, 1600–1850', *Journal of Political Economy*, **76**, September, pp. 953–70.

(1971a), *Institutional Change and American Economic Growth 1607–1860* (with L.E. Davis), Cambridge: Cambridge University Press.

(1971b), *The Economics of Public Issues* (with R.L. Miller), New York: Harper & Row.

(1973), *The Rise of the Western World: A New Economic History* (with R.P. Thomas), Cambridge: Cambridge University Press.

(1981), *Structure and Change in Economic History*, New York: W.W. Norton.

(1990), *Institutions, Institutional Change and Economic Performance*, New York: Cambridge University Press.

(1991), 'Institutions', *Journal of Economic Perspectives*, **5**, February, pp. 97–112.

(1994), 'Economic Performance Through Time', *American Economic Review*, **84**, June, pp. 359–68.

Secondary Literature

Goldin, C. (1995), 'Cliometrics and the Nobel', *Journal of Economic Perspectives*, **9**, Spring, pp. 191–208.

Hill, C. (1980), *The Century of Revolution 1603–1714*, 2nd edn, Wokingham, UK: Van Nostrand Reinhold.

McCloskey, D.N. (1994), 'Fogel and North: Statics and Dynamics in Historical Economics', *Scandinavian Journal of Economics*, **96** (2), pp. 161–6.

Myhrman, J. and B.R. Weingast (1994), 'Douglass C. North's Contributions to Economics and Economic History', *Scandinavian Journal of Economics*, **96** (2), pp. 185–93.

See also   Beaud and Dostaler (1997, pp. 362–3); Blaug (1998, pp. 214–16); Blaug and Vane (2003, pp. 609–10); Nobel Foundation (2004); Pressman (1999, pp. 174–7).

THE 1994 NOBEL MEMORIAL LAUREATES

JOHN HARSANYI,
JOHN NASH JR
AND
REINHARD SELTEN

John C. Harsanyi
(1920–2000)

© The Nobel Foundation

John Harsanyi was born in Budapest, Hungary in 1920. He attended the same school as John von Neumann and showed great early promise in mathematics, winning first prize in a national contest for high-school students in the year of his graduation. Harsanyi's higher educational choices were made in the shadow of Nazism. He had wanted to study philosophy and mathematics but instead – in keeping with his parents' wishes (they owned a pharmacy business) – he became a pharmacy student at the University of Budapest. This allowed him to defer his military service and for a time avoid forced labour in the Hungarian Army that his Jewish origin would otherwise have guaranteed. Following the German occupation of Hungary in 1944, Harsanyi was conscripted into a labour unit but managed to escape as the unit was en route to its destruction in an Austrian concentration camp. He survived the rest of the war in hiding (Nobel Foundation, 2004).

In 1946 Harsanyi re-entered the University of Budapest to study for a doctorate in philosophy. He was awarded his PhD in 1947 and spent the 1947–48 academic year teaching sociology at the university. But there was to be no academic career for him in Hungary. Forced to resign his post because his anti-Marxist political views were unacceptable to the authorities, he and his later wife, Anne, eventually fled Hungary illegally and at no small risk across a thinly guarded stretch of border. They settled in Australia at the end of 1950, where Harsanyi studied economics at the University of Sydney in the evening and did factory work during the day. He was attracted to economics 'because I found the conceptual and mathematical elegance of economic theory very attractive' (Nobel Foundation, 2004). He was awarded an MA in 1953 and took up a post as Lecturer in Economics at the University of Queensland in Brisbane.

On a Rockefeller Fellowship Harsanyi went to Stanford University in 1956, securing a PhD in 1958 that was supervised by Kenneth Arrow, a subsequent Nobel Laureate (see entry on Arrow in this volume). Although Harsanyi then returned to Australia – to a research position at the Australian National University – with the help of Arrow and James Tobin (Nobel Laureate in 1981), he was back in the United States in 1961 as Professor of Economics at Wayne State University, Detroit. In 1964 he moved to the University of California at Berkeley, initially as visiting professor, and then professor in 1965. Harsanyi remained at Berkeley until his retirement in 1990. He died aged 80 on 9 August 2000.

Harsanyi was a member of the National Academy of Sciences, a fellow of both the American Academy of Arts and Sciences and the Econometric Society, and a distinguished fellow of the American Economic Association. In 1994 he was awarded the Nobel Memorial Prize in Economics, together with John Nash and Reinhard Selten, 'for their pioneering analysis of equilibria in the theory of non-cooperative games' (Nobel Foundation, 2004).

Game theory is concerned with analysing strategic interaction between individuals where decision making by each party is conditioned by the choices made by others. This kind of interaction is common in economics and takes place, for example, between competing firms, between countries in their international trade policies, in a whole range of principal–agent relationships, and so on. It also has many applications in political science; for example, in arms control – the context in which game theory was initially funded and applied by the US military during the Cold War. The first modern treatment of game theory in economics was John von Neumann and Oskar Morgenstern's 1944 *Theory of Games and Economic Behaviour*. This study focused on cooperative zero-sum two-person games. Subsequently, Harsanyi's fellow Nobel Laureate John Nash introduced the more widely applicable concept of a non-cooperative finite game where there is no negotiation between players, and identified what has become known as Nash equilibrium – a set of strategies between n-players from which no participant has any personal incentive to deviate (Nash, 1950; 1951).

The best-known interpretation of Nash equilibrium considers it to arise as a result of rational behaviour informed by players' knowledge of each others' preferences within a game. One difficulty here is that, for many actual situations in economics and other contexts, such complete information is seldom available. For example, an oligopolistic firm knows its capabilities and preferences much better than it knows those of a competitor. Harsanyi's contribution to game theory, acknowledged in his Nobel award, was to demonstrate that games with incomplete information can be transformed into games with complete but imperfect information for which Nash equilibria can be defined. His innovation was to conceptualise an incomplete information game as 'type centred', where type refers to type of player. This approach allows an incomplete information game to be specified in probabilistic terms, thus facilitating its conversion into a game with complete information (see Harsanyi, 1995; Royal Swedish Academy of Sciences, 1995; van Damme and Weibull, 1995). Harsanyi's work has enabled game-theoretic methods to be fruitfully applied in a whole range of imperfect information settings (see Gul, 1997). The Prize-winning papers were published in *Management Science* in 1967–68 (Harsanyi, 1967; 1968a; 1968b).

Harsanyi's Nobel citation also acknowledges his work in welfare economics and in economic and moral philosophy. A number of his journal articles have been collected together in two books: *Essays on Ethics, Social Behavior, and Scientific Explanation* (Harsanyi, 1976), and *Papers in Game Theory* (Harsanyi, 1982). These collections are complemented by two other books, one of which Harsanyi co-authored with his fellow Nobel Laureate, Reinhard Selten (Harsanyi, 1977; Harsanyi and Selten, 1988).

Main Published Works

(1967), 'Games with Incomplete Information Played by "Bayesian Players": I. The Basic Model', *Management Science*, **14**, November, pp. 159–82.

(1968a), 'Games with Incomplete Information Played by "Bayesian Players": II. Bayesian Equilibrium Points', *Management Science*, **14**, January, pp. 320–34.

(1968b), 'Games with Incomplete Information Played by "Bayesian Players": III. The Basic Probability Distribution of the Game', *Management Science*, **14**, March, pp. 486–502.

(1976), *Essays on Ethics, Social Behaviour, and Scientific Explanation* (Foreword by K.J. Arrow), Dordrecht: D. Reidel.

(1977), *Rational Behaviour and Bargaining Equilibrium in Games and Social Situations*, Cambridge: Cambridge University Press.

(1982), *Papers in Game Theory*, Dordrecht: D. Reidel.

(1988), *A General Theory of Equilibrium Selection in Games* (with R. Selten), Cambridge, MA: MIT Press.

(1995), 'Games with Incomplete Information', *American Economic Review*, **85**, June, pp. 289–303.

Secondary Literature

Gul, F. (1997), 'A Nobel Prize for Game Theorists: The Contributions of Harsanyi, Nash and Selten', *Journal of Economic Perspectives*, **11**, Summer, pp. 159–74.

Nash, J.F. (1950), 'Equilibrium Points in *n*-Person Games', *Proceedings of the National Academy of Sciences*, **36**, pp. 48–9.

Nash, J.F. (1951), 'Non-Cooperative Games', *Annals of Mathematics*, **54** (2), pp. 286–95.

Royal Swedish Academy of Sciences (1995), 'The Nobel Memorial Prize in Economics 1994', *Scandinavian Journal of Economics*, **97** (1), pp. 1–7.

van Damme, E. and J.W. Weibull (1995), 'Equilibrium in Strategic Interaction: The Contributions of John C. Harsanyi, John F. Nash and Reinhard Selten', *Scandinavian Journal of Economics*, **97** (1), pp. 15–40.

See also   Blaug (1999, pp. 502–3); Nobel Foundation (2004).

John F. Nash Jr
(b. 1928)

© The Nobel Foundation

John Forbes Nash was born in Bluefield, West Virginia, USA in 1928. Both his parents were graduates and they took an active interest in their son's intellectual development. Nash was something of an independent learner and in his early teenage years he was conducting scientific experiments and solving challenging mathematical problems on his own. In 1945 he joined the Carnegie Institute of Technology (now Carnegie-Mellon University) having won a scholarship in the George Westinghouse Competition. He began by studying chemical engineering before switching to chemistry and then mathematics. Because of the notable progress Nash then made, when he graduated in 1948 he was awarded both a BS and an MS. Nash credits this achievement to extra mathematics schooling his parents had arranged for him while he was still in Bluefield. Carnegie also gave him his first brush with economics – an elective he took in international economics that was to lead to both his *Econometrica* paper 'The Bargaining Problem' (Nash, 1950c), and his interest in game theory (Nobel Foundation, 2004).

On the strength of a remarkable recommendation from Carnegie – it read simply 'This man is a genius' – Nash was offered graduate student fellowships by Princeton and Harvard universities (Kuhn et al., 1996). It has been suggested that his preference was for

Harvard, but Princeton offered him more generous terms and seemed keener to attract him; Nash opted for Princeton. His PhD thesis (Nash, 1950a), containing the work that would win him the Nobel Prize, was accepted by Princeton's Mathematics Department in 1950. Nash was 21.

After completing his PhD, Nash stayed at Princeton for a year as an instructor before moving to the Massachusetts Institute of Technology (MIT) as C.L.E. Moore Instructor. For a time he also worked for the RAND Corporation. In 1956–57 he returned to visit Princeton on a sabbatical funded by an Alfred P. Sloan award. Nash remained at MIT until resigning in 1959 because of mental health problems with which he struggled for a long time. He is currently senior research mathematician in the Department of Mathematics at Princeton.

Nash's honours include the award (jointly with Carlton E. Lemke) in 1978 of the John von Neumann Theory Prize by the Operations Research Society of America and the Institute of Management Sciences. In 1999 he received the Leroy P. Steele Prize from the American Mathematical Society. In 1994 Nash was awarded the Nobel Memorial Prize in Economics, together with John Harsanyi and Reinhard Selten, 'for their pioneering analysis of equilibria in the theory of non-cooperative games' (Nobel Foundation, 2004).

Nash's work has been pivotal in the development of game theory and his name is associated with one of its most fundamental concepts: Nash equilibrium. As game-theoretic principles have become central to contemporary economics, Nash can be said to have exerted an enormous influence on the discipline.[15] Indeed, his fellow Laureates Harsanyi and Selten have acknowledged their own debt to his pioneering contributions (see Harsanyi's comments in Nash's Nobel Seminar – Kuhn et al., 1996, p. 166). Nash's work has also been applied in other social science contexts and in evolutionary biology (Kuhn et al., 1996; Milnor, 1998).

Game theory is concerned with analysing strategic interaction between individuals or agents where decision making by each party

---

[15] Leonard (1994, p. 492) argues that 'Any economist who today professes ignorance of game theory implicitly admits to having lost contact with the conceptual structure underpinning many recent developments in microeconomic analysis'. See also Myerson (1999) for an accessible discussion of Nash's influence on the development of economic theory. Rubinstein (1995) offers a short appreciation of Nash as an economic modeller.

is conditioned by the choices made and the actions taken by others. This kind of interaction is common in economic contexts: between competing firms, employers and workers, tax authorities and tax-payers, monetary authorities and economic agents, and so on. The first modern treatment of game theory in economics was John von Neumann and Oskar Morgenstern's *Theory of Games and Economic Behaviour*, first published in 1944. This study focused on zero-sum two-person games that were later characterised by Nash as coop-erative in nature: that is, participants are able to negotiate with each other to reach mutually acceptable outcomes. Nash's PhD thesis (Nash, 1950a) both introduced the more widely applicable concept of a non-cooperative finite game where there is no communication or collusion between players, and identified the notion of what he called 'equilibrium point'. This is the famous Nash equilibrium – a constellation of strategies between n-players from which no partici-pant has an incentive to deviate because none can bring about an individual improvement by changing their personal strategy. Nash also provided proof that at least one such equilibrium always exists. Reporting some of the findings in his PhD thesis, the relevant pa-pers here are Nash (1950b; 1951).

One aspect of Nash equilibrium specifically referenced in Nash's Nobel citation concerns the alternative ways in which equilibrium may be interpreted (Royal Swedish Academy of Sciences, 1995). In his PhD thesis, Nash proposed two interpretations: one based on the concept of rationality and a second reflecting what he called 'mass action' (van Damme and Weibull, 1995). Under the rational interpretation, players are understood to act on the basis of knowl-edge of the full structure of the game, including accurate expecta-tions about the choices of others. Given such conditions, Nash equilibrium emerges as players attempt to maximise their utility in the light of each other's strategic dispositions. This has been the standard interpretation of Nash equilibrium in the literature as it was this that Nash deployed in his earliest published work; the mass-action alternative, resting quietly in his thesis, has been little noticed until recently (Kuhn et al., 1996).

The mass-action interpretation allows that players need be nei-ther rational nor informed about the structure of a repeated game. In these circumstances 'participants ... accumulate empirical infor-mation on the relative advantages of the pure strategies at their disposal' (Nash, quoted in Kuhn et al., 1996, p. 171). Here players are representative of the *group* interests that, Nash argues, characterise certain situations in economics or international politics (see van Damme and Weibull, 1995). The outcome is an equilibrium point arising from the 'average behaviour' in each of the group populations. Games of this form have also been used in biology as a means to understand the processes underpinning natural selection (Royal Swedish Academy of Sciences, 1995).

Nash's other contributions to economics acknowledged by the Royal Swedish Academy include his bargaining solution for cooperative games (Nash, 1950c). As noted, the work for this paper was actually begun while Nash was still an undergraduate at Carnegie and was prompted by his only formal training in economics – the elective he took in international economics. Nash also initiated work that has sought to understand cooperative games by modelling their negotiation using a non-cooperative framework; this approach is known as the 'Nash program' (see Nash, 1951, and for its application, see Nash, 1953; for its significance, see Gul, 1997; Kuhn et al., 1996). Nash's papers have been collected in Nash (1996) and, with editorial introductions, in Kuhn and Nasar (2002). Nash's biographer is Nasar (1998).

Main Published Works

(1950a), 'Non-Cooperative Games', unpublished PhD Thesis, Princeton University.
(1950b), 'Equilibrium Points in *n*-Person Games', *Proceedings of the National Academy of Sciences*, **36**, pp. 48–9.
(1950c), 'The Bargaining Problem', *Econometrica*, **18**, pp. 155–62.
(1951), 'Non-Cooperative Games', *Annals of Mathematics*, **54** (2), pp. 286–95.
(1953), 'Two-Person Cooperative Games', *Econometrica*, **21**, pp. 128–40.
(1996), *Essays on Game Theory* (Introduction by K. Binmore), Cheltenham, UK and Brookfield, USA: Edward Elgar.

Secondary Literature

Gul, F. (1997), 'A Nobel Prize for Game Theorists: The Contributions of Harsanyi, Nash and Selten', *Journal of Economic Perspectives*, **11**, Summer, pp. 159–74.
Kuhn, H.W., J.C. Harsanyi, R. Selten, J.W. Weibull, E. van Damme, J.F. Nash Jr and P. Hammerstein (1996), 'The Work of John Nash in Game Theory', (Nobel Seminar, 8 December 1994), *Journal of Economic Theory*, **69**, April, pp. 153–85.
Kuhn, H.W. and S. Nasar (eds) (2002), *The Essential John Nash*, Princeton, NJ: Princeton University Press.
Leonard, R.J. (1994), 'Reading Cournot, Reading Nash: The Creation and Stabilisation of the Nash Equilibrium', *Economic Journal*, **104**, May, pp. 492–511.
Milnor, J. (1998), 'John Nash and "A Beautiful Mind"', *Notices of the American Mathematical Society*, **45**, November, pp. 1329–32.
Myerson, R.B. (1999), 'Nash Equilibrium and the History of Economic Theory', *Journal of Economic Literature*, **37**, September, pp. 1067–82.

Nasar, S. (1998), *A Beautiful Mind: A Biography of John Forbes Nash Jr.*, New York: Simon & Schuster.

Royal Swedish Academy of Sciences (1995), 'The Nobel Memorial Prize in Economics 1994', *Scandinavian Journal of Economics*, **97** (1), pp. 1–7.

Rubinstein, A. (1995), 'John Nash: The Master of Economic Modeling', *Scandinavian Journal of Economics*, **97** (1), pp. 9–13.

van Damme, E. and J.W. Weibull (1995), 'Equilibrium in Strategic Interaction: The Contributions of John C. Harsanyi, John F. Nash and Reinhard Selten', *Scandinavian Journal of Economics*, **97** (1), pp. 15–40.

See also   Nobel Foundation (2004).

Reinhard Selten
(b. 1930)

© The Nobel Foundation

Reinhard Selten was born in Breslau, Germany (now Wrocław, Poland) in 1930. His childhood cannot have been easy: his father's Jewish origins meant that the family business had to be sold in the mid-1930s and his father passed away a few years later. He had to leave school at 14 and the family became refugees at the end of the Second World War before settling in what was to become West Germany. Selten was then able to complete his school education, developing a pronounced taste for mathematics. He remembers first reading about game theory while still at school. Selten attributes a youthful interest in politics and consequently economics to his experiences 'as a member of an officially despised minority' before and during the war (Nobel Foundation, 2004). Selten enrolled as a student of mathematics at the Johann-Wolfgang-Goethe University of Frankfurt in 1951, and was awarded an MA by the university in 1957. He obtained his PhD, also in mathematics, from the same institution in 1961.

After completing his master's degree, Selten took up a post as research assistant at Frankfurt until 1967 when he moved for a year to the United States as visiting professor at the University of California, Berkeley. He returned to Frankfurt in 1968 where his Habilitation thesis in economics gave him the permission required to teach in German universities (the thesis was published as a book – Selten, 1970). Since then he has held posts in three institutions. From 1969 to 1972 he was professor at the Free University of Berlin, and from 1972 to 1984 professor at the University of Bielefeld. In 1984 he became Professor of Economics at the Rheinische Friedrich-Wilhelms University of Bonn. Since 1996 he has been head of the Laboratorium für experimentelle Wirtschaftsforschung at the University of Bonn.

Selten is a fellow of the Econometric Society and was president of the European Economic Association in 1997. He is a member of the Nordrhein-Westfalische Akademie der Wissenschaften, an honorary member of the American Economic Association and a foreign honorary member of the American Academy of Arts and Sciences. He holds honorary degrees from a number of universities and in 2000 he won the Prize of the State of North-Rhine Westfalia. In 1994 Selten was awarded the Nobel Memorial Prize in Economics, together with John Harsanyi and John Nash, 'for their pioneering analysis of equilibria in the theory of non-cooperative games' (Nobel Foundation, 2004).

As noted in the entries in this volume for John Harsanyi and John Nash, game theory is concerned with analysing interactions between individuals where decision making by each party takes into account the choices made by others. This kind of interaction is common in economics and other branches of social science. The first modern treatment of game theory in economics was John von Neumann and Oskar Morgenstern's *Theory of Games and Economic Behaviour* (1944). This study focused on cooperative zero-sum two-person games. Subsequently, John Nash introduced the more widely applicable concept of a non-cooperative finite game where there is no communication between players, and identified what has become known as Nash equilibrium – a set of optimal strategies for all parties from which, accordingly, no participant has an incentive to deviate.

Although Nash equilibrium is probably the most innovative concept in game theory (we noted in the entry for Harsanyi his and Selten's acknowledgement of their debt to Nash – see Kuhn et al., 1996), it raised some interesting new problems, one of which was solved by Selten. This is the issue of superfluous or 'unreasonable' Nash equilibria that Selten demonstrated could be removed by the application of more stringent equilibrium conditions

(Royal Swedish Academy of Sciences, 1995). His approach here was to emphasise the significance of games in extensive form; that is, where attention is explicitly paid to the timing of moves and to the knowledge of players when they move (Gul, 1997). Before Selten's initial interventions (Selten, 1965a; 1965b), games in extensive and strategic or normal form (where players select their actions simultaneously given expectations about the strategies of others) were thought to be equivalent; Selten suggested that they were not (van Damme and Weibull, 1995). His argument turned on the principle that only *credible* threats should be taken into account as a game in extensive form unfolds. For example, a threat by a large country to engage in unilateralist protectionist trade policy in the face of rising import penetration might not be credible if the costs of such protection in the form of possible retaliatory action by those smaller countries it discriminates against are potentially high. This may constitute a Nash equilibrium as the emptiness of the threat is perceived by all players and it is not carried out. However, if the threat is credible then, as the large country's optimal strategy is to protect and the small countries perhaps perceive that it is in their interests to tolerate the protection, this too is a Nash equilibrium. Selten's point is that relevance of equilibria turns on the credibility of threats and the solution is always 'self-enforcing' (van Damme and Weibull, 1995, p. 24). Selten (1975) labels such equilibria 'subgame perfect', where subgame refers to a stage in a game that is a game in itself. The Royal Swedish Academy of Sciences (1995, p. 5) called Selten's innovation 'the most fundamental refinement of Nash equilibrium' and notes its application to the analysis of economic policy, oligopoly and the economics of information.

Selten (1975) further refined the criteria for Nash equilibria by introducing the concept of 'trembling-hand' perfection. This allows for the possibility that players may make small mistakes in extensive form games. In our example, the credible threat of protection by the large country remains its optimal choice only if the smaller countries tolerate it. If they were to (mistakenly) retaliate, the large country's protection strategy would no longer be optimal. A Nash equilibrium is trembling-hand perfect if it is able to accommodate the probability of such small mistakes. This work has been applied in industrial organisation theory and macroeconomics (Royal Swedish Academy of Sciences, 1995).

Selten's Nobel citation also acknowledges his work in evolutionary games (with Peter Hammerstein), see Selten and Hammerstein
(1984; 1994), as well as experimental game theory, see, for example,
Selten (1990), Selten and Stoecker (1986); Selten et al. (1997). Selten
(1978) is a noted paper on entry deterrence. His books include one
on equilibrium selection with his fellow Nobel Laureate, John
Harsanyi (Harsanyi and Selten, 1988a); Selten (1988b) addresses the
notion of bounded rationality. Many of Selten's most important
papers have been collected together in two volumes in Selten (1999).

Main Published Works

(1965a), 'Spieltheoretishe Behandlung eines Oligopolmodells mit Nachfragetragheit – Teil I
  Bestimmung des dynamischen Preisglieichgewichts', *Zeitschrift für die gesamte Staatswissen-
  schaft*, **121**, pp. 301–24.

(1965b), 'Spieltheoretishe Behandlung eines Oligopolmodells mit Nachfragetragheit – Teil II
  Eigenschaften des dynamischen Preisglieichgewichts', *Zeitschrift für die gesamte Staatswissen-
  schaft*, **121**, pp. 667–89.

(1970), *Preispolitik der Mehrprodukttenunternehmung in der statischen Theorie*, Berlin: Springer-
  Verlag.

(1975), 'Reexamination of the Perfectness Concept for Equilibrium Points in Extensive Games',
  International Journal of Game Theory, **4**, pp. 25–55.

(1978), 'The Chain Store Paradox', *Theory and Decision*, **9**, April, pp. 127–59.

(1984), 'Gaps in Harley's Argument on Evolutionary Stable Learning Rules and in the Logic
  of "Tit for Tat"' (with P. Hammerstein), *The Behavioural and Brain Sciences*, **7** (1), pp. 115–
  16.

(1986), 'End Behaviour in Sequences of Finite Prisoners' Dilemma Supergames' (with R.
  Stoecker), *Journal of Economic Behavior and Organization*, **7** (1), pp. 47–70.

(1988a), *A General Theory of Equilibrium Selection in Games* (with J.C. Harsanyi), Cambridge,
  MA: MIT Press.

(1988b), *Models of Strategic Rationality*, Theory and Decision Library, Series C: Game Theory,
  Mathematical Programming and Operations Research, Dordrecht: Kluwer.

(1990), 'Bounded Rationality', *Journal of Institutional and Theoretical Economics*, **146**, December, pp. 649–58.

(1994), 'Game Theory and Evolutionary Biology' (with P. Hammerstein), in R.J. Aumann
  and S. Hart (eds) *Handbook of Game Theory*, Vol. 2, Amsterdam: Elsevier Science, pp. 929–
  93.

(1997), 'Duopoly Strategies Programmed by Experienced Players' (with M. Mitzkewitz and
  G.R. Uhlich), *Econometrica*, **65**, May, pp. 517–55.

(1999), *Game Theory and Economic Behaviour: Selected Essays*, 2 vols, Cheltenham, UK and
  Northampton, MA, USA: Edward Elgar.

Secondary Literature

Gul, F. (1997), 'A Nobel Prize for Game Theorists: The Contributions of Harsanyi, Nash and
  Selten', *Journal of Economic Perspectives*, **11**, Summer, pp. 159–74.

Kuhn, H.W., J.C. Harsanyi, R. Selten, J.W. Weibull, E. van Damme, J.F. Nash Jr and P.
  Hammerstein (1996), 'The Work of John Nash in Game Theory', (Nobel Seminar, 8 December 1994), *Journal of Economic Theory*, **69**, April, pp. 153–85.

Royal Swedish Academy of Sciences (1995), 'The Nobel Memorial Prize in Economics 1994',
  Scandinavian Journal of Economics, **97** (1), pp. 1–7.

van Damme, E. and J.W. Weibull (1995), 'Equilibrium in Strategic Interaction: The Contributions of John C. Harsanyi, John F. Nash and Reinhard Selten', *Scandinavian Journal of Economics*, **97** (1), pp. 15–40.

See also   Blaug and Vane (2003, pp. 754–5); Nobel Foundation (2004).

THE 1995 NOBEL MEMORIAL LAUREATE
ROBERT LUCAS JR

Robert E. Lucas Jr
(b. 1937)

© The Nobel Foundation

Robert Lucas was born in Yakima, Washington, USA in 1937. As an undergraduate he majored in history and received his BA from the University of Chicago in 1959. Lucas began his graduate studies at the University of California at Berkeley before deciding to switch from history to economics and return to the University of Chicago, where he was awarded a PhD in 1964. In 1963 he was appointed assistant professor at Carnegie Institute of Technology (later renamed Carnegie-Mellon University) and was subsequently promoted to associate professor in 1967, and Professor of Economics in 1970. He returned to the University of Chicago in 1974, first as visiting research professor and then as professor in 1975. In 1980 Lucas became the John Dewey Distinguished Service Professor of Economics at Chicago, a post he still holds. Among his offices and honours, Lucas served as the president of each of the Econometric Society in 1997 and the American Economic Association in 2002. In 1995 he was awarded the Nobel Memorial Prize in Economics 'for having developed and applied the hypothesis of rational expectations, and thereby transformed macroeconomic analysis and deepened our understanding of economic policy' (Nobel Foundation, 2004).

Lucas is best known for his highly influential work in macroeconomics and is widely acknowledged as being the leading figure in the development of new classical macroeconomics and the associated rational expectations revolution. The analytical foundation of the new classical approach to macroeconomics was established in a series of papers written by Lucas (1972; 1973; 1975; 1977), and other prominent new classicists, including Robert Barro, Finn Kydland (see entry in this volume), Edward Prescott (see entry in this volume), Thomas Sargent and Neil Wallace, during the 1970s. The approach is based on the joint acceptance of three main sub-hypotheses, namely: (i) the rational expectations hypothesis – associated with the work of John Muth in the early 1960s – whereby forward-looking agents make the best use of all available information, including information on current and prospective policies, to form their expectations; (ii) the assumption that all markets in the economy continuously clear, in line with the Walrasian tradition; and (iii) the Lucas 'surprise' aggregate supply hypothesis, whereby output deviates from its natural level only in response to an unexpected (surprise) increase in the price level.

In his path-breaking 1972 *Journal of Economic Theory* paper, 'Expectations and the Neutrality of Money', Lucas combined the natural rate hypothesis, which had been developed independently by Edmund Phelps and Milton Friedman (see entry in this volume) in the late 1960s, with the assumption of continuous market clearing and the hypothesis that economic agents form rational expectations. In doing so, Lucas was able to demonstrate that a rational expectations equilibrium model is compatible with a positive (non-exploitable) short-run trade-off between output and inflation, when agents have imperfect information. Central to this result is the distinction between anticipated and unanticipated changes in the money supply (see, for example, Lucas, 1996). While anticipated monetary shocks are neutral, unanticipated monetary shocks will, in the short run, cause output and employment to deviate from their natural levels when agents with incomplete information misperceive a change in the general price level as a change in relative prices. In his 1973 *American Economic Review* paper, 'Some International Evidence on Output–Inflation Tradeoffs', Lucas was able to reach a much larger audience by producing a more accessible paper compared to his highly formal and mathematically complex 1972 *Journal of Economic Theory* paper.

In subsequent work, Lucas (1975; 1977) developed an equilibrium theory of the business cycle based on unanticipated monetary shocks.

Although the early 1980s witnessed the demise of the monetary 'surprise' explanation of the business cycle – in part due to the implausibility of supposed information gaps relating to aggregate price level and money supply data – Lucas's work paved the way for economists like Finn Kydland and Edward Prescott to develop a second phase of new classical equilibrium theorising, which has come to be known as the real business cycle approach.

One insight of Lucas's work in this area involves what is popularly known as the 'Lucas critique', after his seminal paper in which the critique first appeared. Lucas (1976) argued that traditional (Keynesian-dominated) methods of policy evaluation may be misleading as they fail to take into account the impact of policy on expectations. He attacked the then-established practice of using large-scale macroeconometric models to evaluate the consequences of alternative policy scenarios, since the parameters of such models may change as economic agents adjust their expectations and behaviour when policy changes. The Lucas critique has stimulated a continuing research programme that has sought to develop dynamic, stochastic general equilibrium models with parameters that are independent of a change in policy regime. Overall this body of work (Lucas, 1972; 1973; 1975; 1976; 1977) has had a profound effect on macroeconomic model building and policy analysis since the early 1970s. In the latter case, Lucas's insights have reinforced traditional arguments in favour of a rules-based framework for macroeconomic policy making. Many of Lucas's most influential papers on 'rational expectations' macroeconomics are drawn together in his 1981 book *Studies in Business-Cycle Theory* (Lucas, 1981a).

In addition to his highly influential work on macroeconomic modelling and policy evaluation, Lucas has made a number of important contributions to other fields of research, including:

- labour economics (via his 1969 *Journal of Political Economy* article, co-written with Leonard Rapping, in which – in line with the intertemporal labour substitution hypothesis – changes in employment are explained in terms of the 'voluntary' choices of households that change their supply of labour in response to perceived temporary changes in real wages by working more hours when real wages are temporarily high, and vice versa);

- the theory of investment (via his 1971 *Econometrica* article, 'Investment Under Uncertainty', co-written with Edward Prescott);
- the theory of finance (via his 1978 *Econometrica* article, in which he put forward a general equilibrium model of asset pricing with rational expectations);
- rational expectations econometrics (see, for example, the early contributions to this field of research in the book *Rational Expectations and Econometric Practice* (Lucas and Sargent, 1981b), which he co-edited with Thomas Sargent);
- monetary theory (via his 1987 'cash-in-advance' *Econometrica* article, co-written with Nancy Stokey);
- recursive methods in economic dynamics (Lucas et al., 1989, co-written with Nancy Stokey and Edward Prescott); and
- economic growth (for example, via his classic 1988 *Journal of Monetary Economics* article 'On the Mechanics of Economic Development', in which he highlighted the importance of human capital accumulation and learning by doing – Lucas's work in this area, together with that of Paul Romer, has led to a resurgence of interest in the analysis of economic growth and most notably the development of endogenous growth theory).

The above list is far from exhaustive and merely serves to illustrate the breadth and depth of his seminal contributions to numerous fields of research. Lucas is one of the most influential economic theorists of modern times, whose pioneering work, most notably in the 1970s, has transformed macroeconomics.

Main Published Works

(1969), 'Real Wages, Employment and Inflation' (with L.A. Rapping), *Journal of Political Economy*, **77**, September/October, pp. 721–54.

(1971), 'Investment Under Uncertainty' (with E.C. Prescott), *Econometrica*, **39**, September, pp. 659–81.

(1972), 'Expectations and the Neutrality of Money', *Journal of Economic Theory*, **4**, April, pp. 103–24.

(1973), 'Some International Evidence on Output–Inflation Tradeoffs', *American Economic Review*, **63**, June, pp. 326–34.

(1975), 'An Equilibrium Model of the Business Cycle', *Journal of Political Economy*, **83**, December, pp. 1113–44.

(1976), 'Econometric Policy Evaluation: A Critique', in K. Brunner and A.H. Meltzer (eds), *The Phillips Curve and Labour Markets*, Amsterdam: North-Holland, pp. 19–46.

(1977), 'Understanding Business Cycles', in K. Brunner and A.H. Meltzer (eds), *Stabilization of the Domestic and International Economy*, Carnegie-Rochester Conference Series on Public Policy, 5, Amsterdam: North-Holland, pp. 7–29.

(1978), 'Asset Prices in an Exchange Economy', *Econometrica*, **46**, November, pp. 1429–45.

(1981a), *Studies in Business-Cycle Theory*, Oxford: Basil Blackwell.

(1981b), *Rational Expectations and Econometric Practice* (ed. with T.J. Sargent), Minneapolis, MN: University of Minnesota Press.

(1987), 'Money and Interest in a Cash-in-Advance Economy' (with N.L. Stokey), *Econometrica*, **55**, May, pp. 491–514.

(1988), 'On the Mechanics of Economic Development', *Journal of Monetary Economics*, **22**, July, pp. 3–42.

(1989), *Recursive Methods in Economic Dynamics* (with N.L. Stokey and E.C. Prescott), Cambridge, MA: Harvard University Press.

(1996), 'Nobel Lecture: Monetary Neutrality', *Journal of Political Economy*, **104**, August, pp. 661–82.

Secondary Literature

Chari, V.V. (1998), 'Nobel Laureate Robert E. Lucas, Jr.: Architect of Modern Macroeconomics', *Journal of Economic Perspectives*, **12**, Winter, pp. 171–86.

Fischer, S. (1996), 'Robert Lucas's Nobel Memorial Prize', *Scandinavian Journal of Economics*, **98**, March, pp. 11–31.

Hall, R.E. (1996), 'Robert Lucas, Recipient of the 1995 Nobel Memorial Prize in Economics', *Scandinavian Journal of Economics*, **98**, March, pp. 33–48.

Hoover, K.D. (ed.) (1999), *The Legacy of Robert Lucas Jr.*, Cheltenham, UK and Northampton, MA, USA: Edward Elgar.

Snowdon, B. and H.R. Vane (1998), 'Transforming Macroeconomics: An Interview with Robert E. Lucas Jr.', *Journal of Economic Methodology*, **5**, June, pp. 115–46.

Svensson, L.E.O. (1996), 'The Scientific Contributions of Robert E. Lucas, Jr.', *Scandinavian Journal of Economics*, **98**, March, pp. 1–10.

See also Beaud and Dostaler (1997, pp. 325–7); Blaug (1998, pp. 173–5); Blaug and Vane (2003, pp. 511–12); Cate (1997, pp. 380–83); Nobel Foundation (2004); Pressman (1999, pp. 193–7); Snowdon and Vane (2002, pp. 445–52).

THE 1996 NOBEL MEMORIAL LAUREATES

JAMES MIRRLEES
AND
WILLIAM VICKREY

James A. Mirrlees
(b. 1936)

© The Nobel Foundation

James Mirrlees was born in 1936 in Minnigaff, a small village near Newton Stewart in the southwest of Scotland. As a child he was studious and his parents encouraged him to be academically competitive. Mirrlees found he had a vocation for mathematics and through a diet of self-development, and with the help of his teachers, he excelled to the extent that he was entered for a Cambridge University scholarship. Unfortunately, at the time of the examination he was languishing in hospital with a serious illness and consequently he began his undergraduate career at Edinburgh University rather than Cambridge (Nobel Foundation, 2004). He was awarded an MA in mathematics and natural philosophy by Edinburgh in 1957.

Having by now taken and been successful in the Cambridge scholarship examination he had missed, Mirrlees left Scotland to enrol on a second undergraduate degree. At Cambridge he passed Parts II and III of the Mathematical Tripos in 1957 and 1958, respectively; his experience at Edinburgh meant that Part I was waived. It was at this point that Mirrlees decided that he wanted to do economics, despite having the option to go on to do research in mathematics. Why economics? 'because I kept discussing it with economist friends, and they didn't make sense to me; and because poverty in what were then called the underdeveloped countries, seemed to me what really mattered in the world, and that meant economics' (Nobel Foundation, 2004). Mirrlees is another of the more than a few Nobel Laureates drawn to economics out of a desire for wider economic progress and social justice.

With an award to support a PhD, Mirrlees began to study economics. Perhaps, at first, he found the subject a little trickier than mathematics: 'Economics takes a while to learn, even if much of it is in a way quite simple. It is simple to be wrong as well as to be right, and it is none too easy to distinguish between them' (Nobel Foundation, 2004). He was also advised to read Keynes's *General Theory*. In his highly entertaining (as in laugh-out-loud) Nobel autobiography, Mirrlees reflects: 'That may not have been the best advice, but it did no great harm and one day I hope to finish it'. He was awarded a PhD in economics by Cambridge in 1963. One of his supervisors was Richard Stone, Nobel Laureate in 1984, and one of his examiners was a visitor to the university: Kenneth Arrow, Nobel Laureate in 1972.

Although he had a short spell as research assistant to Nicholas Kaldor that led to his first publication (Kaldor and Mirrlees, 1962), Mirrlees's CV records his first academic appointment as adviser with the Massachusetts Institute of Technology (MIT) Center for International Studies in New Delhi, India from 1962 to 1963. In 1963 he received unsolicited job offers from both Cambridge and Oxford universities: 'It seems ridiculous but I have never had a job I applied for. When I do apply, I don't get it, but that is a small sample' (Nobel Foundation, 2004).

Mirrlees took up the offer from Cambridge where he was assistant lecturer, then lecturer, and Fellow of Trinity College from 1963 to 1968. During this period he also acted intermittently as adviser at the Pakistan Institute of Development Economics in Karachi. In 1968, after a sabbatical as visiting professor at MIT, he moved to Oxford as Edgeworth Professor of Economics and Fellow of Nuffield College. Mirrlees stayed at Oxford until 1995, though he held visiting professorships at the University of California at Berkeley in 1986 and Yale University in 1989. In 1995 he returned to Cambridge as Professor of Political Economy and Fellow of Trinity College.

In 1996, Mirrlees was awarded the Nobel Memorial Prize in Economics jointly with William Vickrey 'for their fundamental contributions to the economic theory of incentives under asymmetric information' (Nobel Foundation, 2004).

In his explorations of the role of incentives in the context of asymmetric information, Mirrlees has made path-breaking advances in two specific areas: the analysis of optimal income taxation, and principal–agent contract design. Moreover, these contributions have had a deep – even revolutionary – influence on the economic understanding of both public finance and incentives (Sandmo, 1999). Indeed, some have even gone so far as to suggest that Mirrlees has had as profound an impact on microeconomics as Albert Einstein had on physics (as reported in Dixit and Besley, 1997). How the cheerfully self-deprecating Mirrlees (as he appears in his Nobel autobiography) would react to this paean, the present authors are uncertain.

Economists have long been aware of the distorting effects of redistributive taxation: for example, high marginal income tax rates may well enable governments to promote equity but, given their adverse influence on the incentive to work, they are likely to reduce efficiency. In the mid-1940s, Vickrey attempted to model this problem as conditioned by the presence of asymmetric information: in this instance, that the productivity of individuals is known to them but not the government. How then can the government design an optimum income tax policy when it is ignorant of the economic capabilities of those it wishes to tax and where policy will affect how such capabilities are deployed? Although Vickrey was able to formulate the problem, its complexity defied solution. It was Mirrlees (1971a) who eventually made the breakthrough, and in so doing 'established a paradigm for analysing a broad spectrum of economic issues where asymmetric information is a prime component' (Royal Swedish Academy of Sciences, 1997, p. 174).

Mirrlees approached the problem by thinking about the individual's labour supply decision in relation to the income it generated and the consumption this allowed. His purpose was to capture a set of 'incentive-compatible' allocations of work and consumption within which the more productive individuals would work harder by supplying more labour because – even though their consumption might not increase in proportion to their effort and income – they still had a material incentive to do so. On the assumption that more productive people – with higher wage rates – could always generate more income more easily through work than the less productive, Mirrlees demonstrated that a 'full characterization of incentive-compatible allocations' emerged (Mirrlees, 1997, p. 1317).

He was then able to approach the income tax question by understanding the difference between income and consumption as a tax (Dixit and Besley, 1997).

That incentive-compatible allocations emerge is a result of what is known as the single-crossing property.[16] This ensures that given appropriate incentives, people will in their choices of labour supply, income and consumption, reveal private information about their productivity. In other words, income tax schedules can be designed so that individuals are not tempted to falsely present themselves as lower productivity 'types' because the tax implications of higher productivity – and more work – are perceived to be too severe (Dixit and Besley, 1997; Royal Swedish Academy of Sciences, 1997; Sandmo, 1999).

As noted, a second path-breaking advance to be recognised by the Royal Swedish Academy is Mirrlees's analysis of principal–agent contract design in the context of moral hazard. Mirrlees characterises the principal–agent relationship as less about information asymmetries and more about 'the asymmetry of responsibilities, with the principal moving first, and the agent following' (Mirrlees, 1997, p. 1328). He has shown that optimal incentive design by the principal must take into account the costs associated with incentives, and that such costs will be lower the more sensitive is the agent to penalties and the more discernible the agent's effort in relation to outcomes for which he or she is responsible (Royal Swedish Academy of Sciences, 1997; Sandmo, 1999). The relevant references here are Mirrlees (1974a; 1976).

Other notable contributions highlighted in Mirrlees's Nobel citation include, with Peter Diamond, an analysis of commodity taxes (Diamond and Mirrlees, 1971b; 1971c).[17] This concludes that, to facilitate productive efficiency, taxes should be levied at the consumption stage rather than on factors of production, and that small countries should eschew tariff protection (Dixit and Besley, 1997). With Ian Little, Mirrlees has also published work on project appraisal in developing countries. Their book (Little and Mirrlees,

[16] Mirrlees (1997) notes that this is also called the Spence–Mirrlees condition after its use by Nobel Laureate Michael Spence in his Prize-winning work on signalling in the labour market – see entry on Spence in this volume.
[17] Reflecting on his work with Diamond, Mirrlees writes 'I followed the main principle for academic success: get a good co-author (and also the second: get another)' (Nobel Foundation, 2004).

1974b) has had a 'significant impact' on the development activities of agencies such as the World Bank (Dixit and Besley, 1997, p. 233).

Main Published Works

(1962), 'A New Model of Economic Growth' (with N. Kaldor), *Review of Economic Studies*, **29**, June, pp. 174–92.

(1971a), 'An Exploration in the Theory of Optimum Income Taxation', *Review of Economic Studies*, **38**, April, pp. 175–208.

(1971b), 'Optimal Taxation and Public Production I' (with P.A. Diamond), *American Economic Review*, **61**, March, pp. 8–27.

(1971c), 'Optimal Taxation and Public Production II' (with P.A. Diamond), *American Economic Review*, **61**, June, pp. 261–78.

(1974a), 'Notes on Welfare Economics, Information and Uncertainty', in M. Balch, D. McFadden and S. Wu (eds), *Essays in Equilibrium Behaviour Under Uncertainty*, Amsterdam: North-Holland, pp. 243–61.

(1974b), *Project Appraisal and Planning for Developing Countries* (with I.M.D. Little), London: Heinemann Educational Books.

(1976), 'The Optimal Structure of Incentives and Authority within an Organization', *Bell Journal of Economics*, **7**, Spring, pp. 105–31.

(1997), 'Information and Incentives: The Economics of Carrots and Sticks', *Economic Journal*, **107**, September, pp. 1311–29.

Secondary Literature

Dixit, A. and T. Besley (1997), 'James Mirrlees' Contributions to the Theory of Information and Incentives', *Scandinavian Journal of Economics*, **99** (2), pp. 207–35.

Royal Swedish Academy of Sciences (1997), 'The Nobel Memorial Prize in Economics 1996', *Scandinavian Journal of Economics*, **99** (2), pp. 173–7.

Sandmo, A. (1999), 'Asymmetric Information and Public Economics: The Mirrlees–Vickrey Nobel Prize', *Journal of Economic Perspectives*, **13**, Winter, pp. 165–80.

See also   Blaug (1999, pp. 784–5); Nobel Foundation (2004).

William S. Vickrey (1914–96)

© The Nobel Foundation

William Vickrey was born in Victoria, British Columbia, Canada in 1914. He studied mathematics at Yale University and graduated with a BS in 1935. Vickrey joined Columbia University as a graduate student and was awarded an MA in 1937 and a PhD in 1948. After completing his MA he had jobs with both the National Resources Planning Board and the US Treasury, and, as a conscientious objector during the Second World War,[18] he spent some time working on the development of an inheritance tax for Puerto Rico. In 1946, Vickrey joined Columbia University as Lecturer in Economics. He became professor in 1958 and McVickar Professor of Political Economy in 1972, before retiring as McVickar Professor Emeritus in 1982 (Nobel Foundation, 2004). Vickrey died on 11 October 1996, just three days after the announcement of his Nobel Prize.

Vickrey was a highly active and practical economist. He consulted on a wide range of public services projects from the late 1930s onwards, working on such diverse topics as public utility

---

[18] Vickrey was a Quaker. An obituary fondly remembers that 'his shoes were never leather and his briefcase was always cloth. The money from the Nobel Prize meant little to him' (O'Flaherty, 1996).

pricing, the fare structure on New York's subway system, Japan's tax arrangements and development activities for the United Nations.

Vickrey's offices and honours included election to the National Academy of Sciences and presidency of the American Economic Association, both in 1992. He was a fellow of the Econometric Society and a recipient of the F.E. Seidman Distinguished Award in Political Economy. In 1996, Vickrey was awarded the Nobel Memorial Prize in Economics jointly with James Mirrlees 'for their fundamental contributions to the economic theory of incentives under asymmetric information' (Nobel Foundation, 2004).

Vickrey's Nobel citation makes specific reference to two areas of work: auction theory and optimal income taxation. In both areas, Vickrey understands economic behaviour as the product of incentives operating in the context of asymmetric information. We begin with auction theory. In an auction where ascending bids are openly announced, participants have an incentive not to reveal their private valuations of a sale item: surviving bidders would clearly prefer to *just* outbid their rivals in order to induce them to leave the auction. Vickrey suggested an alternative auction design – a second price sealed-bid auction – in which the winning participant pays a price equal to that offered by the second-highest bidder. In these circumstances 'the optimal strategy for each bidder ... will obviously be to make his bid equal to the full value of the article or contract to himself' (Vickrey, 1961, reprinted in Vickrey 1994, p. 66). As underbidding increases the individual's risk of missing a profitable outcome, the design of the auction encourages all participants to be truthful about their private valuations of the sale item (Laffont, 2003). Accordingly, the Vickrey auction, as it has become known, is both efficient – in the sense that resources are allocated to their most profitable uses – and incentive compatible (Drèze, 1997). Vickrey's insights into auctions (the relevant papers are Vickrey, 1961; 1962) paved the way for other researchers to develop theorisations of the willingness of consumers to pay for the provision of public goods (Royal Swedish Academy of Sciences, 1997; Sandmo, 1999).

Vickrey (1945) also provided the original formulation of the optimum income tax problem that James Mirrlees would eventually solve some 26 years later. As noted in the entry for Mirrlees in this volume, the distorting effects of redistributive taxation are well known: for example, high marginal income tax rates may help governments promote equity but they are likely to reduce efficiency because of their adverse influence on the incentive to work. Vickrey conceptualised the problem as one of asymmetric information between principal and agent: in this instance, workers (agents) know their own productivity but the government (the principal) does not. How then can government design an optimum income tax policy when it is ignorant of the economic capabilities of those it wishes to tax and where policy will affect agents' decisions about work? In other words, what is the optimum income tax balance between efficiency (promoted by reducing the distortion of incentives associated with income tax) and equity (promoted by the redistribution of the revenue raised by income tax)? Although Vickrey was not able to provide a solution to the problem he had posed, this work is widely regarded as path-breaking and far ahead of its time (Arrow, 1994; Atkinson, 1994; Drèze and Arnott, 1994; Laffont, 2003; Sandmo, 1999).

One of the most noted of Vickrey's practical applications of economics concerns his pricing proposals for the New York subway (Vickrey, 1955) in which he investigated the possibilities of marginal cost pricing as a means to improve the subway's efficiency. To Vickrey's lasting regret, his recommendations were never implemented (Laffont, 2003). Vickrey included this study in an overview of what he called his 'innovative failures in economics' (see Vickrey, 1993a). Also included was something Vickrey regarded as his 'proudest accomplishment' (O'Flaherty, 1996): a proposal for the 'cumulative averaging' of taxation which has been called a 'masterstroke of simplification and tax neutralization' (Drèze, 1997, p. 181); the original reference here is Vickrey (1939). According to Atkinson (1994), Vickrey's best-known work on tax is his doctoral thesis *Agenda for Progressive Taxation* (Vickrey, 1947), since revisited in his paper 'Federal Tax Policy for the 1990's' (Vickrey, 1992). A collection of Vickrey's papers that bears testament to the range, depth and practicality of his work is Vickrey (1994). This contains his highly stimulating Presidential Address to the American Economic Association – 'Today's Task for Economists' (first published as Vickrey, 1993b). Two of the editors of his collected papers pay Vickrey the following remarkable tribute:

No other economist exemplifies to the same degree the ability of treating a relevant problem all the way from conceptual clarification, through the careful efficiency analysis, down to the development of a practically implementable solution. In that respect, William Vickrey stands in a class by himself. (Drèze and Arnott, 1994, pp. 5–6)

Main Published Works

(1939), 'Averaging of Income for Income Tax Purposes', *Journal of Political Economy*, **47**, June, pp. 379–97.

(1945), 'Measuring Marginal Utility by Reactions to Risk', *Econometrica*, **13**, October, pp. 319–33.

(1947), *Agenda for Progressive Taxation*, New York: Ronald Press.

(1955), 'A Proposal for Revising New York's Subway Fare Structure', *Journal of the Operations Research Society of America*, **3**, February, pp. 38–69.

(1961), 'Counterspeculation, Auctions and Competitive Sealed Tenders', *Journal of Finance*, **16**, March, pp. 8–37.

(1962), 'Auctions and Bidding Games', in *Recent Advances in Game Theory*, Princeton University Conference, Princeton, NJ: Princeton University Press, pp. 15–29.

(1992), 'Federal Tax Policy for the 1990's', *American Economic Association Papers and Proceedings*, **82**, May, pp. 257–62.

(1993a), 'My Innovative Failures in Economics', *Atlantic Economic Journal*, **21**, March, pp. 1–9.

(1993b), 'Today's Task for Economists', *American Economic Review*, **83**, March, pp. 1–10.

(1994), *Public Economics* (eds R. Arnott, K. Arrow, A.B. Atkinson and J.H. Drèze), Cambridge: Cambridge University Press.

Secondary Literature

Arrow, K. (1994), Introduction to 'Part I, Social Choice and Allocation Mechanisms', in W.S. Vickrey, *Public Economics* (eds R. Arnott, K. Arrow, A.B. Atkinson and J.H. Drèze), Cambridge: Cambridge University Press, pp. 13–14.

Atkinson, A. B. (1994), Introduction to 'Part II, Taxation', in W.S. Vickrey, *Public Economics* (eds R. Arnott, K. Arrow, A.B. Atkinson and J.H. Drèze), Cambridge: Cambridge University Press, pp. 101–14.

Drèze, J. (1997), 'Research and Development in Public Economics: William Vickrey's Inventive Quest of Efficiency', *Scandinavian Journal of Economics*, **99** (2), pp. 179–98.

Drèze, J.H. and R. Arnott (1994), 'William Vickrey', in W.S. Vickrey, *Public Economics* (eds R. Arnott, K. Arrow, A.B. Atkinson and J.H. Drèze), Cambridge: Cambridge University Press, pp. 3–10.

Laffont, J.-J. (2003), 'William Vickrey: A Pioneer in the Economics of Incentives', in T. Persson (ed.) *Nobel Lectures, Economics 1996–2000*, Singapore: World Scientific Publishing.

O'Flaherty, B. (1996), 'Obituary: Professor William Vickrey', *The Independent*, 14 October.

Royal Swedish Academy of Sciences (1997), 'The Nobel Memorial Prize in Economics 1996', *Scandinavian Journal of Economics*, **99** (2), pp. 173–7.

Sandmo, A. (1999), 'Asymmetric Information and Public Economics: The Mirrlees–Vickrey Nobel Prize', *Journal of Economic Perspectives*, **13**, Winter, pp. 165–80.

See also Blaug (1999, p. 1135); Nobel Foundation (2004).

THE 1997 NOBEL MEMORIAL LAUREATES

ROBERT MERTON AND MYRON SCHOLES

© The Nobel Foundation

Robert C. Merton
(b. 1944)

Robert Merton was born in New York City, New York, USA in 1944 and grew up in Hastings-on-Hudson. Merton's father was a renowned professor of sociology at Columbia University, while his mother kept the family home; both parents were important positive influences in his formative years. One thing he got from his father that had a profound effect on Merton's later career was a fascination with the stock market. He remembers:

> As early as 8 or 9 years of age, I developed an interest in money and finance, even at play. I created fictitious banks ... At 10 or 11, I drew up an 'A' list of stocks, and bought my first one, General Motors. In college, I spent time doing some trading, learning tape watching, and hearing the lore of the market from retail traders in brokerage houses. (Nobel Foundation, 2004)

Merton's high school was small but offered a good curriculum and he divided his time there between academic work and sports. His own view is that he was a good rather than exceptional student and an athlete of no great distinction. Outside school and in addition to the stock market, Merton's other interests were initially baseball and then cars. As a teenager he bought and built 'street hot rods' and raced them at drag strips. For a time a place in the automobile industry seemed to be Merton's vocation: he spent his college summers working for the Ford motor company and a career in engineering greatly appealed to him (Nobel Foundation, 2004).

Merton attended Columbia University and studied engineering. He particularly relished his mathematics classes, having since school found the discipline 'fun'. At Columbia he took one introductory economics course, using Paul Samuelson's textbook, little knowing that he would find himself working for Samuelson (see entry in this volume) just a few years later. Merton was awarded a BS (engineering mathematics) by Columbia in 1966.

After graduation, Merton began to study for a PhD in applied mathematics at the California Institute of Technology (Caltech) but, despite finding his work rewarding, he elected to leave Caltech and drop mathematics in favour of economics. In his Nobel autobiography, Merton offers three reasons for this abrupt switch. First, like other Nobel Laureates in economics, he felt drawn to a discipline that appeared to be a force for social progress. This was particularly so in the late 1960s, when the sustained growth and full employment fruits of the postwar boom were widely credited to macroeconomic policy making. Second, Merton's training in mathematics would, he thought (presciently enough), provide him with some advantage in economics. Finally, and, he says, most tellingly, Merton felt that he had an intuitive connection with economics that was stronger than that with the physical sciences. At Caltech he had continued to trade in stocks – even rising in the early morning to get to a local brokerage house to put in a couple of hours before attending classes. In the end, in the battle between his youthful passions, the stock market won out over automobile engineering.

With the support of members of the faculty at Caltech, Merton applied to a number of economics departments but was accepted only by the Massachusetts Institute of Technology (MIT). After taking a mathematics course at MIT offered by Samuelson, he was subsequently recruited by Samuelson as a research assistant. Sharing an interest in the stock market, the two began to work together, producing a paper – part of Merton's PhD thesis – on the theory of warrant pricing in 1969 (see Merton and Samuelson, 1969a). Merton was awarded a PhD in economics by MIT in 1970.

After spending the 1968–70 period as Samuelson's research assistant, and 1969–70 as an instructor in economics at MIT, Merton took up the post of Assistant Professor of Finance at the A.P. Sloan School of Management at MIT from 1970 to 1973. Subsequently, he became associate professor (1973–74) and professor (1974–80), before his appointment in 1980 at the Sloan School as J.C. Penney Professor of Management. After spending 1987 on sabbatical as Visiting Professor of Finance at Harvard University, Merton moved to Harvard in 1988 as the George Fisher Baker Professor of Business Administration. He spent June 1993 as Invited Professor of Finance in France at the University of Nantes. In 1998, Merton was appointed to his current post as the John and Natty McArthur University Professor at Harvard.

Merton's professional appointments include directorships and advisory roles associated with a variety of academic and financial institutions. For example, since 1979 he has been a research associate of the National Bureau of Economic Research; from 1988 to 1996 he was a trustee of the College Retirement Equities Fund; and from 1988 to 1992 he was senior advisor at Salomon Inc. In 1994, Merton, together with Myron Scholes and others, was a co-founder of Long-Term Capital Management, the hedge fund subject to an infamous rescue organised by the Federal Reserve in 1998 (see Edwards, 1999).

Merton has a significant accumulation of offices and honours, among which are honorary degrees from the universities of: Harvard, Chicago, Lausanne, Paris-Dauphine, the National Sun Yat-sen University in Taiwan and the Athens University of Economics and Business. In 1971–72, Merton received the Salgo-Noren Award for Excellence in Teaching at MIT. He was director of the American Finance Association in 1982–84 and 1987–88. He has been a fellow of the Econometric Society since 1983, and a fellow of the American Academy of Arts and Sciences since 1986. Also in 1986, Merton was president of the American Finance Association, and in 1993 vice president of the Society for Financial Studies. He has also been a member of the Honorary Board of the International Raoul Wallenberg Foundation since 1993.[19] In 1993 he received the Financial Engineer of the Year Award from the International Association of Financial Engineers. In 1997 Merton was awarded the Nobel Memorial Prize in Economics jointly with Myron Scholes 'for a new method to determine the value of derivatives' (Nobel Foundation, 2004).

A derivative is a financial instrument that has its price conditioned by the value of some other underlying asset such as a stock

[19] Raoul Wallenberg was a Swedish diplomat credited with saving tens of thousands of Hungarian Jewish lives during the Second Word War.

or currency. Merton and Scholes, together with their colleague Fischer Black who died in 1995,[20] refined a formula for the valuation of a particular form of derivative: the stock option. In the late 1960s and early 1970s, when Black, Merton and Scholes were conducting their research, stock options were rarely used in the financial service industry; shortly after the publication of their findings they became so widespread as to be internationally – now globally – commonplace (see Duffie, 1998; Jarrow, 1999; Nobel Foundation, 2004). As Schaefer (1998, p. 425) notes,

> Many economic theories have affected economic life but most often through their influence on a relatively small group of macro-economic policymakers. But it is surely rare for an advance in the economic sciences to influence the details of the way literally thousands of individuals engaged in financial transactions carry out their analysis and make their decisions.

For a more modest reading of the impact of the Black, Merton and Scholes option-pricing formula that emphasises the need for new financial instruments in the context of the riskier post-Bretton Woods, inflationary and oil-price sensitive economic environment, see Merton (1998).

An option is a contract that provides its owner with the right but not the obligation to purchase or sell a specified quantity of a particular underlying asset – such as stock in a firm – at a specified 'strike' price on a predetermined date in the future. If the right can only be exercised on a given date, the option is known as a European option; if this right can be exercised at any point up to and including the date of maturity, the option is known as an American option. Options are commonly used for risk-management purposes and to facilitate speculative activity. For example, a stockholder who wishes to insure against the possibility of a fall in the value of his or her stock can take out an option to sell it at a given price some time in the future. If the stock does fall in value, the option may be exercised thus insuring its owner against losses. To illustrate the

[20] The Nobel citation for Merton and Scholes specifically acknowledged Black's contribution to the Prize-winning work. In his Nobel Banquet speech at the award ceremony, Merton reflected on Scholes and his friend's absence: 'for us this is also a bittersweet moment for we greatly miss our friend and collaborator, Fischer Black – especially so this special day. We are gratified that the Academy made it quite clear that, were Fischer alive, he too would now be honoured'.

opportunities for speculation provided by options, consider the position of an investor who anticipates that a particular stock will increase in value. Rather than taking the straightforward step of buying a given amount of the stock, he/she could use an equivalent sum to purchase options to buy significantly more stock at a set price in the future. This highly leveraged position both offers the possibility of much greater profit and insures against the possibility that the stock falls in price – if it does the options are simply not exercised and the only cost incurred is their purchase price.

Prior to the work of Black, Merton and Scholes, the development of option-pricing theory had been limited. The major obstacle to progress was an assumed implication of the fact that the price of an option, for example to buy stock, depended upon what happened to the price of the stock up to the maturity of the option (Nobel Foundation, 2004). The supposition was that this meant that the option price had to incorporate a risk premium covering the vagaries of the stock price. Unfortunately, risk premia reflect the subjectivities of individual investors, as well as wider economic fundamentals which are themselves subject to change (Jarrow, 1999). This made the determination of appropriate risk premia difficult and options hard to price.

Black, Merton and Scholes overcame the problems associated with risk-premia decisions by incorporating the risk premium in the stock price. Their widely acclaimed insight into option valuation was to propose that the risk exposure of a call option (the option to buy stock) could be hedged by taking short positions in the stock. Following Jarrow (1999), this meant in practice borrowing the stock from a broker, selling it to a third party, and undertaking to repay the stock at its spot price at a specified time in the future. In these circumstances, if the stock price rises, the value of the call option will increase as the stock price is more likely to be above the strike price when the option matures. However, any gain here is offset because repaying the borrowed stock will cost more. Conversely, if the stock price falls, the decrease in the value of the call option is offset by the fall in the cost of repaying the borrowed stock. The option-stock portfolio thus created – and if perfectly hedged – identifies the option's price. As the portfolio is riskless it must pay the same rate as the risk-free market interest rate, otherwise profits could be made through arbitrage: selling the hedged portfolio and buying the risk-free asset or vice versa. The price of an option can thus be expressed in terms of the underlying stock price and the riskless interest rate. Although the option-pricing formula that emerged from this analysis first appeared in a paper by Black and Scholes (1973), both authors credit Merton with the insight that the hedged position can be managed so that it is riskless (see Duffie, 1998; Schaefer, 1998; Scholes, 1998; also Merton, 1998). Indeed, Black once stated that his paper with Scholes 'should probably be called the Black–Merton–Scholes paper' (quoted in Duffie, 1998, p. 417). In the event, it was Merton (1973a) who elaborated upon several aspects of the option-pricing formula, including proof that the hedged position was riskless, and an extension to allow for the American (early exercise) form of an option (see also Merton, 1998). Merton (1977) is now thought to be the standard version of his analysis (Duffie, 1998).

One of the more immediate applications of the Black, Merton and Scholes breakthrough in option pricing was in the area of corporate finance. Both Black and Scholes (1973) and Merton (1974) recognised that corporate liabilities can be understood as options. For example, the holders of a firm's debt can accept payment on maturity but if the debt cannot be repaid, they have the equivalent of a European call option on the firm's assets (Jarrow, 1999). As Merton (1998, p. 336) argues, this kind of approach to valuation allows a wide variety of instruments for corporate finance to be interpreted as derivative securities and provides 'a unified theory for pricing these liabilities'.

Additional research contributions to financial economics by Merton highlighted in his Nobel citation include the development of a new method for analysing consumption and investment choices over time (Merton, 1969b; 1971), and the generalisation of the capital asset pricing model (for which William Sharpe was awarded the Nobel Prize in 1990 – see entry on Sharpe in this volume) (Merton, 1973b). Many of Merton's earlier papers, including those central to his Nobel award have been drawn together in his 1992 book *Continuous-Time Finance*, which he regards as 'the crowning synthesis of my earlier work' (Nobel Foundation, 2004).

Main Published Works

(1969a), 'A Complete Model of Warrant Pricing That Maximizes Utility' (with P. Samuelson), *Industrial Management Review*, **10**, Winter, pp. 17–46.

(1969b), 'Lifetime Portfolio Selection Under Uncertainty: The Continuous-Time Case, *Review of Economics and Statistics*, **51**, August, pp. 247–57.

(1971), 'Optimum Consumption and Portfolio Rules in a Continuous-Time Model', *Journal of Economic Theory*, **3**, December, pp. 373–413.

(1973a), 'Theory of Rational Option Pricing', *Bell Journal of Economics and Management Science*, **4**, Spring, pp. 141–83.

(1973b), 'An Intertemporal Capital Asset Pricing Model', *Econometrica*, **41**, September, pp. 867–87.

(1974), 'On the Pricing of Corporate Debt: The Risk Structure of Interest Rates', *Journal of Finance*, **29**, May, pp. 449–70.

(1977), 'On the Pricing of Contingent Claims and the Modigliani–Miller Theorem', *Journal of Financial Economics*, **5**, November, pp. 241–9.

(1992), *Continuous-Time Finance*, Cambridge, MA: Basil Blackwell.

(1998), 'Applications of Option-Pricing Theory: Twenty-Five Years Later', *American Economic Review*, **88**, June, pp. 323–49.

Secondary Literature

Black, F. and M.S. Scholes (1973), 'The Pricing of Options and Corporate Liabilities', *Journal of Political Economy*, **81**, May–June, pp. 637–54.

Duffie, D. (1998), 'Black, Merton and Scholes – Their Central Contributions to Economics', *Scandinavian Journal of Economics*, **100** (2), pp. 411–24.

Edwards, F.R. (1999), 'Hedge Funds and the Collapse of Long-Term Capital Management', *Journal of Economic Perspectives*, **13**, Spring, pp. 189–210.

Jarrow, R.A. (1999), 'In Honor of the Nobel Laureates Robert C. Merton and Myron S. Scholes: A Partial Differential Equation That Changed the World', *Journal of Economic Perspectives*, **13**, Fall, pp. 229–48.

Schaefer, S.M. (1998), 'Robert Merton, Myron Scholes and the Development of Derivative Pricing', *Scandinavian Journal of Economics*, **100** (2), pp. 425–45.

Scholes, M.S. (1998), 'Derivatives in a Dynamic Environment', *American Economic Review*, **88**, June, pp. 350–70.

See also   Blaug (1999, pp. 770–71); Nobel Foundation (2004).

Myron S. Scholes
(b. 1941)

© The Nobel Foundation

Myron Scholes was born in Timmins, Ontario, Canada in 1941. His father was a dentist and his mother worked for a time in a family business. While in his teens Scholes suffered heavy losses: the death of his mother and problems with his vision that made reading difficult. His poor eyesight forced Scholes to adjust the way he learned: he had to 'think abstractly and to conceptualise the solution to problems' (Nobel Foundation, 2004). Surgery improved matters but not until ten years later. Scholes developed an interest in economics and finance because of a strong streak of entrepreneurship running through his family. Like fellow Laureate, Robert Merton, with parental encouragement he played the stock market while still at school.

Scholes majored in economics at McMaster University in Ontario, and graduated in 1961 with a BA. He had plans to join his family in business but first entered graduate school at the University of Chicago. As an undergraduate, Scholes had been particularly impressed by the writings of future Chicago Nobel Prize winners George Stigler and Milton Friedman (see entries in this volume). Scholes recalls that his time at Chicago 'changed the direction of my life forever'; there would be no career in the family business (Nobel Foundation, 2004). The turning point was a summer job as a computer programmer at the university. This exposed Scholes to the research work of a series of economists (including the 1990 Laureate Merton Miller); it is not difficult to understand that he found the experience 'empowering'. He became a skilled programmer – 'I must have been one of the first computer nerds' – to the extent that he was even able to offer suggestions about research design to those he was assisting (Nobel Foundation, 2004). At Miller's suggestion, Scholes began work on a PhD. Chicago awarded him an MBA in 1964 and a PhD in 1969.

Scholes's first academic appointment was as Assistant Professor of Finance at the A.P. Sloan School of Management at the Massachusetts Institute of Technology (MIT) in 1969, where he was subsequently promoted to associate professor. At MIT he began to work with Fischer Black, who was then a private consultant, and his new colleague Robert Merton. Scholes returned to the University of Chicago in 1973, first as visiting associate professor and then as professor. Black had become a professor at Chicago in 1972 and Scholes wanted to continue to work with him, Merton Miller, and another economist he knew from his days as a graduate student: Gene Fama (Nobel Foundation, 2004). After a visiting appointment at Stanford University in 1981, Scholes moved there permanently in 1983. Since 1996 he has been Frank. E. Buck Professor of Finance, Emeritus at Stanford.

Scholes's offices and honours include honorary doctorates awarded by three universities: McMaster, Paris-Dauphine and Katholieke Universiteit Leuven in Belgium. Scholes's professional appointments include several directorships; with Robert Merton and others, he was also a co-founder of Long-Term Capital Management, the hedge fund subject to an infamous rescue organised by the Federal Reserve in 1998 (see Edwards, 1999). He is a research associate of the National Bureau of Economic Research. In 1997 Scholes was awarded the Nobel Memorial Prize in Economics jointly with Robert Merton 'for a new method to determine the value of derivatives' (Nobel Foundation, 2004).

In the preceding entry in this volume – for Robert Merton – we review the nature and significance of the option-pricing formula for which Merton and Scholes have been honoured by the Royal Swedish Academy. Rather than covering the same ground in the present entry, we shall instead highlight some of the notable experiences of Scholes and his late colleague Fischer Black during the course of their Prize-winning work; we conclude with some brief references to Scholes's later work.

The history of the paper containing the original Black–Scholes formula for the pricing of an option contract (Black and Scholes, 1973) is both interesting and illuminating (see Black, 1989 for the most commonly cited version). As is well known, Black and Scholes had serious difficulty getting the paper published. An initial submission to the *Journal of Political Economy* in late 1970 was rejected without review, and the editors of the *Review of Economics* and the *Journal of Finance* also agreed that the paper was unsuitable for their readerships (Schaefer, 1998; Scholes, 1998). On the intercession of Merton Miller and Eugene Fama, with whom Scholes has worked at the University of Chicago, the *Journal of Political Economy* accepted the paper after it had been revised and broadened to consider the implications of option contract theory for the analysis of corporate liabilities (see Duffie, 1998; Jarrow, 1999; Schaefer, 1998). Black and Scholes had intended to hold this extension over for inclusion in a later article (Scholes, 1998). This is yet another reminder that even economists capable of Nobel Prize-winning work sometimes suffer in the capricious process that is decision making by journal editors. In a further irony, a paper testing the option-pricing formula (Black and Scholes, 1972) was actually published *before* its theoretical exposition. Our entry on Robert Merton attests to the widespread application and impact of the option-pricing formula following the work of Black, Scholes and Merton. Scholes offers an additional and, in retrospect, amusing anecdote (he must have been at least a little annoyed at the time). In 1974, Texas Instruments produced a calculator that directly used the Black–Scholes model. Scholes asked for royalties but the company claimed the work was in the public domain. When he asked for a calculator they advised him to buy one. He didn't! (See Scholes, 1998.)

In addition to his work on option pricing, Scholes has, with Black and Miller, published notable papers on the impact of dividends on stock valuation (Black and Scholes, 1974; Miller and Scholes, 1978; 1982; see Nobel Foundation, 2004). With Joseph Williams he has done work on the estimation of risk using nonsynchronous data (Scholes and Williams, 1977) and with Mark Wolfson he has written a book bringing together a number of papers on corporate taxation (Scholes and Wolfson, 1992).

Main Published Works

(1972), 'The Valuation of Option Contracts and a Test of Market Efficiency' (with F. Black), *Journal of Finance*, **27**, May, pp. 399–417.

(1973), 'The Pricing of Options and Corporate Liabilities' (with F. Black), *Journal of Political Economy*, **81**, May–June, pp. 637–54.

(1974), 'The Effects of Dividend Yield and Dividend Policy on Common Stock Prices and Returns' (with F. Black), *Journal of Financial Economics*, **1**, May, pp. 1–22.

(1977), 'Estimating Betas from Nonsynchronous Data' (with J. Williams), *Journal of Financial Economics*, **5**, December, pp. 309–27.

(1978), 'Dividends and Taxes' (with M.H. Miller), *Journal of Financial Economics*, **6**, December, pp. 333–64.

(1982), 'Dividends and Taxes: Some Empirical Results' (with M.H. Miller), *Journal of Political Economy*, **90**, December, pp. 1118–41.

(1992), *Taxes and Business Strategy: A Planning Approach* (with M.A. Wolfson), Englewood Cliffs, NJ: Prentice-Hall.

(1998), 'Derivatives in a Dynamic Environment', *American Economic Review*, **88**, June, pp. 350–70.

Secondary Literature

Black, F. (1989), 'How We Came Up With the Option Formula', *Journal of Portfolio Management*, **15**, Winter, pp. 4–8.

Duffie, D. (1998), 'Black, Merton and Scholes – Their Central Contributions to Economics', *Scandinavian Journal of Economics*, **100** (2), pp. 411–24.

Edwards, F.R. (1999), 'Hedge Funds and the Collapse of Long-Term Capital Management', *Journal of Economic Perspectives*, **13**, Spring, pp. 189–210.

Jarrow, R.A. (1999), 'In Honor of the Nobel Laureates Robert C. Merton and Myron S. Scholes: A Partial Differential Equation That Changed the World', *Journal of Economic Perspectives*, **13**, Fall, pp. 229–48.

Schaefer, S.M. (1998), 'Robert Merton, Myron Scholes and the Development of Derivative Pricing', *Scandinavian Journal of Economics*, **100** (2), pp. 425–45.

See also   Nobel Foundation (2004).

THE 1998 NOBEL MEMORIAL LAUREATE

AMARTYA SEN

Amartya K. Sen
(b. 1933)

© The Nobel Foundation

Amartya Sen was born on a university campus in Santiniketan, near Calcutta, India, in 1933. He comes from an academic family – his father taught chemistry at Dhaka University (now the capital of Bangladesh) – and his maternal grandfather was a teacher of Sanskrit and Indian cultural history. Sen says of himself that he has 'not had any serious non-academic job' (Nobel Foundation, 2004).

Although he spent time in Dhaka and Burma as a child, Sen's formative schooling took place in Santiniketan at Visva-Bharati. He remembers that the school had the virtuous emphases of 'fostering curiosity' and embracing cultural diversity; and this at a time when India itself was about to descend into a period of sectarian-based communal violence. Sen relates events around the murder of a Muslim man that he witnessed in his family's predominantly Hindu neighbourhood. The man had simply been looking for work but the search cost him his life. The experience for Sen was 'devastating' but it also made him think about the risks that extreme poverty – a form of 'economic unfreedom' – can force people to take (Nobel Foundation, 2004). As a nine-year-old, Sen was exposed at first hand to the 'harrowing scenes' of the Bengal famine, in which he later estimated almost three million people died. In response to a question about how he became interested in economics, Sen once replied, 'For someone from India, it is not a difficult question to answer. The economic problems engulf us' (Klamer, 1989, p. 136).

Sen's higher education began at Presidency College in Calcutta in 1951. Although he had originally planned to study physics he switched to economics because it 'seemed not only useful and challenging, but also more fun' (Pressman and Summerfield, 2000; Klamer, 1989, p. 136). Sen cites the additional attraction of 'outstanding' teaching and stimulating fellow students. Crediting others for the intellectual environment he has clearly enjoyed and in which he has flourished is a consistent theme in Sen's reflections on his career.

There was a current of left-leaning political activism among the students at Presidency College with which Sen sympathised. This tended to reflect the kinds of economic and social problems in India that he and his friends had grown up observing. He recalls that 'Calcutta itself, despite its immensely rich intellectual and cultural life, provided many constant reminders of the proximity of unbearable economic misery' (Nobel Foundation, 2004). Sen's politics could not find expression in any direct party affiliation as the available groupings – although they expressed laudable commitments to equity and solidarity with the poor – tended to be less tolerant of democratic values. This kind of perspective clashed with the importance, for Sen, of plurality in a culturally diverse society – something he had learned first at school in Santiniketan. Although Sen chose not to embrace conventional political activism, his contribution to economics was to become possessed of a notable ethical underpinning, something specifically recognised in his Nobel citation and which Sen traces directly to the 'concerns that were agitating me most in my undergraduate days in Calcutta' (Nobel Foundation, 2004).

Sen graduated from Calcutta University in 1953 with a BA in economics (major) and mathematics (minor) and moved to Trinity College at the University of Cambridge, UK. Here he enrolled on another BA degree, this time in pure economics, which he completed in 1955. Sen remained in Cambridge for his PhD, which he was awarded in 1959. His thesis supervisor was 'the totally brilliant but vigorously intolerant' Joan Robinson.[21] After conducting his programme of research for only a year, Sen, as he says now, 'was

[21] Robinson had a minor history of somewhat abrasive relationships with subsequent Nobel laureates – see also the entry on Stiglitz in this volume.

bumptious enough' to conclude that he had results that could form a thesis but Cambridge's regulations stipulated that he could not submit for three years. To fill in the time, Sen was granted leave to return to Calcutta, where – at the age of 22 – he was appointed to a chair in economics at the new Jadavpur University and asked to establish a new economics department. This was the beginning of a distinguished academic career.

Sen worked at Jadavpur between 1956 and 1958, before he returning to Cambridge where he had been elected to a prize fellowship at Trinity College. He used the fellowship to embark on the study of philosophy, a discipline in which he has since published widely and which has greatly informed his work in economics (see Arrow, 1999). In 1963 Sen was appointed Professor of Economics at Delhi University in India. He moved back to the UK in 1971, taking up the post of Professor of Economics at the London School of Economics. In 1977 Sen moved to Oxford University, first as Professor of Economics and then, from 1981, as Drummond Professor of Political Economy and Fellow of All Souls College. In 1987 he left the UK for the USA to become Lamont University Professor at Harvard University. He is presently Master of Trinity College, Cambridge, a post held since 1998.

Sen's awards and distinctions include foreign honorary membership of the American Academy of Arts and Sciences. He has been president of each of the Development Studies Association (1982), the Econometric Society (1984), the International Economic Association (1986–89), the Indian Economic Association (1989) and the American Economic Association (1994). He is a past winner of the Mahalanobis Prize (1976), a lifetime achievement award by the Indian government, and in 2000 he became the first ever honorary president of Oxfam. In 1998 Sen was awarded the Nobel Memorial Prize in Economics 'for his contributions to welfare economics' (Nobel Foundation, 2004).

Sen's interest in welfare economics was hugely stimulated by his reading Kenneth Arrow's 'path-breaking study of social choice', *Social Choice and Individual Values* (Arrow, 1951).[22] The book introduced Sen to Arrow's 'stunning "impossibility theorem"' the implication of which is that, in Sen's words, 'no non-dictatorial social

---

[22] Arrow was the 1972 joint Nobel Memorial Laureate – see his entry in this volume.

choice mechanism may yield consistent social decisions' (Nobel Foundation, 2004). For Sen, in a Calcutta riven by inequality, this was an intellectual exploration of the kind of political questions he had been struggling to come to terms with. For example, did the impossibility theorem justify authoritarianism if it permitted some kind of consistent social calculus?

The fundamental problem for welfare economics that Arrow had highlighted was that there was no way to consistently aggregate the preferences of individuals in a society such that unambiguous improvements in social welfare may be consistently reached. This is because there is no method of making interpersonal comparisons of the well-being of different individuals; we simply cannot measure personal utility and therefore, for Arrow, 'interpersonal comparison of utilities has no meaning' (quoted in Sen, 1999, pp. 353–6). This leaves economics with, in Sen's view, the rather limited Pareto criterion for making social decisions. His dissatisfaction with Pareto optimality arises because it 'takes no interest whatever in *distributional* issues, which cannot be addressed without considering conflicts of interest and of preferences' (ibid., p. 352, emphasis in original). It appears then that Arrow's work has an unfortunate and pessimistic implication: the impossibility of social choice beyond Pareto. But, as Sen reflects in his Nobel lecture, this is not the only construction that can be placed on Arrow; the impossibility theorem can and should be read as something that 'invites engagement rather than resignation' (ibid., p. 365; see also Sen, 1970a – a particularly influential contribution according to his Nobel citation). One of Sen's central achievements in economics has been to address the 'impossibility' agenda and to suggest a way forward beyond it; indeed Arrow has characterised Sen as the 'outstanding contributor' to the voluminous literature that has arisen from his own paradigmatic contribution (Arrow, 1999).

Sen's breakthrough was to clarify the theoretical basis for interpersonal comparability and to suggest how the informational base for such comparability may be widened (see Sen, 1999; Arrow, 1999; Atkinson, 1999). In respect of the former consider the following powerful example:

We may ... have no great difficulty in accepting that Emperor Nero's utility gain from the burning of Rome was smaller than the sum-total of the utility loss of all the other Romans who suffered in the fire. But this does not require us to feel confident that we can put everyone's utilities in an exact one-to-one correspondence with each other. (Sen, 1999, p. 356)

Sen argues that such 'partial comparability' provides a basis for social decision making that opens up a richer terrain than that allowed by the alternative Pareto criterion. But he goes further: 'The Pareto principle (i) lists a set of virtues, and (ii) uses dominance of virtues as a criterion. What is in dispute here is the former, not the latter' (Sen, quoted in Atkinson, 1999, p. 177). Sen is arguing that social decisions can indeed be made on the basis of partial comparability – we can be content that Rome was socially impoverished by the fire (the dominance of the utility loss of Roman citizens over Nero's gain) – but he is also clear that the set of 'virtues' upon which comparabilities conventionally rest is open to question.

Welfare economics focuses upon the individual consumption of goods and services: this is how the Pareto criterion judges whether or not there can be an unambiguous improvement in social welfare. But Sen has argued that a person's *capabilities* – what they can be and accomplish – primarily conditions their well-being: individual progress does not reduce to simply increasing the volume of things that can be bought and consumed (Sen, 1982; 1985; 1987; 1999; Sen and Nussbaum, 1993). Capabilities encompass such factors as a person's expectancy of life and health, their education 'and the freedom they have to choose the kind of life they have reason to value' (Nobel Foundation, 2004). This kind of approach to well-being has seen practical application with Sen's involvement in the construction of the United Nations Development Programme's Human Development Index. This measures a country's development in terms of GDP per capita and by reference to literacy and life expectancy; the last two categories are a direct acknowledgement of the significance of capabilities in achieving social progress.

Sen's Nobel citation makes reference to his work on the measurement of poverty (see Sen, 1976; 1982). Sen has been critical of the traditional 'headcount' measure of poverty that simply notes the proportion of a population below a given poverty line (for example, the number of people subsisting on less than a dollar a day). His objection is that the headcount approach is insensitive to the severity of poverty: are people a little way or far below the line? Sen proposed an alternative poverty index which takes into account both the number of people in poverty and how poor they are, with a greater weighting attached to the very poor.

Partly with Jean Drèze, Sen has made important contributions to work on the causation and prevention of famines (Sen, 1981; Drèze and Sen, 1989). He has demonstrated, in the context of a number of catastrophic events, that the common assumption of food shortage as a central causal factor in famine may be misplaced: 'famines can occur even without any major decline – possibly without *any* decline at all – of food production or supply' (Sen, 1999, p. 361, emphasis in original). Instead, the problem generally lies in the distribution of food. Natural events may deprive particular groups of income and the problem then becomes not the supply of food but the absence of an income-based entitlement to it. Sen argues that the 1943 Bengal famine that he witnessed as a child happened because floods deprived wage earners of income.

Sen's other notable contributions to economics include his attempt to demonstrate that the notion of utility maximisation in the context of Pareto optimality conflicts with the liberal tradition that individuals should be free to do as they wish on the understanding that they should not prevent others from doing the same (Sen, 1970b). Finally, in his famous 'Rational Fools' paper, Sen has offered a critique of the traditional interpretation of rationality in economics (Sen, 1977).

Main Published Works

(1970a), *Collective Choice and Social Welfare*, San Francisco: Holden Day.

(1970b), 'The Impossibility of a Paretian Liberal', *Journal of Political Economy*, **78**, January–February, pp. 152–7.

(1976), 'Poverty: An Ordinal Approach to Measurement', *Econometrica*, **44**, March, pp. 219–31.

(1977), 'Rational Fools: A Critique of the Behavioural Foundations of Economic Theory', *Philosophy and Public Affairs*, **6** (4), pp. 317–44.

(1981), *Poverty and Famines: An Essay on Entitlement and Deprivation*, Oxford: Clarendon Press.

(1982), *Choice, Welfare and Measurement*, Oxford: Basil Blackwell.

(1985), *Commodities and Capabilities*, Amsterdam: North-Holland.

(1987), *The Standard of Living* (Tanner Lectures, ed. G. Hawthorne), Cambridge: Cambridge University Press.

(1989), *Hunger and Public Action* (with J. Drèze), Oxford: Clarendon Press.

(1993), *Quality of Life* (ed. with M. Nussbaum), Oxford: Clarendon Press.

(1999), 'The Possibility of Social Choice', *American Economic Review*, **89**, June, pp. 349–78.

Secondary Literature

Arrow, K.J. (1951), *Social Choice and Individual Values*, New York: Wiley.

Arrow, K.J. (1999), 'Amartya K. Sen's Contribution to the Study of Welfare', *Scandinavian Journal of Economics*, **101** (2), pp. 163–72.

Atkinson, A.B. (1999), 'The Contributions of Amartya Sen to Welfare Economics', *Scandinavian Journal of Economics*, **101** (2), pp. 173–90.

Klamer, A. (1989), 'A Conversation with Amartya Sen', *Journal of Economic Perspectives*, **3**, Winter, pp. 135–50.

Pressman, S. and G. Summerfield (2000), 'The Economic Contributions of Amartya Sen', *Review of Political Economy*, **12** (1), pp. 89–113.

See also Arestis and Sawyer (2000, pp. 577–84); Beaud and Dostaler (1997, pp. 402–3); Blaug (1998, pp. 259–61); Blaug and Vane (2003, pp. 755–6); Nobel Foundation (2004); Pressman (1999, pp. 189–93).

THE 1999 NOBEL MEMORIAL LAUREATE

ROBERT MUNDELL

Robert A. Mundell
(b. 1932)

Robert Mundell was born in Kingston, Ontario, Canada in 1932. He obtained a BA from the University of British Columbia in 1953 and an MA from the University of Washington in 1954. After studying at the London School of Economics and the Massachusetts Institute of Technology (MIT) he received his PhD from MIT in 1956. His doctoral thesis concerned aspects of international capital movements, a topic that was to become a focus of much of his subsequent research. Mundell held a Post-Doctoral Fellowship in Political Economy at the University of Chicago (1956–57), taught at Stanford University (Assistant Professor of Economics, 1958–59) and the Johns Hopkins University School of Advanced International Studies in Bologna, Italy (Professor of Economics, 1959–61), before joining the research department of the International Monetary Fund (IMF) as a senior economist (1961–63). The IMF's research department at that time was headed by Marcus Fleming. Subsequent posts included: Visiting Professor of Economics at McGill University (1963–64); Visiting Research Professor of International Economics at the Brookings Institution (1964–65); (summer) Professor of International Economics at the Graduate Institute of International Studies in Geneva, Switzerland (1965–75); Professor of Economics at the University of Chicago (1966–71), where he was editor of the *Journal of Political Economy* (1966–70); and Professor of Economics at the University of Waterloo, Ontario (1972–74). Since 1974, Mundell has been Professor of Economics at Columbia University in New York.

Mundell's many offices and honours have included the award of the title of distinguished fellow of the American Economic Association in 1997 and a fellowship of the American Academy of Arts and Sciences in 1998. In 1999 Mundell was awarded the Nobel Memorial Prize in Economics 'for his analysis of monetary and fiscal policy under different exchange rate regimes and his analysis of optimum currency areas' (Nobel Foundation, 2004).

Mundell's pioneering contributions to open economy or international economics can be divided into three main areas: the development of the so-called Mundell–Fleming model and its implications for the effectiveness of fiscal and monetary policy under different exchange rate regimes; his work emphasising the importance of monetary dynamics; and the development of the concept of an optimum currency area. While these path-breaking contributions (see, for example, the collection of essays gathered together in Mundell, 1968; 1971a) date from the 1960s, their lasting significance is reflected in the key part they still play at the heart of open economy macroeconomic courses. Furthermore, his contributions have provided fertile ground since the 1960s for researchers to extend and refine his original analyses.

The Mundell–Fleming model derives its name from the work of Robert Mundell and Marcus Fleming. Writing independently while at the IMF, both researchers incorporated international trade and capital movements into the IS–LM model of a closed economy (a model initially developed by John Hicks the 1972 Nobel Memorial Laureate). Mundell (1963b) demonstrated that for a *small* open economy, with *perfect* capital mobility, the effects of monetary and fiscal policy critically depend on whether the exchange rate is fixed or flexible. Under a fixed exchange rate the money supply is endogenous and monetary policy becomes totally ineffective in changing the level of domestic economic activity. Any attempt to increase the money supply by open market purchases of securities will merely lead to an offsetting loss of foreign exchange reserves. In contrast, fiscal policy becomes effective as there is no crowding out since the domestic interest rate is tied to the rate ruling abroad. Under a flexible exchange rate the money supply is exogenous and monetary policy becomes effective in changing the level of domestic economic activity. An increase in the money supply *implies* lower interest rates which results in capital outflows and a depreciation of the exchange rate. This in turn causes an increase in aggregate demand (through an increase in net exports) and higher output. In contrast, fiscal policy becomes totally ineffective. An increase in government expenditure puts upward pressure on the domestic interest rate, resulting in an inflow of capital and an appreciation of the exchange rate. As the exchange rate appreciates net exports decrease, completely offsetting the effects of increased government expenditure. In this way fiscal expansion crowds out net exports and there is no change in output.

A second key contribution made by Mundell to open economy macroeconomics relates to his work on the importance of monetary dynamics. This can be seen in three main uses. First, he analysed how persistent international payments imbalances could arise and how they would eventually be eliminated. In his approach, the private sector's money holdings (and thereby its *stock* of wealth) change in response to balance of payments surpluses or deficits (*flows*). For example, under fixed exchange rates with a low degree of capital mobility, an increase in the money supply will reduce interest rates, increase domestic demand and cause a balance of payments deficit. The deficit will result in monetary outflows and a fall in demand until the balance of payments deficit is eliminated. Mundell's approach was subsequently adopted by others and was developed into the monetary approach to the balance of payments. One important conclusion that derives from his analysis is that attempts by the authorities to sterilise balance of payments deficits/ surpluses will disrupt the adjustment mechanism. Second, Mundell (1962) used dynamic principles to solve the so-called 'assignment problem'. Employing a Keynesian model operating under a fixed exchange rate with imperfect capital mobility, he considered the appropriate use of monetary and fiscal policy for internal and external stability. He demonstrated how monetary policy should be assigned to achieve external balance and fiscal policy to achieve internal balance. With the reverse assignment the economy would be dynamically unstable, experiencing progressively rising unemployment and a deteriorating balance of payments situation. The explanation for this is related to his 'principle of effective market classification' (Mundell, 1960), in that policy instruments should be assigned to the objectives on which they have the most direct influence. Third, Mundell's work on monetary dynamics results in his 'incompatibility trinity' whereby, given capital mobility, monetary policy can be directed towards either an external objective (for example, the exchange rate) or an internal objective (for example, inflation) but *not both* at the same time.

The third area in which he has made a major contribution to open economy macroeconomics is in the development of the concept of an optimum currency area. At the time of the Bretton Woods regime of fixed exchange rates, Mundell (1961) posed the then radical and far-sighted question 'when is it advantageous for a number of regions to relinquish their monetary sovereignty in favour of a common currency?'. Addressing this question he considered both the advantages (for example, lower transaction costs) and disadvantages (for example, the problem of maintaining employment when 'asymmetric shocks' necessitate a reduction in real wages in a particular region) of a common currency. He found an optimum currency area to be a set of regions within which the degree of labour mobility is high enough to ensure full employment when one particular region experiences a disturbance. Surprisingly, given Europe's inflexible labour market, Mundell has been a strong supporter of European Monetary Union (see, for example, Mundell, 1973; 1997) and many regard him (inaccurately) as the father of the euro.

In addition to the three main contributions noted above, Mundell has also made a number of other important contributions to macroeconomic theory and the theory of trade. These include: in the former case the 'Mundell–Tobin effect' where a higher rate of inflation may induce people to reduce their real cash balances and invest more in real capital assets (see Mundell, 1963a); and in the latter case the argument that factor mobility tends to equalise goods prices, even if international trade is restricted by trade barriers (Mundell, 1957). In the 1970s, in the field of economic policy, his enthusiasm for tax cuts (see Mundell, 1971b) helped found supply-side economics. Over recent years he has been working on the history of the international monetary system (see Mundell, 2000).

Main Published Works

(1957), 'International Trade and Factor Mobility', *American Economic Review*, **47**, June, pp. 321–35; reprinted in R.E. Caves and H.G. Johnson (eds) (1968), *Readings in International Economics*, Homewood, IL: R.D. Irwin.

(1960), 'The Monetary Dynamics of International Adjustment under Fixed and Flexible Exchange Rates', *Quarterly Journal of Economics*, **84**, May, pp. 227–57.

(1961), 'A Theory of Optimum Currency Areas', *American Economic Review*, **51**, September, pp. 657–65; reprinted in M. Ugur (ed.) (2002), *An Open Economy Macroeconomics Reader*, London: Routledge, pp. 345–53.

(1962), 'The Appropriate Use of Monetary and Fiscal Policy for Internal and External Stability', *IMF Staff Papers*, March, pp. 70–79; reprinted in M. Ugur (ed.) (2002), *An Open Economy Macroeconomics Reader*, London: Routledge, pp. 132–8.

(1963a), 'Inflation and Real Interest', *Journal of Political Economy*, **71**, June, pp. 280–83.

(1963b), 'Capital Mobility and Stabilisation Policy under Fixed and Flexible Exchange Rates', *Canadian Journal of Economics and Political Science*, 29, November, pp. 475–85; reprinted in M. Ugur (ed.) (2002), *An Open Economy Macroeconomics Reader*, London: Routledge, pp. 7–18.

(1968), *International Economics*, New York: Macmillan.

(1971a), *Monetary Theory: Interest, Inflation and Growth in the World Economy*, Pacific Palisades, CA: Goodyear.

(1971b), 'The Dollar and the Policy Mix', *Essays in International Finance*, no. 85, Princeton, NJ: Princeton University Press.

(1973), 'A Plan for a Common Currency', in H. Johnson and A. Swoboda (eds) (1973), *The Economics of Common Currencies*, London: George Allen & Unwin.

(1997), 'Currency Areas, Common Currencies and EMU', *American Economic Review*, **87**, May, pp. 214–16.

(2000), 'The International Monetary System at the Beginning of the New Millennium', *Journal of Economic Research*, **5**, May, pp. 1–15.

Secondary Literature

Dornbusch, R. (2000), 'Robert A. Mundell's Nobel Memorial Prize', *Scandinavian Journal of Economics*, **102**, June, pp. 199–210 and pp. 223–34.

Rose, A.K. (2000), 'A Review of Some of the Economic Contributions of Robert A. Mundell, Winner of the 1999 Nobel Memorial Prize in Economics', *Scandinavian Journal of Economics*, **102**, June, pp. 211–22 and pp. 223–34.

See also   Blaug (1999, pp. 807–9); Cate (1997, pp. 454–6); Nobel Foundation (2004).

Acknowledgement

Adapted from the entry on Robert A. Mundell in B. Snowdon and H.R. Vane (eds) (2002), *An Encyclopedia of Macroeconomics*, Cheltenham, UK and Northampton, MA, USA: Edward Elgar.

THE 2000 NOBEL MEMORIAL LAUREATES

JAMES HECKMAN
AND
DANIEL MCFADDEN

James J. Heckman
(b. 1944)

© The Nobel Foundation

James Heckman was born in Chicago, Illinois, USA in 1944. He spent most of his childhood in Chicago but the family lived in Kentucky and Oklahoma for a few years before settling in Denver, Colorado, where Heckman went to high school. His time in the South, coupled with a later visit in the company of a Nigerian friend, exposed him to the last spasms of institutionalised racial discrimination practised there. This left a lasting impression and kindled a determination to do something to confront the implications of such social degeneration: 'The separate water fountains, park benches, bathrooms and restaurants of the Jim Crow South startled me. These experiences motivated my lifelong study of the status of African Americans, and the sources of improvement in that status' (Nobel Foundation, 2004).

In high school, Heckman was taught by Frank Oppenheimer, whose brother Robert had been leader of the team that developed the first atomic bomb. Frank Oppenheimer was also a physicist but, according to Heckman, he lost his university post because of his membership of the Communist Party. This happened in the early 1950s, a period associated with 'McCarthyism' in the United States, when many Americans suffered professionally because of alleged or sincerely held political beliefs. Eventually Oppenheimer returned to teaching and Heckman won a place in his class. This was an important stage in Heckman's intellectual development. He recollects:

> Under his [Oppenheimer's] guidance I learned the beauty of experimental science and the pleasure of matching theory to evidence. Although I later abandoned physics for economics, my enthusiasm for scientific empirical work guided by theory was born in his classroom. (Nobel Foundation, 2004)

Heckman attended Colorado College, obtaining a BA in mathematics in 1965. After spending a short time at the University of Chicago, he transferred to Princeton University largely because of the presence there of Arthur Lewis. Heckman had first read Lewis at Colorado College and wanted to learn more about his work on economic development (see entry on Lewis – a joint Laureate in 1979 – in this volume). Heckman was awarded an MA in economics by Princeton in 1968. Although he had been drawn to Princeton by the opportunity to study development, Heckman found his interests stimulated by labour economics and econometrics, and a 'lifetime intellectual passion' to bring together theory and evidence in economics was born. He received his PhD from Princeton in 1971 for work on household labour supply and the demand for market goods.

Heckman's first academic post was at Columbia University, where he was assistant professor from 1970 to 1973 and associate professor from 1973 to 1974. In 1972 he was also adjunct professor at New York University. Apart from a very brief period in the mid-1980s, Heckman has enjoyed a long association with the National Bureau of Economic Research where he has been a research associate (1971–85 and 1987–date) and a research fellow (1972–73). In 1973 Heckman moved to the University of Chicago as associate professor before becoming Professor of Economics in 1977 and, in 1985, Henry Schultz Professor. In 1988 he was appointed A. Whitney Griswold Professor of Economics at Yale University before becoming, briefly, Professor of Statistics at Yale in 1990. He returned to the University of Chicago in 1990 as Henry Schultz Professor and also accepted a joint position at the Irving Harris School of Public Policy, also at Chicago. In 1991 Heckman became director of the university's newly founded Center for Evaluation of Social Programs. Since 1995 he has been Henry Schultz Distinguished Service Professor at Chicago.

Heckman's professional activities have included service as a member of: the Social Science Research Council Committee on Research

Methods for Longitudinal Data (1976–79 and 1981–82); the National Science Foundation Evaluation Panel in Economics (1977–79); the National Academy of Sciences Panel on Statistical Assessments as Evidence in the Courts (1982–85); and the National Academy of Sciences Panel on the Status of Black Americans (1985–88).

Heckman's offices and honours include a fellowship at the Center for Advanced Study in the Behavioural Sciences at Stanford University in 1978–79 and, for the same period, a John Simon Guggenheim Memorial Fellowship. He became a fellow of the Econometric Society in 1980 and was awarded the John Bates Clark Medal by the American Economic Association in 1983. In the Fall of 1984, Heckman was Irving Fisher Visiting Professor at Yale University and in 1985 he received the first annual Louis T. Benezet Distinguished Alumnus Award from Colorado College. Also in 1985 he became an elected fellow of the American Academy of Arts and Sciences. Since 1991 he has been a senior research fellow at the American Bar Foundation. Heckman was president of the Midwest Economics Association in 1998 and a fellow of the American Statistical Association in 2001. He became an elected member of the National Academy of Sciences in 1992 and he holds honorary degrees and professorships from a number of universities around the world. In 2000 Heckman was awarded the Nobel Memorial Prize in Economics 'for his development of theory and methods for analysing selective samples' (Nobel Foundation, 2004).

Heckman's most notable contribution to the field of micro-econometrics – the theoretically informed study of individual behaviour using individual data – is methodological. In an enormously influential paper in *Econometrica*, he proposed a means of dealing with the problem of 'selection bias' in statistically-based economic research (Heckman, 1979). This paper was highlighted in Heckman's Nobel award. The selection bias problem arises because the samples investigators work with may not be representative of the populations from which they are drawn. One way in which this can happen is through individuals 'self-selecting' into a sample. Heckman's Nobel citation provides an illustration. An investigation of the effect of education on wages must necessarily focus on a sample whose members have chosen to work: the sample is selective and not representative of the true population that contains both those in work and the unemployed. To address selection bias Heckman proposed a two-stage selection model – what has become known as the

Heckman two-step estimator or 'Heckit' estimator. The first step is to estimate the probability of selection into the sample; the second is to use these probabilities as an independent variable in a least-squares model. The problem of selection bias is, of course, not unique to economics and Heckman's innovations have been taken up in other social science disciplines; indeed, it has been suggested that Heckman's (1979) *Econometrica* paper is the most widely read outside economics ever to have been published in that journal (Heinrich and Wenger, 2002).

Heckman has applied his insights into selection bias to some important economic and social questions. For example, in work with Thomas Lyons and Petra Todd, he has produced a view of the economic progress made by black males in the United States since the Second World War that is, after allowing for selection bias, less sanguine than the norm (Heckman et al., 2000; see also Heckman and Payner, 1989). As he reports in his Nobel lecture, the median American black–white male wage ratio increased between 1940 and 1980 from less than 0.5 to a little above 0.7; after 1980 the ratio stabilised (Heckman, 2001). The problem is that over the whole period, blacks were withdrawing from the labour force at a much faster rate than whites, and this means that they were also withdrawing from the statistics used to measure wages. He finds that

Correcting for the selective withdrawal of low-wage black workers from employment reduces and virtually eliminates black male economic progress compared to that of whites and challenges optimistic assessments of African-American economic progress. (ibid., p. 699)

Heckman's early work in microeconometrics was also characteristically pioneering. The wealth of new microeconomic data that became available to researchers from the 1950s posed significant analytical challenges. As Heckman points out, 'The R^2 (measure of explained fit) of any micro relationship is typically low, so the unobservables account for a lot of ... variability' (ibid, p. 684). This is testament to what he calls the 'pervasiveness of heterogeneity and diversity in economic life' (ibid., p. 674). The challenge was to make scientific and economic sense of data that describes such diversity. This is something Heckman began to do in a series of important papers beginning in the first half of the 1970s. For example, in a widely cited article in *Econometrica*, Heckman modelled labour supply in such a way that the decision to work reflected interrelated choices over hours of work, the reservation wage and constraints on labour force participation (Heckman 1974b; and see Blundell, 2001; Heinrich and Wenger, 2002). He applied this model to consider the effects of the Nixon administration's programmes of child-care support on women's work effort (Heckman, 1974a). Heckman (1976) has also extended his analytical framework to consider the life cycle of labour supply. In the 1980s, with Richard Robb, Heckman produced highly influential methodological advances in the evaluation of training programmes (Heckman and Robb, 1985; 1986), and has since built up a whole body of evaluation work in collaboration with a number of researchers (see, for example, Heckman and Smith, 1997; Cameron and Heckman, 1998a; Heckman et al., 1998b).

Heckman's output is prodigious. His CV lists over 200 journal articles and there is no doubt that, in the words of the Royal Swedish Academy of Sciences, 'His work has had a decisive influence both on subsequent methodological development and on applied research in microeconometrics' (Nobel Foundation, 2004).

Main Published Works

(1974a), 'Effects of Child Care Programs on Women's Work Effort', *Journal of Political Economy*, **82**, March/April, pp. S136–S143; reprinted in T.W. Schultz (ed.), *Economics of the Family: Marriage, Children and Human Capital*, Chicago: University of Chicago Press (for NBER).

(1974b), 'Shadow Prices, Market Wages and Labor Supply', *Econometrica*, **42**, July, pp. 679–94.

(1976), 'A Life-Cycle Model of Earnings, Learning and Consumption', *Journal of Political Economy*, **84**, August, pp. S11–S44.

(1979), 'Sample Selection Bias as Specification Error', *Econometrica*, **47**, January, pp. 47–74.

(1985), 'Alternative Methods for Estimating the Impact of Interventions' (with R. Robb), in J. Heckman and B. Singer (eds), *Longitudinal Analysis of Labour Market Data*, New York: Wiley, pp. 156–256.

(1986), 'Alternative Identifying Assumptions in Econometric Models of Selection Bias' (with R. Robb), in D.J. Slottje (ed.), *Advances in Econometrics*, vol. 5, Greenwich, CT: JAI Press.

(1989), 'Determining the Impact of Federal Anti-Discrimination Policy on the Economic Status of Blacks: A Study of South Carolina' (with B.S. Payner), *American Economic Review*, **79**, March, pp. 138–77.

(1997), 'Making the Most out of Program Evaluations and Social Experiments: Accounting for Heterogeneity in Programme Impacts' (with J. Smith), *Review of Economic Studies*, **64**, October, pp. 487–535.

(1998a), 'Life Cycle Schooling and Educational Selectivity: Models and Choice' (with S. Cameron), *Journal of Political Economy*, **106**, April, pp. 262–333.

(1998b), 'General-Equilibrium Treatment Effects: A Study of Tuition Policy' (with L. Lochner and C. Taber), *American Economic Review*, **88**, May, pp. 381–6.

(2000), 'Understanding Black–White Wage Differentials, 1960–1990' (with T.M. Lyons and P.E. Todd), *American Economic Review*, **90**, May, pp. 344–9.

(2001), 'Microdata, Heterogeneity and the Evaluation of Public Policy', *Journal of Political Economy*, **109**, August, pp. 673–784.

Secondary Literature

Blundell, R. (2001), 'James Heckman's Contributions to Economics and Econometrics', *Scandinavian Journal of Economics*, **103** (2), pp. 191–203.
Heinrich, C.J. and J.B. Wenger (2002), 'The Economic Contributions of James J. Heckman and Daniel L. McFadden', *Review of Political Economy*, **14**, January, pp. 69–89.

See also Blaug and Vane (2003, pp. 360–61); Nobel Foundation (2004).

Daniel L. McFadden
(b. 1937)

© The Nobel Foundation

Daniel McFadden was born in Raleigh, North Carolina, USA in 1937. He grew up in rural isolation as a consequence of his parents' decision to opt for an unconventional life on a remote farm with no electricity or running water. McFadden's mother had been trained as an architect and his father, despite little formal education, had kept the books at a bank. After helping out on the farm and with few other readily available diversions, McFadden relaxed by reading books from his father's library. He remembers being a good student and he pushed beyond the limitations of his high-school curriculum by taking correspondence courses in algebra and geometry. McFadden was helped in this endeavour by his mother who had found work as a high-school mathematics teacher. At age 16 he passed the entrance examination for the University of Minnesota and was awarded a BS in physics with High Distinction in 1957, when he was 19 (Nobel Foundation, 2004).

McFadden continued at Minnesota as a graduate student of physics but in 1958 he secured a place on a Ford Foundation sponsored behavioural science training programme and began a much more eclectic programme of PhD courses in psychology, sociology, economics, anthropology, political science, mathematics and statistics. During this period, McFadden 'developed an interest in mathematical models of learning and choice' and found that some economists at Minnesota – Professors John Chipman and Leo Hurwicz – were working in this area; accordingly, he elected to enrol for an economics PhD (Nobel Foundation, 2004). He was awarded a PhD in behavioural science (economics) in 1962. As part of his doctoral training McFadden spent a summer externship at Stanford University, where he worked for Kenneth Arrow and Marc Nerlove. At Stanford he also 'had a brief interaction with Professor Hirofumi Uzawa that proved to be a pivotal point in my research training, giving me a dissertation topic, and, most importantly, a flash of understanding of how to use mathematics as a research tool' (Nobel Foundation, 2004).

McFadden's first academic post following the completion of his PhD was at the University of Pittsburgh where in 1962–63 he was a Mellon post-doctoral fellow and Assistant Professor of Economics. In 1963 he moved to the University of California at Berkeley as Assistant Professor of Economics. In 1966 he was promoted to Associate Professor of Economics and, following an appointment as visiting associate professor at the University of Chicago in 1966–67, he became Professor of Economics at Berkeley in 1968. In 1977–78 he was Irving Fisher Research Professor at Yale University. McFadden left Berkeley in 1978, taking up the post of Professor of Economics at the Massachusetts Institute of Technology (MIT), where, in 1984, he was given the James R. Killian Chair. In 1986 he became director of the Statistics Center at MIT, a position he held until 1988. After spending 1990 as a Sherman Fairchild Distinguished Fellow at the California Institute of Technology, McFadden left MIT in 1991 to return to Berkeley as Professor of Economics and holder of the E. Morris Cox Chair. At Berkeley he has also been director of the Econometrics Laboratory (1991–95 and 1996–date) and chair of the Department of Economics (1995–96).

McFadden's professional and public service duties have included service on a number of advisory boards including: the Economics Advisory Panel of the National Science Foundation (1969–71); the Advisory Committee on Transportation Models; the Metropolitan Transportation Commission (1975); the National Academy of Sciences (NAS) Committee on Energy Demand Modeling (1983–84); and the NAS Commission on Science, Engineering and Public Policy (1995–date). McFadden was president of the Econometric Society in 1985, vice president of the American Economic Association in 1994 and its president-elect in 2004.

McFadden's offices and honours include election as a fellow of the Econometric Society in 1969 and the award of the John Bates Clark Medal by the American Economic Association in 1975. He was elected to the American Academy of Arts and Sciences in 1977 and received the MIT Outstanding Teacher Award in 1981. In 1986 he was awarded the Frisch Medal by the Econometric Society and won the Richard Stone Prize in Applied Econometrics in 2000–2001. In 2000, McFadden was awarded the Nobel Memorial Prize in Economics 'for his development of theory and methods for analysing discrete choice' (Nobel Foundation, 2004).

In the introduction to his Nobel lecture, McFadden (2001, p. 351) notes that, prior to the 1960s, consumer theory in economics 'was usually developed in terms of a *representative agent*, with market-level behaviour given by the representative agent's behaviour writ large' (emphasis in original). This approach was consistent with an analysis of choice and decision expressed in continuous form as, for example, in the familiarly referenced trade-off between the consumption of guns and butter: more of one can be consumed but only at the expense of forgone consumption of the other. Choice, however, can take discrete as well as continuous forms. Decisions whether or not to work, marry, to live in a particular location, to select a particular mode or mix of transportation, all involve discrete choices: thus, a person is either married or not married, trade-offs between these two states are not possible. McFadden's Nobel award recognises the unique contribution he has made to the empirical study of discrete choice: his work resulted in 'new statistical methods based on a new economic theory of discrete choice' (Nobel Foundation, 2004). Indeed, his 1974 paper, 'Conditional Logit Analysis of Qualitative Choice Behaviour', 'was immediately recognised as a paradigmatic breakthrough', while related work (Domencich and McFadden, 1975a; McFadden, 1975b, 1976) – partly with Thomas Domencich – 'fundamentally changed the way econometricians and empirical researchers thought about the econometric analysis of individual behavior' (Manski, 2001, p. 224).

One of the key milestones in the development of McFadden's work was a request by a Berkeley graduate student, Phoebe Cottingham, for advice on the analysis of data on freeway routing choices by the California Department of Highways. Drawing on work by L.L. Thurstone, Jacob Marschak and R. Duncan Luce, McFadden constructed an econometric model of discrete choice between alternative freeway routes. Although Cottingham's thesis was completed before McFadden's model could be computed, he was later able to use it to analyse her data (McFadden, 2001). Although described in McFadden's (1974) paper as a conditional logit model, it is now generally known as the multinomial logit (MNL) model.

McFadden's analysis of discrete choice was the subject of rapid and wide application. His own research has included travel demand forecasting and his Nobel citation singles out in particular work on the design of the Bay Area Rapid Transport (BART) system in San Francisco (see McFadden et al., 1977; 1978a); more recent research, also acknowledged in his Nobel award, has examined the housing decisions of elderly people (see, for example, McFadden and Feinstein, 1989). Further innovations in econometric modelling have included the development, with Jeffrey Dubin, of a means of analysing discrete and continuous decision making in the context of consumer products (McFadden and Dubin, 1984).

McFadden's approach to economics has been to consistently focus on applied problems. In his Nobel autobiography he reflects that

> [A] common theme of my research has been an emphasis on tightly binding economic theory and the problem of measurement and analysis, and on developing theoretical and statistical tools that expand the options available to applied economists. I have a strong appreciation for elegant and innovative mathematics and statistics, but as a matter of scientific priority try to keep my research focused on concrete applications, and provide templates for applied economists to follow.

There is no doubt that he has been highly successful in the latter endeavour. As Manski (2001) has noted, in addition to those areas McFadden himself has actively researched, his work has been widely applied in fields such as marketing, telecommunications and industrial organisation.

Beyond his work on discrete choice, McFadden has made contributions to a number of other areas of economics, including the analysis of production (McFadden, 1963; Fuss and McFadden, 1978b), economic theory (McFadden, 1969), and growth theory (McFadden, 1973). In addition, with fellow Nobel Laureate Daniel Kahneman and others, he has explored the effects of Kahneman and Tversky's 'anchoring' heuristic on the willingness to pay for public goods (Green et al., 1998; and see entry on Kahneman in the present volume).

As with many other Laureates, McFadden is concerned to acknowledge the importance of the contributions of others to his own success. Notably, like Kahneman, he cites the work of Kahneman's long-time collaborator Amos Tversky. McFadden donated his Nobel Prize money to the East Bay Community Foundation, directing that it should be used for the promotion of arts and education.

Main Published Works

(1963), 'Constant Elasticity of Substitution Production Functions', *Review of Economic Studies*, **30**, June, pp. 73–83.

(1969), 'On Hicksian Stability', in J.N Wolfe (ed.), *Value, Capital and Growth*, Edinburgh: Edinburgh University Press, pp. 329–51.

(1973), 'On the Existence of Optimal Development Programmes in Infinite Horizon Economies', in J. Mirrlees and N.H. Stern (eds), *Models of Economic Growth*, London: Macmillan, pp. 260–82.

(1974), 'Conditional Logit Analysis of Qualitative Choice Behaviour', in P. Zarembka (ed.), *Frontiers in Econometrics*, New York: Academic Press, pp. 105–42.

(1975a), *Urban Travel Demand* (with T. Domencich), Amsterdam: North-Holland; reprinted by The Blackstone Company: Mount Pleasant, MI, 1976.

(1975b), 'The Revealed Preferences of a Government Bureaucracy: Theory', *Bell Journal of Economics and Management Science*, **6**, Autumn, pp. 401–16.

(1976), 'The Revealed Preferences of a Government Bureaucracy: Empirical Evidence', *Bell Journal of Economics and Management Science*, **7**, Spring, pp. 55–72.

(1977), 'Demand Model Estimation and Validation' (with A. Talvitie, S. Cosslett, I. Hasan, M. Johnson, F. Reid, K. Train), in *Urban Travel Demand Forecasting Project*, Final Report, vol. V, Institute of Transportation Studies, University of California, Berkeley.

(1978a), 'Modeling the Choice of Residential Location', in A. Karlqvist, L. Lundqvist, F. Snickars and J. Weibull (eds), *Spatial Interaction Theory and Planning Models*, Amsterdam: North-Holland, pp. 75–96.

(1978b), *Production Economics: A Dual Approach to Theory and Applications*, vols I and II (ed. with M. Fuss), Amsterdam: North-Holland.

(1984), 'An Econometric Analysis of Residential Electric Appliance Holdings and Consumption' (with J. Dubin), *Econometrica*, **52**, March, pp. 345–62.

(1989), 'The Dynamics of Housing Demand by the Elderly: Wealth, Cash Flow, and Demographic Effects' (with J. Feinstein), in D. Wise (ed.), *Issues in the Economics of Aging*, Chicago: University of Chicago Press, pp. 33–87.

(1998), 'Referendum Contingent Evaluation, Anchoring and Willingness to Pay for Public Goods' (with D. Green, K. Jacowitz and D. Kahneman), *Resource and Energy Economics*, **20**, June, pp. 85–116.

(2001), 'Economic Choices', *American Economic Review*, **91**, June, pp. 351–78.

Secondary Literature

Heinrich, C.J. and J.B. Wenger (2002), 'The Economic Contributions of James J. Heckman and Daniel L. McFadden', *Review of Political Economy*, **14**, January, pp. 69–89.

Manski, C.F. (2001), 'Daniel McFadden and the Econometric Analysis of Discrete Choice', *Scandinavian Journal of Economics*, **103** (2), pp. 217–29.

See also Blaug and Vane (2003, pp. 555–6); Nobel Foundation (2004).

THE 2001 NOBEL MEMORIAL LAUREATES

GEORGE AKERLOF, MICHAEL SPENCE AND JOSEPH STIGLITZ

© The Nobel Foundation

George A. Akerlof
(b. 1940)

George Akerlof was born in New Haven, Connecticut, USA in 1940. Akerlof's father, a chemist, held academic and research posts at, among others, Yale University – where he met his future wife (a chemistry graduate student) – and Princeton University. His elder brother followed their father into a career in science but Akerlof developed an interest in social matters such as 'history and, if children can have such interests, economics' (Nobel Foundation, 2004). Akerlof recalls that one of his first significant thoughts about the discipline came at the age of 11 or 12 when, prompted by his father's move from one post to another, he speculated about the wider consequences of his father becoming unemployed and the family having to cut back on its spending. If this caused another father to lose his job, spending to fall further and so on, the economy could falter. Thus Akerlof's professional commitment to Keynesian macroeconomics was prefigured in pre-adolescent reflections about the interdependency of families in their contribution to the maintenance of aggregate demand.

Akerlof attended Yale as an undergraduate and was awarded a BA in mathematics and economics in 1962. In 1966 he received his PhD at the Massachusetts Institute of Technology (MIT). His PhD thesis developed themes that were Akerlof's first attempts 'to base

Keynesian economics on sound microeconomic foundations' (Nobel Foundation, 2004). Perhaps even more significantly, he was shortly to use techniques from his thesis in his 'Market for "Lemons"' paper (Akerlof, 1970).

After graduating from MIT, Akerlof obtained an assistant professorship at the University of California, Berkeley. In 1967–68 he was visiting professor at the Indian Statistical Institute and he spent the summer of 1969 as a research associate at Harvard University. Akerlof subsequently returned to Berkeley where from 1970 until 1977 he was associate professor. In 1977–78 Akerlof was visiting research economist in the Special Studies Section of the Board of Governors of the Federal Reserve System. From the Fed, Alerlof moved to London where he was Cassel Professor with respect to Money and Banking at the London School of Economics between 1978 and 1980. Since 1980, Akerlof has been Koshland Professor of Economics at Berkeley, and since 1994 he has been Senior Fellow at the Brookings Institution, Washington.

Akerlof's awards and distinctions include vice presidency of the Executive Committee of the American Economic Association, 1988–91 and 1995. He is a fellow of the American Academy of Arts and Sciences and has held Guggenheim and Fulbright fellowships. In 2001, Akerlof was awarded the Nobel Memorial Prize in Economics jointly with A. Michael Spence and Joseph E. Stiglitz 'for their analyses of markets with asymmetric information' (Nobel Foundation, 2004).

The 'Market for "Lemons"' is Akerlof's best-known paper. Indeed it 'is probably the single most important contribution to the literature on economics of information' (Löfgren et al., 2002, p. 197) and is the paper for which Akerlof was awarded the Nobel Memorial Prize. Akerlof wrote this paper – 13 pages long – during his first year at Berkeley in 1966–67 when he was 26 years old. As has been the case for other seminal works by Nobel Memorial Prize recipients (see, for example, the entry on Vernon Smith in this volume), the paper found a home only after a fairly protracted struggle by its author. It was rejected in turn by: the *American Economic Review*, the *Review of Economic Studies* and the *Journal of Political Economy*. The first two rejections were on the grounds of triviality, the last was because the argument Akerlof had advanced was, in the view of the *Journal of Political Economy's* referees, simply wrong. The paper was subsequently accepted and published in the *Quarterly Journal of Economics* in 1970.

Akerlof's original intention in developing the 'Lemons' paper (lemon is an American slang word for a poor-quality car) was to try to show that buyers' information uncertainties about the quality of cars in the used-car market would tend to push them into the new-car market. Motivated by the problem of unemployment and 'the financial hardship and the loss of identity that it entails', Akerlof's wider purpose was to understand fluctuations in new car sales as a causal factor in the exacerbation of the business cycle (Akerlof, 2002). Although he struggled to realise his ambition to model the business cycle, Akerlof saw that his insights into asymmetric information in the used-car market would allow him to say something important about conditions in that market. Moreover, he was able to generalise his conclusions to other markets characterised by asymmetric information.

The 'Lemons' paper demonstrated that the presence of asymmetric information in the used-car market would tend to lower the average quality of cars sold and reduce the size of the overall market: essentially – in what Akerlof noted was a modified version of Gresham's Law – the bad cars would drive out the good, leaving an 'adverse selection' of lemons. Because car buyers have less information than sellers, it is difficult for them to discern whether they are getting a lemon or a car of good quality. Accordingly, prices are depressed given the risk of buying a lemon, and sellers of better cars leave the market because they are unable to realise the 'true value' of their cars (Akerlof, 1970).

Akerlof then went on to show that the inferior market outcomes associated with the presence of asymmetric information might arise in the market for insurance, in the employment of minorities and in credit markets in developing countries. He also suggested that his 'Lemons' model could be used to illustrate the full costs of dishonesty in economic transactions. Such costs extend beyond those incurred by the cheated purchaser of a good (say) misrepresented in value, and would additionally encompass losses arising from the desertion of the market by honest traders.

Finally, the 'Lemons' paper considered the range of institutions that have emerged to offset the effects of information imbalances in markets. Akerlof pointed to product guarantees, branding and licensing as mechanisms of reassurance for the uninformed consumer. Presciently he also noted that skilled labour usually carries 'some certification indicating the attainment of certain levels of proficiency

... even the Nobel Prize, to some degree, serves this function' (Akerlof, 1970 p. 500). Akerlof (1976) offers a more discursive review of the implications of asymmetrical information in a range of settings.

Akerlof's other main contributions to economics have centred on the microtheoretic foundations of New Keynesian behavioural macroeconomics (Akerlof, 2002). He has, for example, produced a number of important papers on efficiency wage theory. This seeks to explain why firms may choose to pay above market-clearing wage rates thereby generating involuntary unemployment (see Akerlof, 1980 and 1982; Akerlof and Yellen, 1990).

Using behavioural macroeconomics, Akerlof has also sought to demonstrate, *pace* monetarist and other interpretations, that monetary policy does influence the paths of real variables such as output and employment. In joint work with Janet Yellen, Akerlof proposed 'near-rational' behaviour by firms following money-supply-induced demand shocks that produces intertial price setting (Akerlof and Yellen, 1985). In the presence of sticky prices there is 'a robust relation between changes in the money supply and changes in output' (Akerlof, 2002, p. 418).

Finally, again in joint work, Akerlof has suggested that the behavioural approach to macroeconomics may provide alternative interpretations of the long-run Phillips curve. In particular, when inflation is low it may not be 'salient' and thus inflationary expectations have a negligible role in wage bargaining. The result is that there is a permanent trade-off between inflation and unemployment in the presence of low inflation (see Akerlof et al., 1996; 2000). For Akerlof (2002, p. 422), this in turn gives rise to a further important implication for the contemporary 'rules-based' conduct of monetary policy: 'Most of us think of central bankers as cautious, conservative and safe. But I consider them to be dangerous drivers: to avoid the oncoming traffic of inflation, they drive on the far edge of the road, keeping inflation too low and unemployment too high'.

Main Published Works

(1970), 'The Market for "Lemons": Quality Uncertainty and the Market Mechanism', *Quarterly Journal of Economics*, **84**, August, pp. 485–500.

(1976), 'The Economics of Caste and of the Rat Race and other Woeful Tales', *Quarterly Journal of Economics*, **90**, November, pp. 599–617.

(1980), 'A Theory of Social Customs of Which Unemployment May Be One Consequence', *Quarterly Journal of Economics*, **94**, June, pp. 749–75.

(1982), 'Labour Contracts as Partial Gift Exchange', *Quarterly Journal of Economics*, **97**, November, pp. 543–69.

(1984), *An Economic Theorist's Book of Tales*, Cambridge: Cambridge University Press.

(1985), 'A Near Rational Model of the Business Cycle with Wage and Price Inertia' (with J. Yellen), *Quarterly Journal of Economics*, **100** (supplement), September, pp. 823–88.

(1990), 'The Fair Wage Hypothesis and Unemployment' (with J. Yellen), *Quarterly Journal of Economics*, **105**, May, pp. 255–83.

(1996), 'The Macroeconomics of Low Inflation' (with W.T. Dickens and G.L. Perry), *Brookings Papers on Economic Activity*, **1**, pp. 1–59.

(2000), 'Near-Rational Wage and Price Setting and the Long-Run Phillips Curve' (with W.T. Dickens and G.L. Perry), *Brookings Papers on Economic Activity*, **1**, pp. 1–44.

(2002), 'Behavioural Macroeconomics and Macroeconomic Behaviour', *American Economic Review*, **92**, June, pp. 411–33.

Secondary Literature

Löfgren, K.-G., T. Persson and J.W. Weibull (2002), 'Markets with Asymmetric Information: The Contributions of George Akerlof, Michael Spence and Joseph Stiglitz', *Scandinavian Journal of Economics*, **104** (2), pp. 195–211.

See also Blaug and Vane (2003, p. 10); Nobel Foundation (2004).

A. Michael Spence (b. 1943)

© The Nobel Foundation

Michael Spence was born in Montclair, New Jersey, USA in 1943 while his mother was visiting friends there. He grew up in Canada, mostly in Toronto where he went to school, but received his college education in the United States and the United Kingdom. Spence was awarded a BA in philosophy by Princeton University in 1966. In 1968, as a Rhodes Scholar at Oxford University, he obtained a BA–MA in mathematics. Spence completed his college education at Harvard University and was awarded a PhD in economics in 1972.

Spence's academic career has been split between the universities of Harvard and Stanford. He began teaching at Harvard in 1971 and remained there as assistant professor until 1973 when he moved to Stanford University to take up a post as associate professor. In 1975 he returned to Harvard, first as an honorary research fellow and then visiting professor. In 1977 he became Professor of Economics at Harvard and in 1984, Dean of the university's Faculty of Arts and Sciences. In 1990 Spence moved once again to Stanford University as Dean of the Graduate School of Business, a post he relinquished in 1999. He is presently Professor Emeritus of Management in the Graduate School of Business at Stanford, and a partner in Oak Hill Capital Partners and Oak Hill Venture Partners.

Spence's awards and distinctions include an Honours Thesis Prize in Philosophy from Princeton University. In 1972 he received the David A. Wells Prize for outstanding doctoral dissertation at Harvard University. He has also been awarded the John Kenneth Galbraith Prize for excellence in teaching at Harvard (1978). In 1981, Spence received the John Bates Clark Medal from the American Economic Association, and in 1983 he was elected a fellow of the American Academy of Arts and Sciences. From 1991 to 1997 he was chairman of the United States' National Research Council Board on Science, Technology and Economic Policy. In 2001 Spence, together with George Akerlof and Joseph Stiglitz, was jointly awarded the Nobel Memorial Prize in Economics 'for their analyses of markets with asymmetric information' (Nobel Foundation, 2004).

Spence's Nobel citation makes reference to his pioneering work in the economics of signalling. Spence (1973; 1974) demonstrated that, in markets with incomplete information, there exist incentives for those with more information to signal it to those with less information. The result is the attainment of market equilibria advantageous to the signallers and which would otherwise not occur.

As a graduate student working on the implications of the incompleteness of information in markets, Spence was advised to read fellow Laureate George Akerlof's then recently published 'Market for "Lemons"' paper. Spence reports that he found the paper 'quite electrifying' (Spence, 2002). Akerlof's central contention in the paper was that in a market with asymmetric information, such as that for used cars, buyers have no means of distinguishing the good-quality cars from the bad (the 'lemons'). This presents the sellers of 'lemons' with an opportunity to pass off their cars as better products than they in fact are. The overall effect is that the potentially separate markets for 'lemons' and high-quality cars fuse into a single market but because the equilibrium price in this market may be too low for the sellers of high-quality cars, they consequently withdraw from the market leaving it with only an *adverse selection* of 'lemons'. The central point here is that the presence of informational uncertainty means that trading opportunities are lost and the market does not perform as well as conventional economic theory suggests (see also the entry on Akerlof in this volume).

Spence's response to Akerlof's paper was to identify how potential employees in the labour market can use signals to convey information to employers about their inherent productivity. In the absence of such signals, poorly informed employers are unable to distinguish between the productivity potential of different employees. In the event that employers fail to offer adequate rewards to potentially higher-productivity employees, the latter exit the market and the result is analogous to Akerlof's adverse selection problem (Spence, 2002). Spence published this work in what Blaug (1998, p. 271) has called 'a brilliant and provocative book' (see Spence, 1974). This was a revised version of Spence's prize-winning Harvard doctoral dissertation and made an important contribution to the economics of information (see entry on Stigler in this volume).

Spence supposed that educational attainment could be used by potential employees to signal information about their ability to prospective employers. Moreover, he assumed that for different groups of workers in the labour market, the costs of education differed; in particular, for high-productivity workers, educational costs – measured in terms of effort, time or expense – were lower than for low-productivity workers. In such circumstances, high-productivity workers have both the necessary cost and reward incentives to make the effort to signal their distinctiveness to potential employers. Low-productivity workers on the other hand have neither.

Spence (2002) points out that it is important that employers' beliefs about the relationship between educational attainment and productivity are 'self-confirming'. So long as employers' faith in the reliability of the signals they receive is maintained, they have an incentive to operate a system of differential reward – in effect to *not* underpay workers who have invested in their own education. This means that, overall, signalling acts to preserve what Spence calls 'multiple equilibria'. In other words, the presence of reliable market signals overcomes the adverse selection problem by preventing effectively separate labour markets from collapsing into one another.

In subsequent work, Spence has made important contributions to the theory of industrial organisation; see, in particular, Spence (1976; 1977). Some of the approaches he has developed have subsequently been taken up in, for example, international trade theory; see Spence (1981).

Main Published Works

(1973), 'Job Market Signalling', *Quarterly Journal of Economics*, **87**, August, pp. 355–74.
(1974), *Market Signalling: Informational Transfer in Hiring and Related Screening Processes*, Cambridge, MA: Harvard University Press.

(1976), 'Product Selection, Fixed Costs and Monopolistic Competition', *Review of Economic Studies*, **43**, June, pp. 217–35.

(1977), 'Entry Capacity, Investment and Oligopolistic Pricing', *Bell Journal of Economics*, **8**, Autumn, pp. 534–44.

(1981), 'The Learning Curve and Competition', *Bell Journal of Economics*, **12**, Spring, pp. 49–70.

(2002), 'Signaling in Retrospect and the Informational Structure of Markets', *American Economic Review*, **92**, June, pp. 434–59.

Secondary Literature

Löfgren, K.-G., T. Persson and J.W. Weibull (2002), 'Markets with Asymmetric Information: The Contributions of George Akerlof, Michael Spence and Joseph Stiglitz', *Scandinavian Journal of Economics*, **104** (2), pp. 195–211.

See also   Beaud and Dostaler (1997, pp. 412–13); Blaug (1998, pp. 271–2; 1999, pp. 1053–4); Nobel Foundation (2004).

Joseph E. Stiglitz
(b. 1943)

© The Nobel Foundation

Joseph Stiglitz was born in Gary, Indiana, USA in 1943. Gary harboured the usual mix of difficulties common to industrial cities in postwar America: 'poverty, periodic unemployment and massive racial discrimination'. Stiglitz reports that he grew up in a household where political discussion was commonplace, moulding him as an 'inquiring youngster' who began to wonder about the economic and social problems around him. This background became significant as Stiglitz commenced his studies in economics. He was taught a theoretical canon which predicted outcomes far removed from the reality he had seen growing up: he knew that full employment was not the norm, that poverty was endemic in even the world's richest society and therefore that there might be reasons to suspect the market-clearing models that were unable to assimilate these and other such phenomena (Nobel Foundation, 2004).

Stiglitz's concerns about the 'competitive equilibrium model' were enormously deepened by a period he spent in Kenya in 1969. If economic theory was in some important respects at variance with what could be observed happening in real markets in the developed world, Stiglitz found models of perfect markets 'truly inappropriate' as a means of trying to understand how developing economies functioned. In particular, the developing world exposed

301

the severe limitations of the array of assumptions upon which the competitive model rested. Stiglitz saw that in Kenya the idiosyncrasies of market institutions and inequalities in the distribution of wealth mattered in ways that conventional economics appeared unwilling to acknowledge. For example, agriculture organised around sharecropping happened because of given patterns of land ownership. That this resulted in what amounted to a 50 per cent or more tax on workers' earnings suggested to Stiglitz that the distribution of income in a society could not be simply assumed away (see Stiglitz, 2002a). Insight and critical reflection of this form were to become hallmarks of Stiglitz's career as a professional economist.

Stiglitz attributes the development of his capacity to question to both his family's influence and the kind of schooling he had. From 1960 to 1963 he attended Amherst College in New England, a liberal arts college where he learned 'that what mattered most was asking the right question – having posed the question well, answering the question was often a relatively easy matter' (Nobel Foundation, 2004). From a wide range of possibilities Stiglitz eventually decided to major in economics at Amherst. He recollects, 'I thought it provided an opportunity for me to apply my interests and abilities in mathematics to important social problems, and somehow, I thought it would also enable me to combine my interest in history and writing. I wanted it all and economics seemed to have it all' (Nobel Foundation, 2004). Amen to that.

Stiglitz actually left Amherst without graduating, although the college awarded him a BA in 1964. He opted for graduate studies at the Massachusetts Institute of Technology (MIT) and his teachers at Amherst thought that he should not complete a senior year with them given that he would repeat the same material at MIT. He was awarded a PhD from MIT in 1966, where his teachers included four subsequent Nobel Laureates: Paul Samuelson, Robert Solow, Franco Modigliani and Kenneth Arrow. After a year at MIT, Stiglitz took up an opportunity to edit Samuelson's collected papers (Stiglitz, 1966–77). Stiglitz relates a story that Samuelson once wrote a letter of recommendation on his behalf that included the opinion that he (Stiglitz) was the best economist to come from Gary, Indiana; Samuelson too was from Gary! In 1965–66, having been awarded a Fulbright Fellowship, Stiglitz attended the University of Cambridge, UK where he was tutored by Joan Robinson – with whom he had a 'tumultuous relationship' – and subsequently Frank Hahn. He received an MA from Cambridge in 1970. In the same year Stiglitz was awarded an MA by Yale University; in 1976 he was awarded an MA by the University of Oxford, UK.

Stiglitz is presently Professor of Economics at Columbia University, New York, a post held since 2001. His career record is highly distinguished. The academic highlights include: assistant professor at MIT (1966–67); assistant and then associate professor at the Cowles Foundation, Yale University (1967–70); from 1966 to 1970, Stiglitz was also Tapp Research Fellow at Gonville and Caius College, Cambridge, UK. His work in Kenya was undertaken as a senior research fellow at University College, Nairobi from 1969 to 1971. In 1970 he was appointed Professor of Economics at Yale, a post held until 1974. From 1974 to 1976 Stiglitz moved to Stanford University as Professor of Economics. After Stanford he returned to the UK and from 1976 to 1979 was Drummond Professor of Political Economy at All Souls College, University of Oxford. He became Professor of Economics at Princeton University in 1979 and remained there until 1988 when he moved back to Stanford. He left Stanford in 2001 for his present post at Columbia.

Stiglitz has had an equally dazzling career in economic policy making. He was appointed to US President Bill Clinton's Council of Economic Advisers in 1993 and served as its chairman from 1995 to 1997. From 1997 to 1999 he was chief economist and senior vice president at the World Bank. Stiglitz relinquished his position at the World Bank under somewhat controversial circumstances not unrelated to his capacity to tenaciously question conventions in economics and, in particular, the policy prescriptions that flow from them. We develop this theme below.

Stiglitz's awards and distinctions include a Guggenheim Fellowship in 1969–70. In 1979 he was awarded the American Economic Association's John Bates Clark Medal. In 1988 Stiglitz won the International Prize from the Academia Lincei in Italy and in 1989 the Science Prize given by Universal Academic Press. He holds honorary doctorates from a number of universities around the world. He is a member of the American National Academy of Sciences and fellow of: the American Philosophical Society, the American Academy of Arts and Sciences and the Econometric Society. Stiglitz was also founding editor of the *Journal of Economic Perspectives*. In 2001, he was awarded the Nobel Memorial Prize in Economics jointly with George A. Akerlof and A. Michael Spence 'for their analyses of markets with asymmetric information' (Nobel Foundation, 2004).

Stiglitz's Nobel citation makes reference to a paper with Michael Rothschild (Rothschild and Stiglitz, 1976) that is a 'natural complement' to the key works of his fellow Laureates, Akerlof and Spence (see their entries in this volume). In this paper, Rothschild and Stiglitz consider the information asymmetries in insurance markets where, typically, insurance providers have less information about the risks faced by their customers than do these individuals themselves. More specifically, Rothschild and Stiglitz explore ways in which insurance providers condition the choices faced by their customers so that they purchase policies in accordance with providers' preferences.

In the presence of perfect – and therefore symmetric – information, insurance companies would offer individual customers policies specifically tailored to the level of risk they carry. Riskier customers would pay more; low-risk customers would pay less. But because in reality information is asymmetric, insurance providers offer policy permutations that 'screen' the market such that different risk groups reveal themselves and gravitate towards different policies. Thus Rothschild and Stiglitz demonstrate that information asymmetries are fundamental to an understanding of how this kind of market operates. In their model, high-risk individuals are willing to pay a higher premium on the understanding that they will receive full compensation in the event of a loss which *they* know is more likely. On the other hand, low-risk individuals choose a lower-cost policy but one that carries a deductible or excess charge which, because *they* know they are low risk, they are willing to accept given the attraction of the lower premium. Rothschild and Stiglitz call the outcome that arises from this self-selection process a 'separating equilibrium'. They also show that their model has no 'pooling equilibrium', that is where all individuals opt for the same policy. The case here is analogous to Akerlof's 'lemons' model. In offering a single policy in the market, insurance providers would set a premium too high for low-risk individuals and thus leave themselves with an adverse selection of high-risk customers. Stiglitz's Nobel citation states that the identification of separating and pooling equilibria has led to a paradigmatic shift in general microeconomic theory and information economics (see Löfgren et al., 2002).

Stiglitz's record of publication is prodigious. His Nobel citation suggests that he 'is probably the most cited researcher within the information economics literature – perhaps also within a wider domain of microeconomics'. One explanation of the sheer scale of his output is his method of working. Stiglitz describes his research style as one that addresses problems from a variety of perspectives, leading to the accumulation of models from which insights and conclusions emerge. The gestation period of his papers is consequently sometimes very long. For example, some material first developed in Kenya in 1969 reached the public domain more than 20 years later.

Stiglitz's (1974a) work on the egregious economics of sharecropping, in particular understanding this institutional form as the product of an asymmetric information problem, was one of his earliest contributions to information economics. With Andrew Weiss, he has explored the implications of information asymmetries in credit markets and used these to account for the phenomenon of credit rationing (see Stiglitz and Weiss, 1981). Building upon work first begun during his time in Kenya, he has – with Carl Shapiro – developed the 'shirking' model explanation of efficiency wages, thereby contributing to an important aspect of new Keynesian macroeconomics (see Shapiro and Stiglitz, 1984). With Sanford Grossman he has demonstrated the significance of informational imperfections in financial markets (see Grossman and Stiglitz, 1980). His work with Bruce Greenwald has illustrated that market failures are pervasive in a way not recognised by the competitive model and that these failures rest on informational imperfections or incomplete markets (see Greenwald and Stiglitz, 1986). Stiglitz's Nobel citation also acknowledges important work he has published in other areas of economics, in particular: public economics (Stiglitz and Dasgupta, 1971), industrial organisation (Dixit and Stiglitz, 1977) and the economics of natural resources (Stiglitz, 1974b).

As noted, Stiglitz has worked in the highest echelons of US and international policy making. At the World Bank he was strongly critical of the Washington consensus approach to development promoted by the International Monetary Fund (IMF) and, to Stiglitz's consternation, the US Treasury. In his view, the IMF's policy prescriptions were 'based on an incorrect understanding of economic theory' – one that ignored recent advances, including those in information economics – and 'an inadequate interpretation of the historical data'. Stiglitz's views are summarised in his best-selling book, *Globalization and Its Discontents* (Stiglitz, 2002b).[23]

Main Published Works

(1966–77), *Collected Scientific Papers of Paul A. Samuelson* (ed.), Cambridge, MA: MIT Press.

(1971), 'Differential Taxation, Public Goods and Economic Efficiency' (with P. Dasgupta), *Review of Economic Studies*, **38**, April, pp. 151–74.

(1974a), 'Incentives and Risk Sharing in Sharecropping', *Review of Economic Studies*, **41**, April, pp. 219–55.

(1974b), 'Growth with Exhaustible Natural Resources: Efficient and Optimal Growth Paths', *Review of Economic Studies*, **41** (128), Special Issue pp.123–37.

(1976), 'Equilibrium in Competitive Insurance Markets: An Essay on the Economics of Imperfect Information' (with M. Rothschild), *Quarterly Journal of Economics*, **90**, November, pp. 629–49.

(1977), 'Monopolistic Competition and Optimal Product Diversity' (with A. Dixit), *American Economic Review*, **67**, June, pp. 481–513.

(1980), 'On the Impossibility of Informationally Efficient Markets' (with S. Grossman), *American Economic Review*, **70**, June, pp. 393–408.

(1981), 'Credit Rationing in Markets with Imperfect Information' (with A. Weiss), *American Economic Review*, **71**, June, pp. 393–410.

(1984), 'Equilibrium Unemployment as a Worker Discipline Device' (with C. Shapiro), *American Economic Review*, **74**, June, pp. 433–44.

(1986), 'Externalities in Economies with Imperfect Information and Incomplete Markets' (with B. Greenwald), *Quarterly Journal of Economics*, **101**, May, pp. 229–64.

(2002a), 'Information and the Change in the Paradigm in Economics', *American Economic Review*, **92**, June, 460–81.

(2002b), *Globalization and Its Discontents*, New York: W.W. Norton.

Secondary Literature

Löfgren, K.-G., T. Persson and J.W. Weibull (2002), 'Markets With Asymmetric Information: The Contributions of George Akerlof, Michael Spence and Joseph Stiglitz', *Scandinavian Journal of Economics*, **104** (2), pp. 195–211.

Rosser, J. Barkley (2003), 'A Nobel Prize for Asymmetric Information: The Economic Contributions of George Akerlof, Michael Spence and Joseph Stiglitz', *Review of Political Economy*, **15** (1), pp. 3–21.

See also Beaud and Dostaler (1997, pp. 421–2); Blaug (1998, pp. 279–80); Blaug and Vane (2003, pp. 801–2); Nobel Foundation (2004).

---

[23] At a World Bank sponsored launch of the book, an IMF-based discussant, Kenneth Rogoff, made a splenetic attack on Stiglitz over his criticisms of the IMF (for the full text of this extraordinary speech see www.imf.org/external/np/vc/2002/070202.htm).

THE 2002 NOBEL MEMORIAL LAUREATES

DANIEL KAHNEMAN AND VERNON SMITH

© The Nobel Foundation

Daniel Kahneman
(b. 1934)

Daniel Kahneman was born in Tel Aviv (now in Israel) in 1934 while his mother was visiting family there. His parents were Lithuanian Jews who had emigrated to France in the early 1920s and Kahneman spent his childhood in Paris. Following the German invasion the family fled to Vichy France, though not before Kahneman's father had been interned for a time in the notorious Drancy transit camp. After the war, Kahneman moved to Palestine with his mother and sister. His father had died of diabetes a short time before the Allied invasion of Normandy (Nobel Foundation, 2004).

Kahneman's decision to become a psychologist rested on his youthful interest in questions about faith, human existence and morality. Interestingly, the vocational guidance he received before university suggested that he should study psychology, but economics came a close second. He was awarded a BA in psychology and mathematics at the Hebrew University, Jerusalem in 1954 and a PhD in psychology from the University of California, Berkeley in 1961.

Kahneman was a visiting scientist in the Department of Psychology at the University of Michigan in 1965–66 and Lecturer in Psychology at Harvard University in 1966–67. He worked at the Applied Psychological Research Unit at Cambridge University in 1968–69.

Between 1970 and 1978 he returned to Jerusalem and was first associate professor and then professor at the Hebrew University. In 1978 Kahneman was appointed Professor of Psychology at the University of British Columbia, a post held until 1986. Between 1984 and 1986 he was also an associate fellow of the Canadian Institute for Advanced Research. From 1986 until 1994 Kahneman was Professor of Psychology at the University of California, Berkeley. In 1991–92 he was also a Russell Sage Foundation Visiting Scholar. Kahneman is presently Eugene Higgins Professor of Psychology and Professor of Public Affairs, Woodrow Wilson School; both posts are at Princeton University and have been held since 1993. He is also a fellow at the Center for Rationality at the Hebrew University, a post held since 2000.

Kahneman's awards and distinctions – of which there are more than 20 on his CV at the time of writing – include the award of the Warren Medal by the Society of Experimental Psychologists and the Hilgard Award for Lifetime Contributions to General Psychology, both in 1995. In 2002 he received a Career Achievement Award from the Society of Medical Decision Making and, jointly with Amos Tversky, the Grawemeyer Prize in Psychology. In the same year he was awarded the Nobel Memorial Prize in Economics 'for having integrated insights from psychological research into economic science, especially concerning human judgment and decision-making under uncertainty' (Nobel Foundation, 2004).

Kahneman's work has focused on aspects of bounded rationality. It has contributed to a deeper and more satisfactory understanding of decision making by economic agents. Kahneman has demonstrated the limitations of the economist's traditional attachment to rational behaviour and offered an alternative model – prospect theory – in its stead. Much of Kahneman's writing was done with Amos Tversky. At a press conference in Princeton to mark the announcement of the Nobel Memorial award, Kahneman acknowledged his debt in saying:

> The work for which I'm honoured today is work I did collaboratively with a close friend and a very famous psychologist, Amos Tversky, who died in 1996. Certainly we would have gotten this together, and that's one of the things that this means to me today. There is that shadow over the joy I feel.

In a highly influential paper in *Science*, Tversky and Kahneman (1974) identified a number of valuable heuristics commonly used by individuals to simplify complex tasks of judgement. Their insight was to show that these heuristics, although often leading to reasonable answers, also result in systematic and therefore predictable errors or biases. For economics, this means that assumed rationality is not otiose, rather it is limited in consistent ways: hence the notion of *bounded* rationality. The baby need not be thrown out with the bath water (see Kahneman, 2003).

Tversky and Kahneman considered three heuristics: representativeness, availability, and adjustment and anchoring, and explored a range of problems associated with each. For a fuller review than is given here, see Tversky and Kahneman (1974) and Rabin (2003) (see also Kahneman and Tversky, 1973; 2000 and Kahneman et al., 1982; 2002).

Representativeness involves judgements based on probabilities derived from the resemblance of objects, events or processes to one another: 'For example, when A is highly representative of B, the probability that A originates from B is judged to be high. On the other hand, if A is not similar to B, the probability that A originates from B is judged to be low' (Tversky and Kahneman, 1974, p. 1124). The problem is that representativeness does not encompass several criteria that are important for making probability judgements. One such criterion is identified by Tversky and Kahneman as 'insensitivity to predictability'. This suggests that agents may make inaccurate numerical predictions on the basis of information inappropriate to the purpose of prediction. As an illustration, Tversky and Kahneman suggest that the image of a firm one receives may be suggestive of a predicted profit outcome: a high profit may be representative of a favourable image, a low profit representative of a poor image. But, if there is no information available that has a direct and necessary bearing on profit, there is no basis for different predictions: Tversky and Kahneman suggest that a uniform outcome – such as average profit – should be predicted for all firms.

A second source of bias associated with the representativeness heuristic reflects people's insensitivity to the importance of sample size in making judgements. For example, Tversky and Kahneman (1974) found that subjects assigned the same probability of obtaining an average height of greater than 6 feet to samples of 1000, 100 and 10 men. Rabin (2003) suggests that the tendency to overinfer on the basis of short sequences may provide insights into many economic phenomena. He argues that because we exaggerate the likelihood that, for example, a bad financial analyst will make one poor prediction in three forecasts, we also tend to incorrectly estimate the skill of an analyst who makes three accurate forecasts: 'people ... come to believe in much more variation in skill than in fact exists; somebody who makes successful investments three years in a row may be labelled a financial genius, when in reality she was just lucky' (ibid., p. 162).

When people assess the probability of an outcome or the size of a class with given properties by the ease with which concomitant events or classes can be recalled to mind, they are using a judgemental heuristic that Tversky and Kahneman call 'availability'. As with representativeness, this is a potentially useful means of estimation but because it is influenced by factors beyond probability or the frequency with which a class occurs, it too can lead to predictable biases. Among several examples, perhaps the most evident are those arising from the 'retrievability of instances'. Tversky and Kahneman use this phrase to describe judgements in which more striking evidence is accorded disproportionate weight. For example, one might explain the moral panic over asylum seekers in the UK in 2003 by reference to the disproportionate and sensationalist media coverage of this matter, and the marginalisation in the public mind of, by any objective account, more serious economic and social issues such as drug use.

A third heuristic – adjustment and anchoring – is used when people form estimates on the basis of an initial value to which some adjustment is made to produce a final value. Tversky and Kahneman point out that because, typically, adjustments are insufficient, estimates are biased towards starting values. They call this tendency 'anchoring'. An example of the kinds of bias that can arise from anchoring concerns misperception of the significance of conjunctive and disjunctive events. Tversky and Kahneman take planning as an instance of a conjunctive process. In the development of a new product a series of events must happen but 'even when each of these events is very likely, the overall probability of success can be quite low if the number of events is large'. The result is that estimates of the probability of conjunctive events and that the product will therefore succeed tend to be unjustifiably optimistic. On the other hand, risk evaluation in the context of disjunctive events can lead to the underestimation of risk. Tversky and Kahneman take the example of a nuclear reactor as a complex system dependent on many essential components. The probability that any one component will fail may be low but reactor catastrophe is more likely the greater the number of components involved. Anchoring shifts perceptions onto the likelihood of failure in disjunctive components and therefore the probability of failure tends to be underestimated. Tversky and Kahneman draw the general implication that the direction of anchoring bias may be inferred from the structure of the event: 'the chain-like structure of conjunctions leads to overestimation, the funnel-like structure of disjunction leads to underestimation'.

In Kahneman's view, the importance of the *Science* paper on heuristics was that it engaged the interest of scholars in other disciplines such as economics and philosophy. He also thinks that the paper became so influential not simply because it offered a means to critique the rational-agent model but also because of the way it was written. Directly citing in the text the single question and answer method he and Tversky used to explore human judgement made for a more compelling message than would have a drier more discursive approach. Kahneman also acknowledges that he and Tversky found their wider audience in a rather fortunate way. They did not set out to develop an explicit critique of the rational-agent model. Their purpose was simply to present the evidence they had uncovered on judgement under uncertainty, others then used this as a means to reflect on the shortcomings inherent in rationality (see Nobel Foundation, 2004).

In what was to become a widely cited paper in *Econometrica*, Kahneman and Tversky (1979) offered what they called 'prospect theory' as an alternative to standard utility theory. Prospect theory provides more satisfactory accounts of the observed behaviour of economic agents. Whereas utility theory emphasises satisfaction based on levels of current consumption, prospect theory suggests that agents use references to, for example, past consumption to determine gains and losses in utility. It is the changes in consumption (or wealth) from given reference points that are the 'carriers of utility'. Prospect theory indicates that agents are loss averse and that losses tend to be weighted twice as heavily as gains of the same size. According to Kahneman (Nobel Foundation, 2004), 'Loss aversion is manifest in the extraordinary reluctance to accept risk that is observed when people are offered a gamble in which they might lose $20, unless they are offered more than $40 if they win'.

Kahneman considers loss aversion to be his and Tversky's most useful contribution to the study of decision making.

An interesting aside: why *prospect* theory? Kahneman relates that he and Tversky agreed on the name because it was 'meaningless'. They supposed that the distinctiveness of the label would be its most valuable characteristic should the theory gain ground (Nobel Foundation, 2004).

An important dimension of loss aversion was identified by an economist, Richard Thaler (Thaler, 1980). This – the endowment effect – suggests that people become more attached to an item of wealth once they own it. Thaler illustrated the endowment effect using the example of the owner of a bottle of vintage wine who would refuse to sell it for $200 but would not pay $100 to replace it if it was smashed (cited in Nobel Foundation, 2004). The point being that ownership of the bottle increases its perceived value. Once the good is lost, its value premium disappears. Jointly with Thaler and another economist, Jack Knetsch, Kahneman published the results of experiments with real goods that confirmed the endowment effect and its roots in loss aversion (Kahneman et al., 1990). As Kahneman and others have pointed out, loss aversion working through the endowment effect can have important implications in economics: for example, in explaining the sluggishness of property markets when prices are low: owners are reluctant to sell when the market value does not match their own endowment-inflated valuation of their property (Rabin, 2003; and see Genesove and Mayer, 2001).

In continued collaboration with Tversky, Kahneman published work that demonstrated how the structure of equivalent sets of questions about a given problem could influence the choice of solution; this phenomenon is known as framing. Tversky and Kahneman (1986a) asked 152 subjects to choose between two public health programmes as responses to a hypothetical epidemic that is expected to kill 600 people. The first programme saves 200 lives. The second programme gives a one-third probability that 600 people will be saved and a two-thirds probability that no one will be saved. Seventy-two per cent of subjects preferred the first programme (see also Kahneman and Tversky, 1984).

A different group of 155 subjects was presented with an identical problem but framed in a different way: if the first programme is adopted, 400 people will die; if the second programme is adopted, there is a one-third probability that no one will die and a two-thirds probability that 600 people will die. In this case, 78 per cent of subjects preferred the second programme. In Kahneman's view, the potency of framing demonstrates a boundary to both cognitive power and, by implication the rational-agent model. Rationality requires a consistent or, in Tversky and Kahneman's phrase, an 'invariant' response to sets of questions such as those summarised above.

Kahneman has also published research that explores the perception of fairness in economic transactions (Kahneman et al., 1986b). Rabin (2003) suggests that this work illustrates the most important application of framing in economics: it explains aspects of money illusion. Rabin offers a simple example by way of illustration:

> [A] nominal wage increase of 5 per cent in a period of 12 per cent inflation offends people's sense of fairness less than a 7 per cent decrease in a time of no inflation. More generally, people react more to decreases in real wages when they are also nominal decreases, and react negatively to nominal price increases even if they represent no increase in real prices. (Rabin, 2003, p. 175)

Another aspect of Kahneman's work explores the practice of 'contingent valuation'. For example, in the questions around the provision of public goods, 'the translation of attitudes into dollars involves the almost arbitrary choice of a scale factor, leading some people to state very different values of their willingness to pay, for no good reason' (Nobel Foundation, 2004; and see Kahneman and Knetch, 1992; Kahneman et al., 1999).

Kahneman's current research focuses on the study of 'experienced' utility – a Benthamite conception of utility (see, for example, Kahneman, 1994; Kahneman et al., 1997). Kahneman argues that because agents are not rational, they have no innate capacity for utility maximisation. Whether or not utility is maximised thus becomes a question open to empirical resolution; this has led Kahneman to explore new approaches to the measurement of well-being and welfare.

Main Published Works

(1973), 'On the Psychology of Prediction' (with A. Tversky), *Psychological Review*, **80** (4), pp. 237–51.

(1974) 'Judgment Under Uncertainty: Heuristics and Biases' (with A. Tversky), *Science*, **185**, pp. 1124–31.

(1979), 'Prospect Theory: An Analysis of Decisions Under Risk' (with A. Tversky), *Econometrica*, **47**, March, pp. 263–91.

(1982), *Judgment Under Uncertainty: Heuristics and Biases* (ed. with P. Slovic and A. Tversky), Cambridge: Cambridge University Press.

(1984), 'Choices, Values and Frames' (with A. Tversky), *American Psychologist*, **39** (4), pp. 341–50.

(1986a), 'Rational Choice and the Framing of Decisions' (with A. Tversky), *Journal of Business*, **59**, October, S251–S278.

(1986b), 'Fairness as a Constraint on Profit Seeking: Entitlements in the Market' (with J. Knetsch and R. Thaler), *American Economic Review*, **76**, September, pp. 728–41.

(1990), 'Experimental Tests of the Endowment Effect and the Coase Theorem' (with J. Knetsch and R. Thaler), *Journal of Political Economy*, **98**, December, pp. 1325–48.

(1991), 'The Endowment Effect, Loss Aversion and Status Quo Bias' (with J. Knetsch and R. Thaler), *Journal of Economic Perspectives*, **5**, Winter, pp. 193–206.

(1992), 'Valuing Public Goods: The Purchase of Moral Satisfaction' (with J. Knetsch), *Journal of Environmental Economics and Management*, **22**, January, pp. 57–70.

(1994), 'New Challenges to the Rationality Assumption', *Journal of Institutional and Theoretical Economics*, **150**, March, pp. 18–36.

(1997), 'Back to Bentham? Explorations of Experienced Utility' (with P.P. Walker and R. Sarin), *Quarterly Journal of Economics*, **112**, May, pp. 375–405.

(1999), 'Economic Preferences or Attitude Expressions? An Analysis of Dollar Responses to Public Issues' (with I. Ritov and D. Schkade), *Journal of Risk and Uncertainty*, **19**, August, pp. 220–42.

(2000), *Choices, Values and Frames* (ed. with A. Tversky), Cambridge: Cambridge University Press and New York: Russell Sage Foundation.

(2002), *Heuristics and Biases: The Psychology of Intuitive Judgment* (ed. with T. Gilovich and D. Griffin), Cambridge: Cambridge University Press.

(2003), 'Maps of Bounded Rationality: Psychology for Behavioural Economics', *American Economic Review*, **93**, December, pp. 1449–75.

Secondary Literature

Genosove, D. and D. Mayer (2001), 'Loss Aversion and Seller Behaviour: Evidence from the Housing Market', *Quarterly Journal of Economics*, **116**, November, pp. 1233–60.

Rabin, M. (2003), 'The Nobel Memorial Prize for Daniel Kahneman', *Scandinavian Journal of Economics*, **105** (2), pp. 157–80.

Thaler, R. (1980), 'Towards a Positive Theory of Consumer Choice', *Journal of Economic Behaviour and Organization*, **1**, March, pp. 39–60.

See also Blaug and Vane (2003, pp. 438–40); Nobel Foundation (2004).

© The Nobel Foundation

Vernon L. Smith
(b. 1927)

Vernon Smith was born in Wichita, Kansas, USA in 1927. He was awarded a BS in electrical engineering by the California Institute of Technology (Caltech) in 1949. As an undergraduate, Smith recalls attending lectures given by visiting scholars such as Robert Oppenheimer and Bertrand Russell. His interest in economics was stimulated by a course he took in the subject at Caltech. Wider reading acquainted Smith with a number of different approaches to economics, some of which complemented the methodologies of physics and engineering with which he was already familiar. To discover whether or not he might have a career appetite for economics, Smith returned to Kansas and studied for a master's degree. He was awarded an MA in economics by the University of Kansas in 1952. In his Nobel Memorial Prize autobiographical notes, Smith remembers being particularly influenced by a course in the development of economic thought taken as part of his master's programme. The material he encountered allowed him 'to acquire knowledge of all the supporting structure, tools and primary sources of inspiration' in economics (Nobel Foundation, 2004). Smith's commitment to the discipline was by now confirmed and he moved to Harvard University, completing a PhD in 1955. Here he was taught by, among others, Alvin Hansen and Wassily Leontief; he also took courses from Paul Samuelson at nearby Massachusetts Institute of Technology.

Smith's first teaching post after leaving Harvard was in Indiana at Purdue University, where he remained until 1967. At Purdue he was assistant professor (1955–56), associate professor (1957–59) and professor (from 1961). In 1961–62 he was visiting associate professor at Stanford University. In 1967, Smith took up a professorship at Brown University, leaving the following year for a similar post at the University of Massachusetts where he worked until 1975. From 1974–75, Smith was visiting professor at Caltech. In 1975 he moved to the University of Arizona at Tucson as Regents' Professor of Economics. Since 2001 Smith has been Professor of Economics and Law at George Mason University, Arlington, Virginia.

Smith's awards and distinctions include past presidencies of the Public Choice Society, the Economic Science Association and the Western Economic Association. He has been a Sherman Fairchild Distinguished Scholar at Caltech, a Ford Foundation fellow and a fellow of the Center for Advanced Study in the Behavioural Sciences. He is a fellow of the Econometric Society, the American Association for the Advancement of Science and the American Academy of Arts and Sciences. In 2002, Smith was awarded the Nobel Memorial Prize in Economics 'for having established laboratory experiments as a tool in empirical economic analysis, especially in the study of alternative market mechanisms' (Nobel Foundation, 2004).

In his first teaching post at Purdue University, Smith 'found it a challenge to convey basic microeconomic theory to students. Why/ how could any market approximate a competitive equilibrium?' (Nobel Foundation, 2004). While at Harvard, Smith had participated in E.H. Chamberlin's class-based experimental demonstration that markets need *not* produce the equilibrium outcomes predicted by economic theory because they are imperfectly structured. Chamberlin assigned buyer and seller roles to students in class to produce his results. This method proved to be Smith's inspiration but he modified it for use at Purdue in two important ways: first, he refined the institutional setting to make it more open and competitive and, second, he allowed for several successive 'trading days', so that participants could learn from their experiences in the experimental marketplace.

Smith found his results quite staggering: instead of confirming Chamberlin's work, they contradicted it. Equilibrium rapidly emerged in accordance with the strictures of price theory and this continued to happen regardless of nuances in the design of the basic experiment. Even when the number of agents was limited to single figures, equilibrium was still reached. Smith had certainly found a powerful means to illustrate the simple elegance of the market mechanism to his students. Getting his work accepted by his peers proved a rather more difficult proposition. These early experiments were eventually reported in a paper in the *Journal of Political Economy* (Smith, 1962), though only 'after two revisions, four negative referee reports and an initial rejection' (Nobel Foundation, 2004). Even economists who will one day win the Nobel Memorial Prize sometimes have it tough.

Further experiments investigated the influence of actual financial rewards on the behaviour of student subjects as economic agents. Smith found that paying subjects according to their 'success' in the marketplace was a powerful means of ensuring that their motives reflected those the investigator was trying to reproduce. He also discovered that the greater the reward, the faster the emergence of 'rational' behaviour among subjects (Smith, 1964).

Smith's growing interest and expertise led him to offer a graduate seminar in economic experimentation at Purdue starting in 1963. His lecture notes from this period would later form the basis of a paper in the *American Economic Review* on induced valuation (Smith, 1976a). The Nobel Memorial citation for Smith declares that this paper as 'a practical and detailed guide to the design of economic experiments in the laboratory and a motivation for these guidelines … serves as a paradigm for experimental scholars in economics' (Nobel Foundation, 2004).

In collaboration with others, Smith demonstrated that the institutional form assumed by a market may have an important bearing on the way it functions (see, for example, Plott and Smith, 1978; Smith and Williams, 1981). This confirmed the implication from Smith's earlier refinement of Chamberlin's original model that the design of a market could be tested and improved in the laboratory. Experiments clearly facilitate forms of research in economics that cannot be accomplished by the observation of field data from actual markets. One further application of this approach by Smith has been to test the efficiency of alternative designs for public goods delivery mechanisms (see, for example, Smith, 1980a).

Smith's Nobel Memorial citation includes specific reference to his work on auctions (Nobel Foundation, 2004). Although auctions have recently become big business, sometimes yielding immense sums to governments if not the economists advising them (see Binmore and Klemperer, 2002), Smith has been applying the methodology of experimental economics to auction theory for a long time (see, for example, Smith, 1965). With colleagues, he has uncovered a series of regularities associated with different auction forms (see, for example, Smith, 1976b; Coppinger et al., 1980b).

In his highly stimulating Nobel Memorial Prize Lecture, Smith employs a distinction between 'constructivist' and 'ecological' rationality to help explain the significance of experimental economics. Constructivism embraces the familiar perfectly knowledgeable rational agent who is situated in an institutional context suited to his or her capacities and motivations. But this conceptualisation is 'unlikely to approximate the level of ignorance that has conditioned either individual behaviour, or our evolved institutions' (Smith, 2003, p. 506). In contrast, following Adam Smith, ecological rationality understands economic behaviour and institutional forms to possess a social-grown and multiply-determined 'emergent order'. Agents need not be all-knowing or consistently act in an immediately self-interested fashion; nor must institutions be immediately fully formed and complete: economic order and progress still happens. Smith argues that experimental economics can bridge the gap between these two interpretations of rationality. For example, designs for economic systems or institutions might be produced using constructivist rationality: we propose what we think might work. It then becomes possible to mirror the process of an emergent order by employing the methodology of experimental economics to test, modify and rework these designs. This use of the laboratory as a design 'wind tunnel' is also highlighted in Smith's Nobel Memorial citation.

In addition to his pioneering work in experimental economics, Smith has also made important contributions to a number of other areas including: the theory of investment and production (see, for example, Smith, 1959; 1961) and natural resource economics (see, for example, Smith 1968; 1971; 1975). For a collection of key papers in experimental economics the reader is referred to Smith (1979; 1982; 1985; 1991).

Main Published Works

(1959), 'The Theory of Investment and Production', *Quarterly Journal of Economics*, **73**, February, pp. 61–87.

(1961), *Investment and Production*, Cambridge, MA: Harvard University Press.

(1962), 'An Experimental Study of Competitive Market Behaviour', *Journal of Political Economy*, **70**, April, pp. 111–37.

(1964), 'Effect of Market Organization on Economic Behaviour', *Quarterly Journal of Economics*, **87**, May, pp. 181–203.

(1965), 'Experimental Auction Markets and the Walrasian Hypothesis', *Journal of Political Economy*, **73**, August, pp. 387–93.

(1968), 'Economics of Production from Natural Resources', *American Economic Review*, **58**, June, pp. 409–31.

(1971), *Economics of Natural and Environmental Economics*, New York: Gordon & Breach.

(1975), 'Economics of the Primitive Hunter Culture with Application to Pleistocene Extinction and the Rise of Agriculture', *Journal of Political Economy*, **83**, July–August, pp. 727–55.

(1976a), 'Experimental Economics: Induced Value Theory', *American Economic Review*, **66**, May, pp. 274–9.

(1976b), 'Bidding and Auctioning Institutions: Experimental Results', in Y. Amihud (ed.), *Bidding and Auctioning for Procurement and Allocation*, New York: New York University Press.

(1978), 'An Experimental Examination of Two Exchange Institutions' (with C. Plott), *Review of Economic Studies*, **45**, February, pp. 133–53.

(1979), *Research in Experimental Economics*, vol. 1 (ed.), Greenwich, CT: JAI Press.

(1980a), 'Experiments with a Decentralised Mechanism for Public Goods Decisions', *American Economic Review*, **70**, September, pp. 584–99.

(1980b), 'Incentives and Behaviour in English, Dutch, and Sealed-Bid Auctions' (with V.M. Coppinger and J.A. Titus), *Economic Enquiry*, **18**, pp. 1–18.

(1981), 'On Nonbinding Price Controls in a Competitive Market' (with A.W. Williams), *American Economic Review*, **71**, June, pp. 467–74.

(1982), *Research in Experimental Economics*, vol. 2 (ed.), Greenwich, CT: JAI Press.

(1985), *Research in Experimental Economics*, vol. 3 (ed.), Greenwich, CT: JAI Press.

(1991), *Papers in Experimental Economics*, New York and Melbourne: Cambridge University Press.

(2003), 'Constructivist and Ecological Rationality in Economics', *American Economic Review*, **93**, June, pp. 465–508.

Secondary Literature

Bergstrom, T.C. (2003), 'Vernon Smith's Insomnia and the Dawn of Economics as Experimental Science', *Scandinavian Journal of Economics*, **105** (2), pp. 181–205.

Binmore, K. and P. Klemperer (2002), 'The Biggest Auction Ever: The Sale of the British 3G Telecom Licenses', *Economic Journal*, **112**, March, C74–C96.

See also Blaug and Vane (2003, pp. 785–6); Nobel Foundation (2004).

THE 2003 NOBEL MEMORIAL LAUREATES

ROBERT ENGLE
AND
CLIVE GRANGER

Robert F. Engle
(b. 1942)

© The Nobel Foundation

Robert Engle was born in Syracuse, New York, USA in 1942. He grew up near Philadelphia, Pennsylvania and attended Williams College; he graduated from Williams with a BS in 1964, achieving highest honours in physics. From a young age he had a strong interest in science – his father had a PhD in chemistry – and Engle elected to continue with physics in graduate school at Cornell University. He was awarded an MS by Cornell in 1966. However, even before starting graduate school, he felt his attachment to physics was weakening. At Williams, Engle had filled up his senior-year programme with an elective in economics that he had enjoyed and, before completing his MS, he approached the Economics Department at Cornell to ask about the possibility of changing disciplines. The department offered him a PhD fellowship and he accepted it, taking undergraduate classes in economics while he completed his master's in physics. Cornell awarded Engle a PhD in economics in 1969. In an interview in *Econometric Theory*, Engle reflected on the advantages a background in physics can lend to an econometrician given the emphasis on the integration of theory and data common to both subjects; however, interestingly, he has also acknowledged the difficulties of his late discipline switch: 'It was probably ten years before I really absorbed the economic way of thinking' (see Diebold, 2003; Nobel Foundation, 2004).

Engle's first academic post was in 1969 as assistant, later associate, professor at the Massachusetts Institute of Technology (MIT). At Cornell he had developed an interest in time-series econometrics but this was not much of a focus for the economists at MIT and Engle found his place there 'complicated' (Nobel Foundation, 2004). Involvement with the Boston Redevelopment Authority allowed him to develop his skills in economic modelling and he became an urban economist. With the encouragement of his fellow Laureate Clive Granger, Engle left MIT in 1975 for the University of California at San Diego (UCSD), where he was appointed associate professor, and where he continued to teach urban economics. At the time Granger was professor at UCSD. Engle was promoted to Professor of Economics at UCSD in 1977. In 1999 he moved as professor to the Stern School of Business at New York University, and since 2003 he has been Michael Armellino Professor in the Management of Financial Services in the Stern School.

Engle's honours and awards include fellowships of the Econometric Society (1981), the American Academy of Arts and Sciences (1995), and the American Statistical Association (2000). He has been a research associate of the National Bureau of Economic Research since 1987 and received an Excellence in Teaching Award from the MIT Graduate Economics Association in 1974–75. Jointly with Clive Granger, Engle was awarded the 2003 Nobel Memorial Prize in Economics 'for methods of analysing economic time series with time-varying volatility (ARCH)' (Nobel Foundation, 2004).

In honouring Engle with a Nobel Prize, the Royal Swedish Academy of Sciences highlighted the contribution of his 1982 *Econometrica* paper, 'Autoregressive Conditional Heteroscedasticity with Estimates of the Variance of United Kingdom Inflation', to econometric method. In this paper, Engle announced his discovery of a model – known by the acronym ARCH – that facilitated the measurement of uncertainty in an economic process, where uncertainty was itself subject to change. In developing ARCH, Engle's purpose had been to try to test Milton Friedman's proposition that business cycles were rooted in entrepreneurial uncertainties over *future* rates of inflation: trepidation about what might happen to prices could make businesses cautious and reluctant to invest, thus prompting an economic downturn. As Engle (2004, p. 406) notes, for Friedman to be right, uncertainty 'had to be changing over time'. It turned out that, though there was variation in the uncertainty in inflation forecasts for both the UK and, as Engle subsequently found, for the United States, it did not appear to have business-cycle implications in either context. Engle suggests that this may reflect the multiple determination problem common in macroeconomics which renders uncertainty one among several factors of influence. He also points to the differences associated with relatively low-frequency data in macroeconomic time series. However, if the deployment of ARCH in macroeconomics was not particularly fruitful, Engle found the field of finance much more receptive: here, uncertainty over the returns on assets is a clear imperative in decision making, and high-frequency data are readily to hand to underpin the modelling process. Engle (1987a), in collaboration with David Lilien and Russel Robins, is his first application of ARCH to finance.

The balance between risk and reward is central to financial economics. Engle's ARCH model provides a means to evaluate the volatility of the returns on assets – such as shares – and hence their associated risks. A common approach to risk assessment has been to assess 'historical volatility' by using the standard deviation of returns over a given time period (Engle, 2004). But then the question becomes over what period should volatility be measured? The difficulty is that returns are subject to 'volatility clustering' (Engle, 2001). In other words, to reprise an earlier point, uncertainty – here over returns – is itself subject to change. For example, for most share indices, large movements in returns are typically followed by further large movements, and small fluctuations tend to be similarly tracked by equally modest changes. The ARCH model resolves the problem of choosing the 'right' period over which to measure volatility by taking weighted averages of past squared forecast errors generated by a statistical analysis (Engle, 2004). Such weights assign more importance to recent information – acknowledging clustering – and less to information that is dated. The whole analysis turns on the treatment of heteroscedasticity – meaning that uncertainty is time-varying – not as a statistical problem of least squares but as something that can be tested for and fruitfully modelled (Engle, 2001). Once this has been done it becomes possible to measure and forecast volatility as an aid to risk analysis and as a means of tackling other financial problems such as options pricing, an area to which Engle has also contributed (see Engle et al., 1994a). ARCH has been generalised, and its acronym consequently extended to GARCH, by Tim Bollerslev, a student of Engle's. Although not carrying any new insights, GARCH is useful, and popular, given that it permits relatively parsimonious specification (Nobel Foundation, 2004).

ARCH has spawned a voluminous literature. Notable works by Engle here include explanations of volatility rooted in the impact of turbulence in early-closing markets on markets that close later (see Engle et al., 1990). More recently Engle, with Jeffrey Russell, has proposed the autoregressive conditional duration (ACD) model, which uses the clustering of market trades to forecast the arrival probability of the next trade (Engle and Russell, 1998). Other work by Engle acknowledged by the Royal Swedish Academy includes pivotal research on cointegration with his fellow Nobel Laureate, Clive Granger. Engle and Granger (1987b) 'is perhaps the most cited paper in the history of econometrics' (Diebold, 2004, p. 166). Other important papers by Engle include those on exogeneity, for example, Engle et al., (1983). Engle has also jointly edited books on cointegration (Engle and Granger, 1991), and econometrics (Engle and McFadden, 1994b). Finally, Engle (1995) is a collection of papers on ARCH.

Main Published Works

(1982), 'Autoregressive Conditional Heteroscedasticity with Estimates of the Variance of United Kingdom Inflation', *Econometrica*, **50**, July, pp. 987–1007.

(1983), 'Exogeneity' (with D.F. Hendry and J.-F. Richard), *Econometrica*, **51**, March, pp. 277–304.

(1987a), 'Estimating Time-Varying Risk Premia in the Term Structure: the ARCH-M Model' (with D.M. Lilien and R.P. Robins), *Econometrica*, **55**, March, pp. 391–407.

(1987b), 'Co-integration and Error-Correction: Representation, Estimation and Testing' (with C.W.J. Granger), *Econometrica*, **55**, March, pp. 251–76.

(1990) 'Meteor Showers or Heat Waves – Heteroscedastic Intradaily Volatility in the Foreign-Exchange Market' (with T. Ito and W.L. Lin), *Econometrica*, **58**, May, pp. 525–42.

(1991), *Long-Run Economic Relationships: Readings in Cointegration* (ed. with C.W.J. Granger), Oxford: Oxford University Press.

(1994a), 'Forecasting Volatility and Option Prices of the S&P 500 Index' (with J. Noh and A. Kane), *Journal of Derivatives*, **2**, Fall, pp. 17–31.

(1994b), *Handbook of Econometrics*, vol. 4 (ed. with D. McFadden), Amsterdam: North-Holland.

(1995), *ARCH: Selected Readings* (ed.), Oxford: Oxford University Press.

(1998), 'Autoregressive Conditional Duration: A New Model for Irregularly Spaced Transaction Data' (with J.R. Russell), *Econometrica*, **66**, September, pp. 1127–62.

(2001), 'GARCH 101: The Use of ARCH/GARCH Models in Applied Econometrics', *Journal of Economic Perspectives*, **15**, Fall, pp. 157–68.

(2004), 'Risk and Volatility: Econometric Models and Financial Practice', *American Economic Review*, **94**, June, pp. 405–20.

Secondary Literature

Diebold, F.X. (2003), 'The ET Interview: Professor Robert F. Engle', *Econometric Theory*, **19**, December, pp. 1159–93.

Diebold, F.X. (2004), 'The Nobel Memorial Prize for Robert F. Engle', *Scandinavian Journal of Economics*, **106** (2), pp. 165–85.

Royal Swedish Academy of Sciences (2004), 'The Nobel Memorial Prize in Economics 2003', *Scandinavian Journal of Economics*, **106** (2), pp. 163–4.

See also   Blaug and Vane (2003, p. 232); Nobel Foundation (2004).

Clive W.J. Granger
(b. 1934)

© The Nobel Foundation

Clive Granger was born in Swansea, Wales, in 1934. In his Nobel autobiography Granger takes the self-deprecating view that his life has been conditioned by a series of 'lucky breaks', the first of which took his family to Nottingham when he was still a boy and pitched him into school with able and enthusiastic mathematics teachers. He subsequently studied mathematics at Nottingham University, where he was awarded a BA in 1955 and a PhD in 1959. Granger entered university as a student of both economics and mathematics but dropped economics after a year. His PhD was in statistics and his thesis explored economic time series, a topic chosen because it seemed promisingly underdeveloped: Granger could find only one relevant book in the university library (Nobel Foundation, 2004).

Granger's academic career began in 1955 as a result of another serendipitous event. He had applied for a junior lectureship in statistics at Nottingham, but as a makeweight to save the university the embarrassment of interviewing only one candidate. Not expecting to get the job, he had a relaxed and enjoyable interview; his rival did not and Granger was offered the post (Nobel Foundation, 2004). He was promoted to a lectureship in economics in 1958. In 1959 he was visiting professor at Princeton University, working for a year with Oscar Morgenstern on time series, and in 1963 he was visiting profes-

327

sor at Stanford University. Returning to Nottingham, Granger became Reader in Mathematics in 1964 and, from 1965 to 1974, Professor of Applied Statistics and Econometrics. In 1974 he moved as Professor of Economics to the University of California at San Diego (UCSD), a post he still holds. Granger has also been visiting professor at the Australian National University (1977) and visiting fellow of All Souls College, Oxford (1994) and Trinity College, Cambridge (1996).

Granger's honours and awards include fellowships of the Econometric Society in 1972 and the American Academy of Arts and Sciences in 1994. He became a distinguished fellow of the American Economic Association in 2002, and was president of the Western Economic Association in 2002–03. He became a foreign member of the Finnish Society of Arts and Science in 1997 and a corresponding fellow of the British Academy in 2002. Jointly with Robert Engle, Granger was awarded the 2003 Nobel Memorial Prize in Economics 'for methods of analysing economic time series with common trends (cointegration)' (Nobel Foundation, 2004).

Granger's work on time series has had a paradigmatic influence on macroeconomic research and policy analysis (Hendry, 2004). His development of the concept of cointegration has provided for a hugely fruitful blending of long-run equilibrium macro relationships with short-run perspectives (Nobel Foundation, 2004). The resultant framework is equally satisfactory in terms of economic theory and econometric method.

A key milestone in this work was research done by Granger with his colleague, Paul Newbold. Their 1974 *Journal of Econometrics* paper, 'Spurious Regressions in Econometrics', showed that the application of standard statistical methods to the non-stationary time series that are common in macroeconomics could produce fundamentally misleading results, suggesting the presence of significant relationships between variables when in fact none existed. Non-stationary series exhibit no tendency to return to a given trend or value: short-term disturbances affect longer-term outcomes, as, for example, in the cases of output or employment. Granger (2004, p. 423) notes that his and Newbold's findings 'led to a great deal of re-evaluation of empirical work, particularly in macroeconomics, to see if apparent relationships were correct or not. Many editors had to look again at their list of accepted papers'.

A way around the problem of non-stationarity suggested by Granger and Newbold was to pose econometric models using first differences of variables (their rates of increase) rather than their levels (see Hendry, 2004; Nobel Foundation, 2004). This is because first differences of variables are usually stationary – that is they *do* tend to observe a given trend – and are thus amenable to analysis using standard statistical methods. Spurious results can therefore be avoided. Unfortunately, however, while such an approach is statistically robust in capturing shorter-run economic relationships, it is less satisfactory in terms of economic theory because this usually specifies relationships between the longer-run levels of variables rather than first differences (Nobel Foundation, 2004). Granger's great contribution was to leap over this seeming impasse between what was desirable from the viewpoint of economic theory and what was necessary for valid statistical method. The key was his discovery that a linear combination of a pair of non-stationary variables may be stationary. This property – which Granger (1981) labelled 'cointegration' – facilitates standard statistical analysis but, importantly, it also makes a desirable connection to longer-run economic theorisation – something missing from the purely first differences solution to the problem of non-stationarity just discussed. Cointegration has been widely deployed in macroeconomic research and policy making using the 'error correction model' first proposed by Dennis Sargan (Granger, 2004). With Andrew Weiss, Granger also devised a test for cointegration between non-stationary variables (Granger and Weiss, 1983). Finally, in what Diebold (2004, p.166) has called 'perhaps the most cited paper in the history of econometrics', Granger, in collaboration with his fellow Nobel Laureate Robert Engle (Engle and Granger, 1987), provided a two-step estimation procedure for cointegrated variables.

Other notable work by Granger includes a book on spectral analysis (written in association with Michio Hatanaka; see Granger and Hatanaka, 1964); and, with J.M. Bates, research on the superiority of pooled forecasts (Bates and Granger, 1969a). His associations with Oscar Morgenstern and Paul Newbold resulted in two books – Granger and Morgenstern (1970) and Granger and Newbold (1977); and he has also edited a volume with Robert Engle on cointegration (Engle and Granger, 1991). In Granger (1969b) he offered an influential interpretation of causality – now referred to as 'Granger causality' – and he has also undertaken important research with Roselyn Joyeux, among others, on long-memory models (see, for example, Granger and Joyeux, 1980). With Timo Terasvirta he has written an overview of non-linear time-series modelling (Granger and Terasvirta,

1993). Finally, among Granger's most recent work is his contribution to a multi-author study of the future of the Amazon rainforest in Brazil (Granger et al., 2003).

Main Published Works

(1964), *Spectral Analysis of Economic Time Series* (in association with M. Hatanaka), Princeton, NJ: Princeton University Press.

(1969a), 'The Combination of Forecasts' (with J.M. Bates), *Operations Research Quarterly*, **20**, pp. 451–68.

(1969b), 'Investigating Causal Relationships by Econometric Models and Cross-Spectral Methods', *Econometrica*, **37**, July, pp. 424–38.

(1970), *Predictability of Stock Market Prices* (with O. Morgenstern), Lexington, MA: D.C. Heath.

(1974), 'Spurious Regressions in Econometrics' (with P. Newbold), *Journal of Econometrics*, **2**, July, pp. 111–20.

(1977), *Forecasting Economic Time Series* (with P. Newbold), New York: Academic Press, 2nd edn 1986.

(1980), 'An Introduction to Long-Memory Time Series Models and Fractional Differencing' (with R. Joyeux), *Journal of Time Series Analysis*, **1**, pp. 15–30.

(1981), 'Some Properties of Time Series Data and Their Use in Econometric Model Specification', *Journal of Econometrics*, **16**, May, pp. 121–30.

(1983), 'Time Series Analysis of Error Correction Models' (with A. Weiss), in S. Karlin, T. Amemiya and L.A. Goodman (eds), *Studies in Econometrics, Time Series, and Multivariate Statistics*, New York: Academic Press, pp. 255–78.

(1987), 'Co-integration and Error-Correction: Representation, Estimation and Testing' (with R.F. Engle), *Econometrica*, **55**, March, pp. 251–76.

(1991), *Long-Run Economic Relationships. Readings in Cointegration* (ed. with R.F. Engle), Oxford: Oxford University Press.

(1993), *Modelling Nonlinear Economic Relationships* (with T. Terasvirta), Oxford: Oxford University Press.

(2003), *The Dynamics of Deforestation and Economic Growth in the Brazilian Amazon* (with L. Andersen, E. Reis, D. Weinhold and S. Wunder), Cambridge: Cambridge University Press.

(2004), 'Time Series Analysis, Cointegration and Applications', *American Economic Review*, **94**, June, pp. 421–5.

Secondary Literature

Diebold, F.X. (2004), 'The Nobel Memorial Prize for Robert F. Engle', *Scandinavian Journal of Economics*, **106** (2), pp. 165–85.

Hendry, D.F. (2004), 'The Nobel Memorial Prize for Clive W.J. Granger', *Scandinavian Journal of Economics*, **106** (2), pp. 187–213.

Royal Swedish Academy of Sciences (2004), 'The Nobel Memorial Prize in Economics 2003', *Scandinavian Journal of Economics*, **106** (2), pp. 163–4.

See also Blaug and Vane (2003, pp. 312–13); Nobel Foundation (2004).

THE 2004 NOBEL MEMORIAL LAUREATES

FINN KYDLAND
AND
EDWARD PRESCOTT

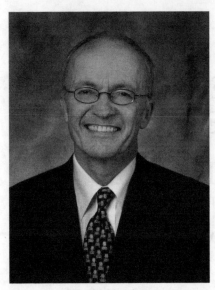

© The Nobel Foundation

Finn E. Kydland
(b. 1943)

Finn Kydland was born in Gjestal, near Stavangar, Norway in 1943. He studied economics at the Norwegian School of Economics and Business Administration (NHH) in Bergen, graduating in 1968 with the Norwegian Siviløkonom. He remained at NHH as a research scholar for a time before moving to Carnegie-Mellon University, where he was awarded an MS in 1972 and a PhD in 1973. Kydland's PhD adviser at Carnegie-Mellon was his fellow Laureate, Edward Prescott.

Kydland's academic career began in 1973 when he took up the post of assistant professor at NHH. In 1976 he returned to the United States, first as visiting scholar at the University of Minnesota in Minneapolis, before moving in 1977 to Carnegie-Mellon as visiting fellow. In 1978 he was appointed associate professor at Carnegie-Mellon, becoming Professor of Economics in 1982. In 2004, a few months before the award of his Nobel Prize, Kydland took up his present post as the Henley Professor of Economics at the University of California, Santa Barbara.

Kydland's professional work includes research associate affiliations with the Federal Reserve Banks of Cleveland, Dallas and St Louis, and he has been a member of the editorial board of *Macroeconomic Dynamics* since 1996. His honours and awards include the

John Stauffer National Fellowship in Public Policy from the Hoover Institution at Stanford University (1982–83), and the Alexander Henderson Award for the best work in economic theory from Carnegie-Mellon in 1973. In 2004, Kydland and Edward Prescott were jointly awarded the Nobel Memorial Prize in Economics 'for their contributions to dynamic macroeconomics: the time consistency of economic policy and the driving forces behind business cycles' (Nobel Foundation, 2004).

During the early 1970s when Kydland and Prescott began to work together, first at Carnegie-Mellon and then in Norway, where Prescott had taken up an NHH visiting professorship, macroeconomic theory was in a state of distressed flux. The established Keynesian certainties over the efficacy of discretionary government intervention tuned to particular circumstances were giving way to worrying doubts that conventional macroeconomic policy was not only proving increasingly ineffective as a means to address its traditional objective – the preservation of full employment – it was also fast becoming associated with the emergence of inflation on a new grand scale. Economies were suffering from both rising unemployment *and* inflation – so-called 'stagflation' – and traditional Keynesian responses seemed either inadequate or, according to some, actually culpable. It was against this backdrop that Robert Lucas (see entry in this volume) formulated his now famous critique of traditional macroeconomic policy evaluation. Lucas convincingly argued that Keynesian macroeconometric models that specified general theoretical and empirical relationships between central macroeconomic variables could not be effectively used in policy evaluation since their parameters might be altered as economic agents adjust their expectations and behaviour in response to a given policy change. In other words, the policy to be evaluated may itself fatally undermine the evaluation process: a macroeconomic 'Catch 22'.

The Lucas critique posed a serious problem for what Kydland and Prescott in their path-breaking 1977 *Journal of Political Economy* paper, 'Rules Rather Than Discretion: The Inconsistency of Optimal Plans', refer to as 'optimum control theory'. In economic policy making this, in essence, involves selecting a best response in each eventuality. How, though, can a best response be determined given the flaw in the policy evaluation process identified by Lucas? What Kydland and Prescott showed was that an optimal control approach to macroeconomic intervention could be consistent in the sense that policy makers were in each particular set of circumstances indeed selecting the best policy, *but* the economic performance thereby achieved could be suboptimal. The ultimate conclusion of their analysis is that governments should forgo the discretion to select optimal policies in favour of a set of rules for economic policy from which it would be hard to deviate. A rules-based approach answers the Lucas critique in that it absolves the government of both the opportunity and the obligation to pursue optimal plans that are time inconsistent.

Kydland and Prescott use the trade-off between inflation and unemployment as one illustration of their argument. A government that wishes to reduce inflation to some socially preferable lower rate could achieve its objective by an announced policy of monetary contraction. In the new classical view, if the policy is credible, agents will revise their inflationary expectations downwards and inflation will fall without any evident implications for the rate of unemployment. This is an optimal policy 'given the current situation and a correct evaluation of the end of period position' (Kydland and Prescott, 1977, p. 473). However, a new situation and new optimal policy that is also socially preferable now arises: if the government increases the rate of monetary growth – reneging on its previous commitment and creating a 'monetary surprise' – it may engineer a reduction in the rate of unemployment below the natural rate. Unfortunately, this is unsustainable as agents will again revise their inflationary expectations, upwards this time, and discount the surprise. The outcome is that the economy returns to the vicinity of its position prior to the first policy change; this is clearly suboptimal given the earlier achievement of a lower inflation rate and an unchanged rate of unemployment. However, there is one other crucial difference following the implementation of such time-inconsistent optimal plans: the government's credibility will have been damaged and future monetary policy announcements are unlikely to be believed. Kydland and Prescott (1977, p. 481, emphases in original) are at pains to point out here that they are not charging governments with myopia – their actions are after all appropriate in each set of prevailing circumstances and, moreover, they are consistent with social preferences – rather the suboptimal outcome 'arises because there is no mechanism to induce *future* policymakers to take into consideration the effects of their policy, via the expectations mechanism, upon *current* decisions of agents'. The mechanism they have in mind is the conduct of macroeconomic policy by rules, the point of which is to make macroeconomic governance both time consistent and optimal. In terms of the example, rules that focused on the attainment of a low and stable rate of inflation would be the equivalent of the implementation of the 'first optimal' policy without the possibility of any subsequent and damaging volte-face. Kydland and Prescott's paper stimulated a large and influential literature, one of the practical results of which has been the embodiment of a rules-inspired approach in the institutional architecture of macroeconomic policy making – for example, in the increasing reliance on independent central banking arrangements in Europe and elsewhere (Nobel Foundation, 2004).

The second contribution for which Kydland and Prescott were awarded the Nobel Prize was their 1982 *Econometrica* paper, 'Time to Build and Aggregate Fluctuations'. This offered new ways to conceptualise, model and interpret business cycles, and proved enormously influential: in the view of the Royal Swedish Academy of Sciences (2004, p. 25), it 'transformed the academic research on business cycles'. Kydland and Prescott's approach was to integrate what had for a long time been two rather distinct areas of study: growth theory and business cycle theory. Long-run economic growth had been interpreted largely as a supply-side reflection of technological change. On the other hand, short-run fluctuations around the long-run growth trend – the business cycle – were widely thought to be linked to changes in aggregate demand. The latter interpretation offered policy makers the opportunity to respond to business cycle fluctuations by manipulating aggregate demand. However, during the 1970s, the stable relationships between macroeconomic aggregates that gave rise, for example, to the Phillips curve had evidently broken down and issues around the business cycle were reopened to debate. As noted, Robert Lucas was an early contributor. As well as offering his critique of the traditional form of policy evaluation, Lucas also introduced a 'monetary surprise' explanation of the business cycle in which unanticipated changes in the money supply caused errors in agents' price expectations and moved output and employment temporarily away from their natural levels. However, Lucas also recognised that, in its exclusive focus on economy-wide aggregates, macroeconomic theory *as a whole* was neglectful of the microeconomic structures, processes and decisions that ultimately underpin macroeconomic performance. In providing a new approach to understanding business cycles, Kydland and Prescott's 1982 paper also contributed new micro foundations to the study of macroeconomic phenomena.

Kydland and Prescott's working hypothesis was that both long-run growth and the business cycles were driven by the same real force of technological change. A supply-side explanation of the business cycle was novel to economics after Keynes, but perhaps the paper's most innovative characteristic was its explicit micro-theoretic foundation. Kydland and Prescott identified a link between technological change and fluctuations in output and employment that centred on the responses of rational agents, in their labour supply and consumption decisions, to the altered structure of relative prices prompted by a technology shock. A positive technology shock will raise productivity, real wages and labour demand, thereby directly (via a productivity effect), and indirectly (as a result of higher labour input) boosting output. In turn, some of this increased output will be consumed and the rest invested, the relevant proportions reflecting agents' preferences and expectations (Royal Swedish Academy of Sciences, 2004). Kydland and Prescott used the Solow residual as a measure of the rate of technological progress and in a later paper (Kydland and Prescott, 1991a) found that about 70 per cent of the variance in US output in the post-1945 period could be accounted for by variations in the residual. One of the most notable implications of Kydland and Prescott's 1982 paper has been the restoration of the view that in the matter of economic fluctuations, the supply side is important. Regardless of the economic perspective considered, their work demands that the micro-theoretic components of the macroeconomic canvas are given explicit treatment.

Other notable work by Kydland includes, with Edward Prescott, further research on business cycles and a methodological discussion (Kydland and Prescott, 1991a; 1991b; 1996). Partly with David Backus and Patrick Kehoe, he has reflected on international business cycle questions (Kydland, 1992b; Backus et al., 1992a). With William Gavin, Kydland has done work on the neutrality of money (Gavin and Kydland, 1999), and with Paul Gomme and Peter Rupert he has introduced refinements to the real business cycle model (Kydland et al., 2001). Kydland (1995) has also edited a collection of essays on business cycle theory.

Main Published Works

(1977), 'Rules Rather Than Discretion: The Inconsistency of Optimal Plans' (with E.C. Prescott), *Journal of Political Economy*, **85**, June, pp. 473–92.

(1982), 'Time to Build and Aggregate Fluctuations' (with E.C. Prescott), *Econometrica*, **50**, November, pp. 1345–70.

(1991a), 'Hours and Employment Variation in Business Cycle Theory' (with E.C. Prescott), *Economic Theory*, **1**, January, pp. 63–81.

(1991b), 'The Econometrics of the General Equilibrium Approach to Business Cycles' (with E.C. Prescott), *Scandinavian Journal of Economics*, **93** (2), pp. 161–78.

(1992a), 'International Real Business Cycles' (with D. Backus and P. Kehoe), *Journal of Political Economy*, **100**, August, pp. 745–75.

(1992b), 'On the Econometrics of World Business Cycles', *European Economic Review*, **36** (2), pp. 476–82.

(1995), *Business Cycle Theory* (ed.), Aldershot, UK and Brookfield, US: Edward Elgar.

(1996), 'The Computational Experiment: An Econometric Tool' (with E.C. Prescott), *Journal of Economic Perspectives*, **10**, Winter, pp. 69–85.

(1999), 'Endogenous Money Supply and the Business Cycle' (with W. Gavin), *Review of Economic Dynamics*, **2**, April, pp. 347–69.

(2001), 'Home Production Meets Time to Build' (with P. Gomme and P. Rupert), *Journal of Political Economy*, **109**, October, pp. 1115–31.

Secondary Literature

Royal Swedish Academy of Sciences (2004), 'Finn Kydland and Edward Prescott's Contribution to Dynamic Macroeconomics: The Time Consistency of Economic Policy and the Driving Forces Behind Business Cycles', available from http://nobelprize.org.

See also Blaug and Vane (2003, pp. 475–6); Nobel Foundation (2004).

© The Nobel Foundation

Edward C. Prescott
(b. 1940)

Edward Prescott was born in Glens Falls, New York, USA in 1940. He graduated from Swarthmore College in 1962 with a BA in mathematics, and was awarded an MS in operations research by the Case Institute of Technology (now Case-Western Reserve University) in 1963. He then attended Carnegie-Mellon University and was awarded a PhD in economics in 1967.

Prescott's academic career began in 1966 when he was appointed lecturer in the Department of Economics at the University of Pennsylvania. He was promoted to assistant professor in 1967. Prescott moved back to Carnegie-Mellon in 1971 as Assistant Professor of Economics, becoming Associate Professor of Economics in 1972, and Professor of Economics in 1975. He spent 1974–75 as Visiting Professor of Economics at the Norwegian School of Economics and Business Administration in Bergen, where he worked with his fellow Laureate Finn Kydland on the first of the two papers that would later win them the Nobel Prize: 'Rules Rather Than Discretion: The Inconsistency of Optimal Plans', published in 1977 in the *Journal of Political Economy*. In 1980 Prescott left Carnegie-Mellon to take up a professorial post at the University of Minnesota. He moved to the University of Chicago as Professor of Economics in 1998 but returned to Minnesota the following year. In 2003 he took up his present post as W.P. Carey Chair of Economics at Arizona State University. Prescott has also held visiting professorial positions at the University of Chicago (1978–79) and Northwestern University (1979–80 and 1980–82).

Prescott's professional affiliations include the posts of senior advisor (1980–2003) and senior monetary advisor (since 2003) at the Federal Reserve Bank of Minneapolis, and he has been a research associate of the National Bureau of Economic Research since 1988. Prescott was president of the Society of Economic Dynamics and Control from 1992 to 1995, and president of the Society for the Advancement of Economic Theory from 1992 to 1994.

Prescott's awards and honours include fellowships of the Econometric Society (1980) and the American Academy of Arts and Sciences (1992). He was a Brookings Economic Policy Fellow in 1969–70, and a Guggenheim Fellow in 1974–75. In 2004, Edward Prescott and Finn Kydland were jointly awarded the Nobel Memorial Prize in Economics 'for their contributions to dynamic macroeconomics: the time consistency of economic policy and the driving forces behind business cycles' (Nobel Foundation, 2004).

In the preceding entry in this volume – for Finn Kydland – we reviewed the nature and significance of the two strands of work for which Prescott and Kydland have been jointly honoured by the Royal Swedish Academy of Sciences. Rather than cover the same ground in the present entry, we shall instead briefly discuss some of the constructions placed on this analysis by Prescott (1986); we conclude with some references to Prescott's more recent work.

A notable implication of Kydland and Prescott's 1982 *Econometrica* paper, 'Time to Build and Aggregate Fluctuations', the second of the two papers cited in their Nobel award, concerns the conceptual significance of business cycles: are they independent phenomena distinct from the long-run growth process as economists for a long time believed? Prescott (1986) argues that they are not. His and Kydland's pioneering research provided an integrated approach to understanding growth and cyclical fluctuations and demonstrated that large movements in output and employment over relatively short time periods are what standard neoclassical theory predicts. Indeed, it 'would be puzzling if the economy did not display these large fluctuations in output and employment' (Prescott, 1986, p. 9). In Prescott's view there is a message here for economic policy. He considers business cycles or economic fluctuations to be 'optimal responses to uncertainty in the rate of technological change' (Prescott, 1986, p. 21); they should not be construed as forms of aberrant behaviour in need of correction by government. This argument is consistent with the main finding of Kydland and Prescott's other Nobel cited paper (Kydland and Prescott, 1977), that optimal control theory and discretionary policy should be abandoned in favour of a rules-based approach to macroeconomic governance.

Other notable work by Prescott with Kydland includes further research on business cycles and a methodological discussion (Kydland and Prescott, 1991a; 1991b; 1996). With Robert Lucas (see entry in this volume) he has produced important papers on investment and unemployment (Lucas and Prescott, 1971; 1974). With Ellen McGratten he has considered issues around the valuation of the US and UK stock markets (McGratten and Prescott, 2000a); with Fumio Hayashi he has explored the reasons behind the poor performance of the Japanese economy in the 1990s (Hayashi and Prescott, 2002a); and he has reflected more generally on depressions (Prescott, 2002b). Finally, with Stephen Parente, Prescott has written a book explaining the obstacles to economic development that confront the world's poorer economies (Parente and Prescott, 2000b).

Main Published Works

(1971), 'Investment Under Uncertainty' (with R.E. Lucas), *Econometrica*, **39**, September, pp. 659–81.

(1974), 'Equilibrium Search and Unemployment' (with R.E. Lucas), *Journal of Economic Theory*, **7**, February, pp. 188–209.

(1977), 'Rules Rather Than Discretion: The Inconsistency of Optimal Plans' (with F.E. Kydland), *Journal of Political Economy*, **85**, June, pp. 473–92.

(1982), 'Time to Build and Aggregate Fluctuations' (with F.E. Kydland), *Econometrica*, **50**, November, pp. 1345–70.

(1986), 'Theory Ahead of Business Cycle Measurement', *Federal Reserve Bank of Minneapolis Quarterly Review*, **10**, Fall, pp. 9–22.

(1991a), 'Hours and Employment Variation in Business Cycle Theory' (with F.E. Kydland), *Economic Theory*, **1**, January, pp. 63–81.

(1991b), 'The Econometrics of the General Equilibrium Approach to Business Cycles' (with F.E. Kydland), *Scandinavian Journal of Economics*, 93 (2), pp. 161–78.

(1996), 'The Computational Experiment: An Econometric Tool' (with F.E. Kydland), *Journal of Economic Perspectives*, **10**, Winter, pp. 69–85.

(2000a), 'Is the Stock Market Overvalued?' (with E.R. McGratten), *Federal Reserve Bank of Minneapolis Quarterly Review*, **24**, Fall, pp. 20–40.

(2000b), *Barriers to Riches* (with S.L. Parente), Cambridge, MA: MIT Press.

(2002a), 'The 1990s in Japan: A Lost Decade' (with F. Hayashi), *Review of Economic Dynamics*, **5**, January, pp. 206–35.

(2002b), 'Prosperity and Depressions', *American Economic Review*, **92**, September, pp. 1205–17.

Secondary Literature

Royal Swedish Academy of Sciences (2004), 'Finn Kydland and Edward Prescott's Contribution to Dynamic Macroeconomics: The Time Consistency of Economic Policy and the Driving Forces Behind Business Cycles', available from http://www.nobelprize.org.

See also Blaug and Vane (2003, pp. 664–5); Nobel Foundation (2004); Snowdon and Vane (2005, pp. 344–56).

Glossary of Selected Associations, Awards, Institutions and Societies

American Academy of Arts and Sciences

The American Academy of Arts and Sciences was founded in 1780. An international learned society, with a current membership of 4000 American fellows and 600 foreign honorary members, the academy is based in Cambridge, Massachusetts. Members, who have demonstrated 'exceptional achievement', and who are drawn from 'science, scholarship, business, public affairs, and the arts', engage in a wide variety of multidisciplinary studies of problems in society. For more information, see the American Academy of Arts and Sciences website at: http://www.amacad.org/.

American Economic Association (AEA)

The AEA was organised in 1885 at Saratoga, New York. Currently based at Nashville, Tennessee, its present-day objectives include: (i) 'the encouragement of economic research'; (ii) 'the issue of publications on economic subjects'; and (iii) 'the encouragement of perfect freedom of economic discussion' – partly facilitated by an annual meeting. Among its publications are the prestigious *American Economic Review* (first published in 1911), the *Journal of Economic Literature* (first published in 1969) and the *Journal of Economic Perspectives* (first published in 1987). Today, the AEA has approximately 18,000 members. Over half its membership is associated with academic institutions, approximately 15 per cent with business and industry, and the balance largely with federal, state and local government agencies. Past presidents of the AEA include Nobel Memorial Laureates (with year of presidency in brackets): Simon Kuznets (1954), Theodore Schultz (1960), Paul Samuelson (1961), George Stigler (1964), Milton Friedman (1967), Wassily Leontief (1970), James Tobin (1971), Kenneth Arrow (1973), Franco Modigliani (1976), Lawrence Klein (1977), Tjalling Koopmans (1978), Robert Solow (1979), Arthur Lewis (1983), Gary Becker (1987), Gerard Debreu (1990), William Vickrey (1992), Amartya Sen (1994), Robert Fogel (1998) and Robert Lucas (2002). For more information, see the AEA website at: http://www.vanderbilt.edu/AEA.

American Finance Association (AFA)
The AFA was planned in 1939 at a meeting in Philadelphia. Currently based at Berkeley, California, the association is 'devoted to the study and promotion of knowledge about financial economics'. Today it has more than 8000 members and sponsors an annual meeting. Among its publications is the *Journal of Finance* (first published in 1946). For more information, see the AFA website at: http://www.afajof.org/.

American Political Science Association (APSA)
The APSA was founded in 1903. Based in Washington, DC, it is a professional organisation for the study of politics with more than 14,000 members. Among its publications is the *American Political Science Review*. For more information, see the APSA website at: http://www.apsanet.org/.

American Psychological Association (APA)
The APA is a scientific and professional organisation that represents psychology in the USA. It is based in Washington, DC, and has more than 150,000 members. For more information, see the APA website at: http://www.apa.org/.

American Statistical Association (ASA)
The ASA was founded in Boston in 1839. A scientific and educational society, with more than 16,000 members, its mission is to 'promote excellence in the application of statistical science across the wealth of human endeavour'. Among its publications is the *Journal of the American Statistical Association*. For more information, see the ASA website at: http://www.amstat.org/.

Brookings Institution
The Brookings Institution was founded in 1927, following the consolidation of the Institute for Government Research, the Institute of Economics and the Robert Brookings Graduate School. Named in honour of Robert Somers Brookings (1850–1932), a St Louis businessman, civil leader and philanthropist, it is based in Washington, DC. In addition to its educational activities the institution conducts research into economics, foreign policy, governance and metropolitan policy. Among its publications is the prestigious *Brookings Papers on Economic Activity* (first published in 1970). For

more information, see the Brookings Institution website at: http://www.brook.edu/.

Council of Economic Advisers (CEA)

The CEA was set up under the Employment Act of 1946 to provide advice to the US President on such matters as stabilisation policy, economic regulation and international economic policy. The council, which consists of a small team of three economists, is supported by a professional staff of about ten senior staff economists (usually professors on leave from their universities), ten junior staff economists (usually advanced graduate students) and four permanent economic statisticians. One of the main tasks of the council is to help the President prepare his annual Economic Report to Congress. For more information, see the CEA website at: http://www.whitehouse.gov/cea/.

Cowles Commission/Foundation

The Cowles Commission for Research in Economics was founded in 1932 by the economist and businessman Alfred Cowles. Initially located in Colorado Springs, the commission moved, in 1939, to the University of Chicago and again, in 1955, to its present home at Yale University, where it was renamed the Cowles Foundation for Research in Economics. Its purpose is the 'conduct and encouragement of research in economics, finance, commerce, industry and technology'. For more information, see the Cowles Foundation website at: http://www.cowles.econ.yale.edu/.

Development Studies Association (DSA)

With more than 800 members, the aim of the DSA is to 'promote the advancement of knowledge on international development; disseminate information on development research and training; and encourage interdisciplinary exchange and cooperation'. For more information, see the DSA website at: http://www.devstud.org.uk/.

Econometric Society

The Econometric Society was founded in 1930 by Irving Fisher (who became its first president) and Ragnar Frisch (the joint recipient of the first Nobel Memorial Prize in Economics in 1969). The main purpose of the society is 'to promote studies that aim at a unification of the theoretical–quantitative and empirical–quantitative approach to economic problems and that are penetrated by constructive and rigorous thinking similar to that which has come to dominate in the natural sciences'. Its main activities include organising meetings in six regions (North America, Europe and Other Areas, Latin America, Australasia, the Far East and India–Southeast Asia) and, every five years, a World Congress. It also publishes a monograph series and the prestigious journal *Econometrica* (since 1933), which is widely acknowledged as one of the world's leading journals in economics. Past presidents of the Econometric Society include Nobel Memorial Laureates (with year of presidency in brackets): Jan Tinbergen (1947), Ragnar Frisch (1949), Tjalling Koopmans (1950), Paul Samuelson (1952), Wassily Leontief (1954), Richard Stone (1955), Kenneth Arrow (1956), Trygve Haavelmo (1957), James Tobin (1958), Lawrence Klein (1960), Franco Modigliani (1962), Robert Solow (1964), Gerard Debreu (1971), James Mirrlees (1982), Amartya Sen (1984), Daniel McFadden (1985) and Robert Lucas (1997). For more information, see the Econometric Society website at: http://www.econometricsociety.org.

History of Economics Society

The History of Economics Society was founded in 1974 at the University of North Carolina, Chapel Hill, USA. It is an international organisation which seeks to 'promote interest in and inquiry into the history of economics and related parts of intellectual history; facilitate communication and discourse among scholars working in the field of the history of economics; and disseminate knowledge about the history of economics'. For more information, see the History of Economics Society website at: http://www.eh.net/HE/HisEcSoc/.

International Economic Association (IEA)

The IEA was founded in 1950. Its aims are 'to promote personal contacts and mutual understanding among economists in different parts of the world through the organization of scientific meetings, through common research programmes and by means of publications of an international character on problems of current importance'. Past presidents of the association include Nobel Memorial Laureates: Paul Samuelson (1965–68), Kenneth Arrow (1983–86), Amartya Sen (1986–89) and Robert Solow (1999–2002). For more information, see the IEA website at: http://www.iea-world.com/.

John Bates Clark Medal

Instituted in 1947 by the American Economic Association, the John Bates Clark Medal (named after the American economist John Bates Clark, 1847–1938) is awarded every two years to an American economist under the age of 40 who is adjudged to have made 'a significant contribution to economic thought and knowledge'. As noted in the opening chapter, to date of the 28 economists who have been awarded the Medal (no award was made in 1953), 11 have subsequently been awarded the Nobel Memorial Prize, namely (with year of Medal award followed by year of Memorial Prize award): Paul Samuelson (1947, 1970); Milton Friedman (1951, 1976); James Tobin (1955, 1981); Kenneth Arrow (1957, 1972); Lawrence Klein (1959, 1980); Robert Solow (1961, 1987); Gary Becker (1967, 1992); Daniel McFadden (1975, 2000); Joseph Stiglitz (1979, 2001); Michael Spence (1981, 2001); and James Heckman (1983, 2000).

John von Neumann Theory Prize

The John von Neumann Theory Prize is awarded by the Operations Research Society of America and the Institute of Management Sciences (ORSA/TIMS) for contributions to the theory of operations research and management science. Past recipients of the prize include Nobel Memorial Laureates (with the year of the award of the John von Neumann Theory Prize in brackets): John Nash (1978), Kenneth Arrow (1986) Herbert Simon (1988) and Harry Markowitz (1989).

Legion of Honour

First created in 1802 by Napoleon Bonaparte, the Legion of Honour is the highest civilian award given by the French government for outstanding service to France. The award has five classes of distinction namely: Knights (Chevaliers), Officers, Commanders, Grand Officers and Grand Crosses.

Mont Pelerin Society

The Mont Pelerin Society was founded in 1947 by a group of scholars brought together for its first meeting at Mont Pelerin, Switzerland by Friedrich Hayek. The society's objective is to facilitate 'an exchange of ideas between like-minded scholars in the hope of strengthening the principles and practice of a free society and to study the workings, virtues, and defects of market-orientated economic systems'. Past presidents of the Mont Pelerin Society include Nobel Memorial Laureates: Friedrich Hayek (1947–61), Milton Friedman (1970–72), George Stigler (1976–78), James Buchanan (1984–86) and Gary Becker (1990–92). For more information, see the Mont Pelerin Society website at: http://www.montpelerin.org/.

National Bureau of Economic Research (NBER)
Founded in 1920, the NBER is a private, non-profit, non-partisan research organisation whose main aim is 'to promote a greater understanding of how the economy works [by] undertaking and disseminating unbiased economic research among policymakers, business professionals, and the academic community'. Its publications include the *NBER Macroeconomics Annual*. In the early years, research undertaken at the NBER concentrated on the macro economy and included pioneering work by Simon Kuznets (the 1971 Nobel Memorial Laureate) on the development of national income accounts; Wesley Mitchell on business cycles; Milton Friedman (the 1976 Nobel Memorial Laureate) on the theory of the consumption function; and Milton Friedman and Anna Schwartz on money and business cycles. Today the bureau's empirical research is focused on four main areas: developing new statistical measurements, estimating quantitative models of economic behaviour, assessing the effects of public policies on the US economy, and projecting the effects of alternative policy proposals. For more information, see the NBER website at: http://www.nber.org/.

National Medal of Science
The National Medal of Science is a US presidential award first established by Congress in 1959. Recipients of the Medal are 'deserving of special recognition by reason of their outstanding contributions to knowledge in the physical, biological, mathematical, or engineering sciences'. In 1980, Congress extended such recognition to include the social and behavioural sciences. Past recipients of the Medal include Nobel Memorial Laureates (with the year of the award of the Medal in brackets): Herbert Simon (1986), George Stigler (1987), Milton Friedman (1988), Paul Samuelson (1996), Robert Solow (1999) and Gary Becker (2000).

Royal Economic Society (RES)
Originally founded in 1890 as the British Economic Association, the RES assumed its current title in 1902, when it was granted a royal charter. The main purpose of the society is 'to promote the encouragement of the study of economic science in academic life, government service, banking, industry and public affairs'. Among its publications is the prestigious *Economic Journal* (first published in 1891), widely acknowledged as one of the world's leading economics journals. The society has more than 3000 individual members, 60 per cent of whom live outside the United Kingdom. Past presidents of the RES include Nobel Memorial Laureates: John Hicks (1960–62), James Meade (1964–66), and Richard Stone (1978–80). For more information, see the RES website at: http://www.res.org.uk/.

References

Arestis, P. and M. Sawyer (eds) (2000), *A Biographical Dictionary of Dissenting Economists*, 2nd edn, Cheltenham, UK and Northampton, MA, USA: Edward Elgar.

Arrow, K.J. (1999), 'Amartya K. Sen's Contribution to the Study of Welfare', *Scandinavian Journal of Economics*, **101** (2), pp. 163–72.

Atkinson, A.B. (1999), 'The Contributions of Amartya Sen to Welfare Economics', *Scandinavian Journal of Economics*, **101** (2), pp. 173–90.

Beaud, M. and G. Dostaler (1997), *Economic Thought Since Keynes: A History and Dictionary of Major Economists*, London: Routledge.

Blaug, M. (1998), *Great Economists Since Keynes: An Introduction to the Lives and Works of One Hundred Modern Economists*, 2nd edn, Cheltenham, UK and Lyme, USA: Edward Elgar.

Blaug, M. (ed.) (1999), *Who's Who in Economics*, 3rd edn, Cheltenham, UK and Northampton, MA, USA: Edward Elgar.

Blaug, M. (2001), 'No History of Ideas, Please, We're Economists', *Journal of Economic Perspectives*, **15**, Winter, pp. 145–64.

Blaug, M. and H.R. Vane (eds) (2003), *Who's Who in Economics*, 4th edn, Cheltenham, UK and Northampton, MA, USA: Edward Elgar.

Cate, T. (ed.) (1997), *An Encyclopedia of Keynesian Economics*, Cheltenham, UK and Lyme, USA: Edward Elgar.

Grubel, H.G. (1979), 'Citation Counts for Leading Economists', *Economic Notes*, **2** (Monte Dei Paschi di Siena Journal), pp. 134–45.

Lindbeck, A. (1985), 'The Prize in Economic Science in Memory of Alfred Nobel', *Journal of Economic Literature*, **23**, March, pp. 37–56.

Lindbeck, A. (2001), 'The Sveriges Riksbank (Bank of Sweden) Prize in Economic Sciences in Memory of Alfred Nobel 1969–2000', in A.W Levinovitz and N. Ringertz (eds) *The Nobel Prize: The First 100 Years*, London: Imperial College Press and World Scientific Publishing.

Nasar, S. (1998), 'Economist Wins Nobel Prize for Work on Fairness and Poverty', *New York Times*, 15 October, section C, p. 1.

National Bureau of Economic Research (2004), Official Web Site, www.nber.org/.

Nobel Foundation (2004), Official Web Site, www.nobel.se.

Pressman, S. (1999), *Fifty Major Economists*, London: Routledge.

Pressman, S. and G. Summerfield (2000), 'The Economic Contributions of Amartya Sen', *Review of Political Economy*, **12** (1), pp. 89–113.

Quandt, R.E. (1976), 'Some Quantitative Aspects of the Economics Journal Literature', *Journal of Political Economy*, **84**, August, pp. 741–55.

Snowdon, B. and H.R. Vane (1999), *Conversations with Leading Economists: Interpreting Modern Macroeconomics*, Cheltenham, UK and Northampton, MA, USA: Edward Elgar.

Snowdon, B. and H.R. Vane (eds) (2002), *An Encyclopedia of Macroeconomics*, Cheltenham, UK and Northampton, MA, USA: Edward Elgar.

Snowdon, B. and H.R. Vane (2005), *Modern Macroeconomics: Its Origins, Development and Current State*, Cheltenham, UK and Northampton, MA, USA: Edward Elgar.

Name Index

Subject Index